COLLEGE FOR HUMAN SERVICES
LIBRARY
345 HUDSON STREET
NEW YORK, N.Y. 10014

Clinical Assessment of Learning Problems

Model, Process, and Remedial Planning

Marion Sanders, Ed.D.

BROOKLINE
BOOKS

Copyright © 1983 by Marion Sanders. All rights reserved. No part of this book may be reproduced in any form, electronic or mechanical, including photocopy, recording, or any information storage and retrieval system without permission in writing from the publisher.

Originally published by Allyn and Bacon, Inc.

Library of Congress Cataloging in Publication Data

Sanders, Marion.
    Clinical assessment of learning problems.

    Reprint. Originally published: Boston: Allyn and Bacon, ©1979.
      Bibliography: p.
      Includes index.
      1. Remedial teaching. 2. Learning ability.
3. Handicapped children — Education. 4. Learning disabilities.   I. Title. [DNLM: 1. Learning disorders — Diagnosis. 2. Remedial teaching. LC 4704 S215e]
LB1029.R4S26   1984   371.9   83-26146
ISBN 0-914797-03-4

Printed in the United States of America at Braun-Brumfield, Inc.

Published by
Brookline Books, Inc.
460 Broadway
Cambridge, MA 02138

TO
REBECCA M. SANDERS

AND TO THE MEMORY OF
ALEXANDER W. SANDERS

Contents

Preface		vii
Chapter 1	Introduction	1
Chapter 2	Biological Determinants of Learning Problems	15
	Mental Retardation 19	
	Learning Disability 22	
	Maturational Lag 48	
Chapter 3	Psychological Determinants of Learning Problems	51
	Psychological Disturbance and Learning Problems 53	
	Interpersonal and Task Orientations in Learning 71	
	Learning and Aggression 76	
Chapter 4	Social Determinants of Learning Problems	83
	The Family 85	
	The Culture 99	
	The School 112	
Chapter 5	Clinical Assessment: Interviews	117
	Parent Interviews 121	
	Teacher Interviews 130	
Chapter 6	Clinical Assessment: Testing	141
	Intellectual Assessment 143	
	The WISC-R 144	
	Copying Tests 164	

Assessing Expressive Language Skills 166
Diagnostic Assessment of Basic Academic Skills 168
Learning Disabilities Testing 174
Personality Testing 178
Referral for Medical or Paramedical Evaluation 180

CHAPTER 7   CASE ILLUSTRATIONS   187

Three Boys—Danny, Chip, and George 189
Mr. Meyer and Mr. Rossi—Adults with Learning Disabilities 200
Four Girls 207
Susan 215

CHAPTER 8   REMEDIATION   221

Some Basic Issues in Remediation 223
A Sampling of Learning Problems and Remediation Approaches 235
The Teacher-Student Relationship in Remediation 248
Some Clinical Issues in Remedial Planning 252
A Final Note 261

APPENDICES
I. POSSIBLE QUESTIONS TO TEACHERS REGARDING THE CHILD'S SCHOOL BEHAVIOR AND ACADEMIC PERFORMANCE   263
II. DESCRIPTIONS OF THE ITPA, THE DETROIT TESTS, AND THE FROSTIG DEVELOPMENTAL TEST OF VISUAL PERCEPTION   268

INDEX   286

Preface

This book presents a framework for the comprehensive assessment of learning problems, taking into account possible biological, intrapsychic, and environmental determinants. It is modeled after Erikson's case study method, which he first presented in *Childhood and Society*, published in 1950. In this book, the learning problems of school age children are the main focus of attention, but case material on preschool children and adults is also included. There is a special emphasis on understanding the relatively new field of learning disabilities, and on integrating that understanding into a comprehensive, psychodymanic assessment. The book is directed towards those persons responsible for uncovering the sources of learning difficulties in children and for recommending or planning remedial intervention. The specific target audience includes clinical child psychologists, school psychologists, and graduate students in these fields, but anyone involved with children who have learning disorders may find it useful—special educators, school guidance counselors, and other mental health professionals who work with children and their families.

With the growing awareness and concern about learning difficulties, and the variety of theories about etiology from numerous medical, educational, psychological, and mental health professionals, the assessment of learning problems has become an increasingly complex affair. The number of possible determinants of learning difficulties requires that the assessing clinician have a sufficiently broad and organized conceptual framework for considering why a particular child is having trouble learning.

The first section, following an introductory overview chapter, discusses the biological, intrapsychic, and environmental determinants that are frequently related to learning problems. The second section includes two chapters on the assessment process, covering interviewing and testing, and a third chapter presenting case studies. The final chapter is devoted to remediation, though illustrations of remedial planning and teaching occur throughout the book. The intention is to consider remediation from the perspective of the evaluating clinician, who recommends and plans for remedial intervention, rather than to summarize the principles and practices of a demanding educational specialty.

I am grateful to Joan Hornsby and Lucille Kohlberg who read and commented on the manuscript. Dr. Jeffrey Rosen was very helpful in his close reading of chapter 2 and his constructive comments. I particularly want to thank Dr. Ellen Berger and Dr. Betty North who read the entire manuscript and gave generously of their time, suggestions, and encouragement.

Finally, I am happy to express my deepest appreciation to my teachers, particularly William Steinhoff of the University of Michigan, who taught me about writing, and Dr. Charles Hersch, who taught me about clinical child psychology, and to the many students and patients who have taught me so much of what appears here.

M.S.

1

Introduction

Assessing learning problems is one of the most complex tasks confronting teachers and psychologists who work with children. Over the last thirty to forty years, we have become increasingly aware of a variety of factors that influence learning, without becoming as skilled at sorting them out or assessing their interaction. Even in regard to influences we recognize, such as economic and cultural disadvantage, intrapsychic pressures, and neurological dysfunction, we are far from being able to accurately characterize them or measure their effects in every instance. In the past, we have witnessed great progress in many academic and professional fields associated with children's learning problems, including special education, clinical child psychology, developmental and social psychology, pediatric neurology, neuropsychology, child psychiatry, psycholinguistics, optometry and ophthalmology, and audiology. This list could go on but more striking than its length is the fact that many of these specialty areas did not even exist forty years ago.

As each new specialty emerges and develops, it generates new vocabulary, methodology and doctrine, adherents and adversaries. In writing this book, my goal has not been to discuss and integrate the theories and practices of all the involved areas. However, this book does present one way of structuring the evaluation of learning problems so as to strengthen the likelihood that major, relevant determinants will be incorporated into a comprehensive assessment.

There have always been children with learning problems, those who have not learned as much or as easily as most children. History, literature, and folklore are filled with references to the lazy who would not, and the dullards who could not, learn. Diagnosis did not enter the picture until early in this century when Alfred Binet developed an intelligence test to identify children whose mental development was retarded to the extent of requiring special education. Since then, intelligence tests and IQ scores have been used (and, unfortunately, often misused) as the first sorting instruments for children who present learning problems. Children who score low enough on the intelligence test to be labeled "mentally retarded" often do not receive further diagnostic attention aimed at understanding the cause or nature of their learning difficulties. It is felt that the label is sufficient explanation. Children deemed to be of average or higher intelligence, on the basis of testing or more subjective judgments, evoke a variety of possible explanations for their learning problems, depending to a large extent on the background and theoretical orientation of the observer, which is, in turn, often dependent on the prevailing zeitgeist.

The current zeitgeist has followed certain scientific and historical developments, and it is instructive to look back at how learning problems have been perceived and dealt with over time. From the time that Binet developed the intelligence test until after World War II, intelligence was commonly considered to be the only major determinant of learning ability. An intelligent child was assumed to be an able child; if he did not perform according to expectations, he was lazy.

The development of mental health services for children burgeoned after World War II. As a result, learning problems were forcefully brought to the attention of mental health professionals since a high percentage of the children coming for treatment had some form of poor school performance among their presenting complaints. (Kessler, 1966, estimates that academic difficulties prompt the referral of at least 75 percent of the children brought to mental health facilities.) In standard child guidance practice, once the presence of good intelligence and the absence of obvious brain damage was established, the learning problem was interpreted as a manifestation of emotional disturbance, and the prescribed treatment was psychotherapy. Parents were asked to involve themselves in parallel treatment, as patients; and teachers and school officials were often ignored, or at best offered support, reassurance, and sometimes consultation on how to cope with the disturbed and disturbing behavior of the child. There was rarely an attempt to deal with the actual learning problem itself. It was assumed that when the child was ready to learn, he would do so, and that readiness would come as a result of a healthier emotional adjustment. In many instances, however, even where psychotherapy was perceived to have successfully treated the child's affective and behavior problems, the school learning problems persisted.

The "learning disability" field developed in the United States during the 1960s and 1970s. The term is used here to include all labels for learning handicaps based on presumed brain dysfunction (or neurogenic disorder), including minimal brain damage, minimal brain dysfunction, dyslexia, specific language disability, specific learning disability, minimal neurological dysfunction, and perceptual-motor handicap. While to date there is no final agreement on a specific definition of learning disability (Meyers & Hammill, 1976), many, including Johnson and Myklebust (1967), Lerner (1971), Bryan and Bryan (1975), and Wepman, Cruickshank, Deutsch, Morency, and Strother (1975) do agree that it is a neurogenic disorder affecting perceptual, perceptual-motor, and basic language skills. It is in this sense that the term is used throughout this book. All other terms used, including learning problems, learning difficulties, and learning disorders, refer to any situation in which, for whatever reason, a child has difficulty with school work.

The term *learning disability* is meant to refer to a neurogenic difficulty, one that stems to a significant degree from some neurological dysfunction or inefficiency. The presence of neurogenic difficulty is sometimes established upon neurological or electroencephalographic examination; more often it is presumed on the basis of poor performance in various neuropsychological functions. These functions, as well as the concept, history, and current working definitions of learning disability are discussed at length in chapter 2.

The response to the development of the learning disabilities field has been enthusiastic in many quarters, particularly among parents and teachers. Many parents feel more comfortable with a diagnostic label indicating physical rather than psychological problems; there is no guilt attached to it, and they feel they are dealing with something relatively concrete. Also, parents are often able to contribute to the remedial process and feel like competent facilitators rather than patients.

On the other hand, the desire for a learning disability diagnosis may create problems when children do in fact have some emotional problems (either in addition to or instead of a learning disability) that the parents cannot acknowledge or accept. For many parents, "learning disability" has become the diagnosis of choice, providing an acceptable cover for individual and family problems that continue to fester and debilitate. The development of the learning disability field is thus a mixed blessing, for while it has contributed greatly to the understanding and remediation of children's learning problems, it has also provided a new distraction for parents unable to acknowledge psychogenic emotional problems in their children or in themselves.

Teachers have also received a vote of confidence from the learning disabilities movement. When the presumed causes of learning problems were largely emotional, the primary role of teachers was to be patient and understanding. Now, since much of the diagnostic and almost all of the remedial procedures for learning disabilities fall within the educational rather than the clinical domain, teachers are in a position to be more active and effective change agents in their daily work with children.

The response to learning disabilities in mental health circles has been mixed. Clinicians in public mental health agencies and psychiatrists and psychologists in private practice have become increasingly aware of the possibility of mild as well as major neurogenic involvement in the learning problems of children, but there is a tendency to attempt differential diagnosis so as to categorize children as learning disability cases or emotional problem cases. The concepts of comprehensive assessment and interaction between physical and emotional factors have not taken hold in a practical way, although most clinicians would honor the theoretical constructs. More troubling is the fact that some clinicians still treat learning problems by considering only psychodynamics once retardation and marked organic damage are ruled out.

At the opposite end of the psychology spectrum is another approach to learning problems, which also rapidly developed in the 1960s and 1970s, *behavior modification.* Behavior modification does not require the assessment of physical or intrapsychic aspects of learning problems. It focuses on descriptions of environmental conditions that elicit and reinforce certain behaviors, and then, through techniques based on learning theory, attempts to extinguish undesirable behaviors and reinforce desirable ones. To the extent that school and family conditions contributing to learning problems are scrutinized and analyzed, the practice of behavior modification contributes to learning problem assessment. In the main however, it appears that the greatest contributions have been in the area of remediation, which will be discussed in more detail in chapter 8.

During the 1960s, still another perspective on learning problems developed, focusing not on the problems within the child, but on cultural disadvantage and deprivation, which can so adversely affect learning ability that a child, whose basic endowment would otherwise equip him to learn successfully, enters school at a distinct disadvantage and falls farther and farther behind other children. Individual assessment of children with learning problems has not been characteristic of this approach. Instead, the aim is to provide all children from socially disadvantaged areas and strata of society, such as lower-class neighborhoods, migrant worker groups, and ghettos, with a compensatory educational program to stimulate verbal or cognitive development, provide remediation in school subjects, and develop educational and cultural interests and talents (Deutsch, Katz, & Jensen, 1968; Hellmuth, 1970).

The apparent failure of compensatory programs to provide lasting improvement in the disadvantaged child's ability to do well at school has contributed to the generation of a number of additional hypotheses and explanations of learning failure. These include theories of genetic differences in intellectual ability between racial groups (e.g., Jensen, 1969), lasting physiological effects on learning capacities due to poor nutrition and health care in early years (Birch & Gussow, 1970), motivational differences between lower and middle class children (Douvan, 1956; Gordon, 1970), and the detrimental attitudes of teachers working with lower class and black children (Clark, 1973).

There also exists a rather strict educational view of learning problems, attributing learning difficulties to some aspect of the child's educational program, such as class size, teacher personality, teaching methods, curriculum, and degree of classroom structure and formality. One of the best-known and most articulate proponents of this view is John Holt (1964). To the extent that such a view does not consider the program in relation to the child's specific character or problems but rather assumes that a given educational program can by itself create learning problems it constitutes a separatist approach. This view essentially affirms that there is no need to assess the child, since a certain kind of educational program has created the learning problems. It also suggests that some other kind of program would relieve these problems or at least prevent their occurrence in other children.

Historical and scientific developments have had great influence in how learning problems are perceived and understood, but individual attitudes and experience continue to be important and often counter prevailing practice or new developments. There were those who saw reading problems as reflective of neurological deficit long before the recent surge of activity in the field (Morgan, 1896; Orton, 1925). There are many psychiatric and psychological clinicians today who are essentially unimpressed and unchanged by recent developments in the area of learning disabilities. There are behavior psychologists, social action workers, and educators who believe that the environment is primarily responsible for creating problems in learning, and that the road to improvement is planned environmental change. Thus, no matter what particular historic and scientific balance prevails today in the abstract, one can find among the many professionals dealing with learning problems a wide array of attitudes, perspectives, biases, and beliefs as to what causes learning problems and what to do about them.

These differences are also reflected among the general public and other professional people, such as pediatricians and school administrators, who have contact with children experiencing learning problems and feel a responsibility to refer them for evaluation and treatment. Many parents turn to such professionals for referral, or to friends and relatives. What they often receive is a recommendation that embodies a "hidden diagnosis"; the choice of child guidance clinic, learning disability program, neurologist, optometrist, or new experimental school tacitly expresses an assumption that the problem is either psychological, physical, or educational.

In order to cope conceptually with the array of influences on learning, and to avoid the pitfalls of any single perspective on learning problems, it is helpful to draw upon Erikson's case study model as first presented in *Childhood and Society* (Erikson, 1950/1963). Erikson's approach revived in a fresh and dramatic way two old truisms in the study of human development: first, that one must constantly keep in mind the total life situation of the person being considered; and second, that this total life situation or human life can be usefully trichotomized for purposes of conceptualization and scientific endeavor into biological, psychological, and social sectors. Erikson used the case study model to demonstrate how the processes of these three sectors interact to produce specific human behavior, and how the meaning and importance of an "item" in one sector is codetermined by its relevance to items in the others.

In *Childhood and Society* Erikson demonstrates the usefulness of the bio-psycho-social model in analyzing a neurological crisis in a child and a combat crisis in an adult. In the case of the child Sam, age three, the etiology of three convulsive seizures within a four-month period was traced by Erikson to a constellation of factors and events, including a constitutionally lowered threshold for convulsive explosiveness; the recent death of Sam's grandmother; his teasing and counterphobic disposition; a recent move to a new neighborhood in which acceptance seemed to require that he control his active, inquisitive, and retaliatory mode of response; and Sam's developmental stage, in which physical restraint and blocked curiosity are particularly intolerable (Erikson, 1963, pp. 25-37). One of the major objectives of the present volume is to demonstrate the usefulness of this approach—that is, of ferreting out critical biological, psychological, and social items for evaluation and integration—in the assessment of learning problems.

The term "assessment" rather than "diagnosis" is used advisedly, for the goal is not to isolate the cause of a problem but to identify the combinations and interactions of strengths and weaknesses in aspects of human functioning that have particular relevance to learning. These aspects can be dealt with conceptually as processes, structures, and events in the biological, psychological, and social sectors.

With this perspective, rather than diagnosing or ruling out "learning disability," for example, the neurologically based skills involved in learning are appraised as part of the biological self that the child brings to his efforts to learn, and an assessment is made about the extent to which they help or hinder these efforts. Similarly, the presence of neurotic inhibitions or conflicts about learning do not constitute a diagnosis but are seen as significant parts of the psychological processes involved in the child's learning; and the possible effects of cultural deprivation, family pressure, or indifference are important considerations in the social or environmental sphere. Strengths as well as weaknesses are sought out in every sphere, and the relationships of various relevant items within and between spheres are analyzed in order to clearly understand what determines the child's current status as a learner. This permits planning for the most effective changes, which are likely to involve curriculum, school and family attitudes and expectations, participation of the child in the planning and implementation of his remedial program, and perhaps psychotherapy.

An actual case may serve to illustrate this viewpoint. Joel is a 14-year-old boy living in an Israeli kibbutz, a cooperative farming and industrial community. Here children are raised communally with their age-mates while still maintaining close affective ties with their parents and siblings, whom they see daily. Joel is the third of five children and all are reported to have some kind of learning problem, as does their father, who never learned to read well.

Joel was referred to the kibbutz child guidance clinic with the complaint of long-standing difficulties with school work; he seemed unable to organize his work, tended to clown a bit in class, and had particular difficulties with written assignments. At the time of referral he was just entering the regional kibbutz high school. The referral was made by his former tutor in elementary school, and was mostly an afterthought, precipitated by the fact that she had decided to refer Joel's younger brother, whom she was then tutoring, for testing. She believed the younger boy to be very alert and intelligent despite a specific problem in spelling, and she wanted to know how to help him with spelling so that it would not interfere with his otherwise excellent academic performance. Joel, on the other hand, was perceived by her and the family as being not very bright; and although she did not know how the clinic evaluation might help, she felt that he deserved an evaluation too.

Joel was described as a well-liked, good-hearted boy,

somewhat lacking in self-confidence. His mother tended to nag him to work harder so as not to end up like his father, who had never mastered the basic academic skills. His father was the kibbutz electrician, and for years Joel had been collecting odds and ends of electrical equipment such as pieces of wire, fuses, and tools. At the time of referral, Joel was resisting the efforts of his high school tutor to help him with spelling and handwriting.

Testing revealed that Joel was of high average intelligence, with a fairly serious deficit in visual memory. His spelling was very poor, and his handwriting so jerky and rough it was often illegible. His reading and comprehension were fine, and he demonstrated very good powers of reasoning and judgment.

Testing also showed Joel to be somewhat impulsive in response to stress, to be anxious when presented with certain kinds of intellectual tasks, and to defend against the anxiety and threatened loss of self-esteem by expressing scorn for the tasks. By contrast, when given a difficult task that he felt he did have the ability to master, he worked diligently and patiently, and was visibly pleased with his success.

A variety of items from the biological, psychological, and social sectors are relevant to Joel's learning difficulty. The problem in visual memory, the poor handwriting, and the history of learning problems in the family suggest biological and quite likely genetic factors. Joel's identification with his father, who has a severe learning problem, and his highly vulnerable self-esteem suggest emotional issues around learning. His family's and teacher's perception of him as being not too bright, and the prevailing kibbutz ethic of maintaining respect and being an accepted member of one's group are social or environmental factors that may well relate to Joel's face-saving, scornful reactions and subsequent problems in school.

A learning disability specialist, or an optometrist, noting Joel's visual and visual-motor difficulties, would not be wrong in diagnosing some degree of learning disability and treating accordingly; but the picture would not be complete. If psychological and environmental factors were not also noted and dealt with, there would probably be little if any change. An analogous situation would occur were Joel to be seen by a psychoanalytically oriented psychologist or psychiatrist who noted only the psychological issues, the high IQ, and the family dynamics. Unless the visual memory problem was noted, related to the spelling problems, and dealt with appropriately, improvement would be hard to achieve.

This is not to say that one-area diagnoses and treatment programs are never effective. Some children are so afflicted in one area of functioning that by comparison other aspects of the learning problem are insignificant. In these instances, labeling and treating the outstanding problem is sufficient to bring the child to an adequate level of performance, with perhaps some attention to any secondary problems that have developed largely as a consequence of the major handicap. Sometimes, only after the major handicap is ameliorated is it possible to examine the rest of the system and see what subtle problems may have been coexistent or interwoven with, but masked by, the overriding difficulty. A hyperactive child who responds well to medication and can then begin to be taught; the identification of a family crisis situation that enables a teacher to adjust her work with a certain child according to what she now understands about his reactions; the diagnosis of a severe auditory disability in a child who is being taught by a system depending almost entirely on that skill are examples of these situations. In such cases, coexistent or interrelated difficulties do not necessarily have to be identified and dealt with in order that significant improvement be achieved.

Experience suggests, however, that most children with learning problems do not present one outstanding symptom, the alleviation of which is sufficient to allow for successful learning. Rather, like Joel, they present a variety of items related to learning difficulty from all three sectors of human functioning that converge, accumulate, and interact, then finally result in a learning problem. In such cases, it often appears that any of the significant items occurring in isolation would not by itself have created a serious difficulty, but in combination with other factors it becomes insurmountable. If Joel, for example, had had a visual memory problem but no conflict about being like or unlike his father in regard to learning, and no related problems of self-esteem, he might well have overcome the spelling difficulty by himself or by more readily accepting the help of his teachers. Conversely, in the absence of a visual memory problem, conflict resulting from identification with his father or a problem with self-esteem might have been avoided altogether or might have found expression in some area other than learning.

Because the majority of children with learning problems are not easily divided into categories labeled *learning disability, emotional problems, cultural deprivation,* or something else, it is essential that the persons responsible for the assessment of a child be aware of the interaction of the various influences on learning, even if they themselves cannot adequately assess all the variables involved. It is not necessary that any person become a multidisciplinary expert on learning problems. It is necessary that one has enough information about the major influences on learning processes so as to better understand the information received from one's own test and interview material, and to more advisedly recommend additional assessments from other disciplines. It is also important that the person be able to apply the clinician's understanding of behavioral processes. Finally, one must be able to translate the clinical assessment into an educational plan.

The following material is presented in three main sections. In the first, biological, psychological, and social determinants which, according to research and clinical practice, are most frequently associated with learning problems are reviewed. The second section deals directly with the issues, methods, and results of clinical assessment, with a discussion of diagnostic instruments and methods and a presentation of illustrative case material. In the final chapter an additional problem is discussed. This problem stems from the fact that the assessment of learning problems is generally done in clinical settings while the treatment or remediation must ultimately be carried out in educational settings. The result is a gap between assessment and educational planning which can defeat the best and most comprehensive assessment. In order to be useful, clinical findings must be tied to the specific academic and social behavior of the child in school and translated into actual educational practices. In an attempt to bridge this gap, some of the major issues of remediation and ways clinicians can assist in planning realistic, effective remedial programs are discussed in the final chapter.

In concluding this introductory chapter, a few comments on the general direction and character of the book are in order. It was stated earlier that one of the reasons for writing this book is to demonstrate the applicability and usefulness of a bio–psycho–social approach to the understanding of learning problems. There is another objective, that of clarifying the concept of learning disabilities for psychodynamically oriented clinicians working with children. During the course of our training, few, if any of us, received instruction or even exposure in this area. It is too new, and too firmly rooted in the discipline of special education to have crossed over into clinical child psychology, although in some places it begins to appear in school psychology programs. Until clinicians have some working understanding of learning disabilities, they cannot adequately consider the biological aspects of a comprehensive learning problem assessment.

Presenting learning disabilities to clinicians has necessarily resulted in some inconsistency of emphasis in the material that follows. A major part of the chapter on biological determinants is devoted to learning disabilities, and in subsequent chapters the material on Wechsler test interpretation and case studies sometimes presents the learning disability aspects in greater detail, not because they are more important, but because it is assumed that clinicians are familiar enough with psychosocial issues to allow for a briefer and more condensed discussion of these topics. However, the resulting imbalance does seem justifiable in view of the current needs of clinical psychologists engaged in learning problem assessments.

2

Biological Determinants of Learning Problems

When dealing with learning problems, the biological determinants under consideration are those relating to the formation, development, and operation of a healthy and well-functioning brain. These determinants can be usefully grouped according to Cattell's (1950) four categories of biological contribution to development. They are listed below in such an order that each term comprises the preceding ones, and adds new determinants.

Hereditary contributions are those derived from the normal genetic transmission of information from the parents' genes. Examples of hereditary disorders are phenylketonuria (PKU) and Tay-Sachs disease, both of which stem from metabolic defects that are transmitted via the combination of a recessive gene from each parent.

Innate contributions include both the hereditary and also the genetic effects of gene mutations and chromosomal anomalies. Down's syndrome (mongolism) is perhaps the most familiar condition resulting from a chromosomal anomaly that has a global effect on intellectual functioning.

Congenital contributions are all those occurring between conception and birth. In addition to normal and anomalous genetic material, they include the effects of conditions during pregnancy and the birth process. Among the conditions capable of affecting intelligence are maternal malnutrition, maternal illness (e.g., German measles or toxemia), drugs, irradiation, and the blockage of oxygen to the brain at the time of birth (Achenbach, 1974).

Constitutional contributions to development include all of the foregoing, as well as any alteration of body state by life experience (Cattell, 1950). There are numerous examples of life experiences capable of altering the body state and thereby affecting intelligence. Malnutrition (Winick, Rosso, & Waterlow, 1970) and sensory deprivation (Cassler, 1968) can impede brain development, in some cases irreversibly. Automobile accidents, falls, and direct blows can cause brain damage, as can inflammations resulting from encephalitis and meningitis. In addition, the immature brain is susceptible to damage from lead-based paint and other poisons commonly found in household substances such as cleaning materials and insecticides (Achenbach, 1974).

While it is not within the scope of this book to deal in depth with the highly complex issues concerning the nature of intelligence, it is important in view of the material that follows to note the position taken here on two of those issues: (1) the respective contributions of hereditary and environmental factors; and (2) whether intelligence is, as Tyler (1969) has phrased it, a "unitary trait or only a name for a combination of loosely related, separately developed aptitudes for special kinds of thinking" (p. v).

While it is the interaction of hereditary and environmental factors that ultimately determines the level of intellectual performance that will be achieved by any individual, this chapter focuses on hereditary and other biological factors in the interaction. In addition, the assumption is that an undetermined but important proportion of the variance in manifest intelligence is attributable to heredity. As Zigler (1966) has noted, "Studies of parent-child resemblances in intelligence, sibling resemblances, a variety of twin studies, and studies of children in foster homes have made it clear that inherited intellectual endowment is a much more important factor in intelligence than those who are environmentally oriented would have us believe" (p. 118). Achenbach (1974) reaches the same conclusion in his review of the research.

In regard to the second issue, that of unitary versus specific trait aptitudes, intelligence is perceived as a complex of many abilities that can be considered globally, in clusters, or as separate entities, depending on the aspect of intelligence under consideration. Within this chapter, for example, when specific, known genetic factors affecting intelligence are discussed, intelligence is dealt with as a global quality; when discussion centers on neuropsychological factors that have differential effects on various kinds of thinking and thereby limit intelligent behavior, intelligence is construed as comprising diverse aptitudes. (For fuller treatment of these issues, see Butcher, 1968; Cancro, 1971; Tyler, 1969; and Wechsler, 1975.)

According to present day perspectives on impeded intellectual development stemming from biological factors, three general forms emerge:

1. Mental retardation, a global intellectual deficit, persistent over time and ranging from mild to profound in degree
2. Learning disability, which by definition involves discrepancies among various aspects of intellectual functioning and is not a function of mental retardation (see Chalfant & Scheffelin, 1969; Lerner, 1971)

3. Maturational lag (or developmental delay), in which the rate of development of some intellectual abilities is delayed, and which carries the assumption that with time and further maturation the unevenness will level off

MENTAL RETARDATION

The conventional criterion for mental retardation is essentially a psychometric one. The distribution of intelligence in the population is assumed to follow the normal or Gaussian curve, with the lower three percent of the distribution comprising those who are retarded and the upper three precent those gifted or superior. The 1973 edition of the *Manual on Terminology and Classification in Mental Retardation* (Grossman, 1973) presents a definition of mental retardation as "significantly subaverage general intellectual functioning existing concurrently with deficits in adaptive behavior, and manifested during the developmental period" (p. 11). Subaverage general intellectual functioning is defined as performance two or more standard deviations from the mean of the test measuring intelligence (p. 11). The criterion of two or more standard deviations below the mean is coincidental to the performance of the lower three percent of the population, and makes the cutoff score 70 on Wechsler tests.

In fact, according to population studies, there is a bulge in the lower end of the curve, with somewhat over 3% scoring below 70. As both Achenbach (1974) and Zigler (1966) have pointed out in reviewing the literature on population genetics and mental retardation, a two group theory of mental retardation will account for that bulge and also contribute some conceptual clarity to the field of retardation. The two groups are the cultural–familial retardate group, who shows no sign of physiological defect, and the pathological group, whose mental retardation is clearly linked to a physiological defect. Since cultural-familial retardates rarely score below 50, it is suggested that they constitute the lower end of the normal curve of which the IQ range is 50 to 150. The distribution of intelligence within the defective group produces a somewhat normal curve of its own, with a mean of 35 and a range of 0 to 70 (Zigler, 1966).

The cause of retardation within the defective group may stem from any of the four categories noted above. Hereditary conditions include *epiloia* marked by skin and brain tumors and transmitted by a single dominant gene (and occasionally by new gene mutations);

phenylketonuria (PKU), a metabolic disorder transmitted through recessive genes; most cases of microcephaly; and others (cf. Gunzberg, 1972). Innate, nonhereditary conditions resulting from genetic mutation or chromosomal abnormality include Down's and Klinefelter's syndromes. Both of these involve the presence of extra chromosomes, Down's involving three rather than two number 21 chromosomes, and Klinefelter's involving an extra X sex chromosome. Congenital, non-innate conditions include hydrocephalus and cerebral palsy. Constitutionally determined mental retardation resulting from head injury, malnutrition, infection, and poison ingestion after birth may be mild to severe. This may be the hardest to accurately diagnose because of the dependence on history rather than visible signs. Such cases are more likely to be reported with unknown or uncertain etiology, or mistaken for cultural-familial retardation.

The majority of those in the defective group do not present the usual problems in learning disorder assessment and remediation. In most instances their IQs are below 50 and traditional academic learning is severely curtailed or ruled out. Their education is aimed at developing life skills and as high a measure of social adaptation as possible. Nevertheless, inclusion in the defective group does not automatically imply a noneducable status, and there can be wide variability in the capabilities of children with the same condition. This is well illustrated in the Down's syndrome group, with some children being very severely handicapped intellectually and others achieving good levels of work and academic performance. A moving illustration of the level that can be attained can be found in *The World of Nigel Hunt* (Hunt, 1967), an autobiographical account by an adolescent with Down's syndrome.

According to most estimates, the cultural–familial group comprises about 75% of the cases of mental retardation. This group is the subject of continuing debate on two major counts. The first concerns the heredity-environment dilemma. While there is agreement that mental retardation is found to be "passed on" within families, and that it is overrepresented among lower socioeconomic groups, there is as yet no generally accepted explanation of "the independent action of, or the relationship between, genetic and cultural factors in the etiology of cultural-familial mental retardation" (Heber, 1961, p. 40). A widely accepted model of hereditability is a polygenic one, maintaining that intelligence is regulated by more than one gene and that the combination actually transmitted determines the parameters within which environmental determinants will operate. Such a model is easily accepted by most; the argument arises over the presumed narrowness or breadth of the inherited parameters.

The second major argument about cultural-familial retardation concerns the nature of the lower intellectual ability. Some maintain that cultural-familial retardates are normal individuals of low intelligence, and that they are able to develop intellectually along normal developmental lines, albeit more slowly and with a lower ceiling to their ultimate achievements. Others hold that cultural-familial retardates do carry some physiological defect, which we are unable to determine because of the primitive nature of our assessment techniques. Several theories have been advanced as to the nature of this defect, most of them having to do with the anatomy or chemistry of the brain, some with the development of cognitive structures. The reader is referred to Achenbach (1974), Gunzberg (1972), and Zigler (1966) for reviews and discussions of the various theories currently being researched.

One consistent finding is that when retarded and normal children are matched for mental age, the retarded children still tend not to perform as well or at least differently. While this appears to support the arguments that the cultural-familial retardate suffers from a physiological or cognitive defect, there is another line of argument of which Zigler (1971) has been a major proponent. He argues that experiential and motivational differences can explain the poorer performance of the retarded, and cites the experimentally demonstrated evidence that retarded children are more *outer-directed* in their approach to problem solving, depending on cues provided by other people.

It has also been experimentally demonstrated that failure experience increases the outer-directedness and cue dependency in normal as well as retarded children (Sanders, Zigler, & Butterfield, 1968; Turnure & Zigler, 1964), and that the strategy of using superficial cues, which work against effective problem solving, is employed by some normal children as well (Achenbach, 1970, 1971). Thus, the argument runs as follows: retarded children, because of their slower rate of intellectual development, suffer considerable failure experience as they are continually confronted by overly difficult tasks in the normal course of daily life. Like all children with frequent failure experience, they tend to become increasingly dependent on cues from others in their problem-solving strategies and fail to develop a more independent, creative, and self-directed style. It is on this basis that Zigler and his associates have argued that the difference between cultural-familial retarded children and normal children of the same mental age is motivational, based on early and persistent experience with failure and the resultant outer-directedness, and not physiological.

LEARNING DISABILITY

The concept of learning disability is difficult to define since it is relatively new and still emerging from the work of theoreticians, clinicians, and researchers from numerous disciplines. (The concepts of mental retardation and maturational lag are also complex and subject to theoretical argument and debate, but in those two instances there is general agreement about the semantic meaning of the terms.) In this section, I shall briefly review the major theoretical and clinical constructs that contribute to current conceptions of learning disability, consider a number of theoretical and practical problems, and finally present a framework for considering learning disabilities that I have found useful in clinical assessment and remedial planning.

A Schematic History of Learning Disability

Several diagnostic and etiological constructs are embodied in the current notions of learning disability. Prominent among these are developmental dyslexia, brain injury (or Strauss syndrome), minimal brain damage, perceptual handicap, and perceptual-motor handicap.

Developmental dyslexia was first. It was referred to as congenital word-blindness for many years, beginning in 1896 with an English ophthalmologist (Morgan, 1896). Subsequently, Hinshelwood (1917) and Orton (1925, 1928, 1937) wrote extensively about this condition; and Orton (1928) coined the term strephosymbolia, meaning twisted symbols, and introduced the idea that problems in cerebral dominance were a major causal factor (1937). Since that time, *developmental dyslexia* or simply *dyslexia* has become the predominant term for referring to a condition in children whose reading problems are neurogenic, although it received little attention from child mental health and educational professionals until the 1960s.[1] In addition, there are parallel terms

[1] It should be noted that the term dyslexia is still not used by everyone to indicate only neurogenic etiology. Gibson and Levin (1975) and Bannatyne (1971) for example, include emotional, cultural, and educational determinants as sources of dyslexia whether or not they affect central nervous system operations in some specific way.

to describe presumed neurogenic problems in writing and spelling (dysgraphia) and in arithmetic (dyscalculia), which were identified and labeled first in brain-damaged adults, and then extended by analogy to children with no known brain pathology.

In 1947, Strauss and Lehtinen published *Psychopathology and Education of the Brain-Injured Child*, creating a new category of exceptionality to be distinguished from other categories, particularly from mental retardation and emotional disturbance. They describe the brain-injured child as follows:

> The brain-injured child is the child who before, during or after birth has received an injury to or suffered an infection of the brain. As a result of such organic impairment, defects of the neuromotor system may be present or absent; however, such a child may show disturbances in perception, thinking, and emotional behavior, either separately or in combination. This disturbance can be demonstrated by specific tests. These disturbances prevent or impede a normal learning process. Special educational methods have been devised to remedy these specific handicaps. (p. 4)

Strauss emphasized that the brain injury involved was exogenous rather than genetically determined, and had affected a potentially normal and structurally sound brain. He thus ruled out any genetically based retardation, including cultural-familial retardation. Many of the cases in his studies were children with severe behavior disturbances, and in attributing their distractible, perseverative, and uninhibited behavior to brain injury he was implying that neither faulty child rearing practices nor internalized psychological conflict could be responsible for the disturbed behavior. While some of the children in his studies are described as having visual-perceptual disorders or conceptual problems, learning problems are not a necessary condition for their inclusion in this group of children. The criterion for inclusion is presumed brain damage, occurring either before, during, or after birth. Strauss reasoned that although many of the children did not evidence signs of brain damage upon neurological testing, their behavior was similar to that of children who were known to have experienced brain damage. Strauss and Lehtinen recommended specific educational techniques for such children, with particular emphasis on cutting down distracting stimuli and directing motor activity into more productive and less disturbing activities.

While there was general appreciation for the pioneering efforts of Strauss and Lehtinen in identifying a category of children with unusual behavior who did not fit into other exceptional child categories, there was also dissatisfaction with their terminology. This was largely because of the confusion and anxiety it generated. To diagnose brain damage without any neurological findings and to convey that nonspecific and frightening term to parents disturbed many professional workers. The official statement of dissatisfaction with Strauss–Lehtinen terminology was the 1966 publication of a task force report from the National Institute of Neurological Diseases and Blindness (Clements, 1966). The report noted 38 terms from the literature; some focused on etiology (e.g., organic brain disease, minimal cerebral injury, organic behavior disorder), and others focused on behavior segments or consequences (e.g., hyperkinetic behavior syndrome, dyslexia, clumsy child syndrome, learning disabilities). The term "minimal brain dysfunction syndrome" was then recommended.

> The term "minimal brain dysfunction syndrome" refers in this paper to children of near average, average, or above average general intelligence with certain learning or behavioral disabilities ranging from mild to severe, which are associated with deviations of function of the central nervous system. These deviations may manifest themselves by various combinations of impairment in perception, conceptualization, language, memory, and control of attention, impulse, or motor function.
>
> Similar symptoms may or may not complicate the problems of children with cerebral palsy, epilepsy, mental retardation, blindness, or deafness. (pp. 9-10)

The minimal brain dysfunction syndrome (MBD) is similar to the Strauss syndrome in that learning problems are not a necessary criterion for diagnosis. The syndromes differ in that (1) the task force report took pains to separate MBD from major brain syndromes such as the cerebral palsies, the epilepsies, mental retardation, autism, blindness, and deafness; and (2) MBD etiology is not limited to exogenous brain damage. In addition to including genetic variations among possible etiologies, "the definition also allows for the possibility that early severe sensory deprivation could result in central nervous system alterations which may be permanent" (Clements, 1966, p. 10).

While the term MBD is still used, the tendency is to use it in medical, and particularly in neurology settings. MBD has become associated more and more often with hyperactive problems or the "hyperkinetic syndrome." In the meantime, the concept of learning disability, which had been developing almost simultaneously with the concept of minimal brain damage throughout the 1950s and 1960s, was focusing more directly on academic skill acquisition rather than behavior, although associated behavior difficulties were often noted. Samuel Kirk seems to have been the first to use the term (Chalfant & Scheffelin, 1969; Lerner, 1971), defining it in 1962 as follows:

> A learning disability refers to a retardation, disorder, or delayed development in one or more of the processes of speech, language, reading, spelling, writing, or arithmetic resulting from a possible cerebral dysfunction and/or emotional or behavioral disturbance and not from mental retardation, sensory deprivation, or cultural or instructional factors. (p. 261)

Those who subsequently defined learning disability tended to include emotional or behavioral disturbance among the *non*causal factors. Otherwise, the 1962 Kirk definition is a reasonable prototype for the prevailing concept of learning disability. It should be noted that the learning disability definition, unlike the Strauss syndrome and MBD syndrome definitions, has as a sine qua non some language or learning disorder.

Research in more focused areas of children's intellectual processes had contributed to the formulation of Kirk's definition. Particularly significant and representative were the groundbreaking efforts of Kephart, Frostig, Wepman, and Myklebust. Each pioneered investigations that continue to this day: Kephart in motor and perceptual-motor development and control; Frostig and her associates in visual perception; Wepman in auditory perception and aphasia; and Myklebust in language development. It seems fair to say that were it not for the investigations and clinical work taking place in specific areas such as these, the concept of learning disability (as distinguished from the more behavioral concepts of MBD and hyperactivity) could not have been developed.

Towards a Definition of Learning Disability

In 1975, as part of a larger effort to sort out problems in the classification of children (Hobbs, 1975), Wepman, Cruickshank, Deutsch, Morency, and Strother (1975) jointly authored an article on learning disability containing the following definition:

> *Specific learning disability*, as defined here refers to those children of any age who demonstrate a substantial deficiency in a particular aspect of academic achievement because of perceptual or perceptual-motor handicaps, regardless of etiology or other contributing factors. The term *perceptual* as used here relates to those mental (neurological) processes through which the child acquires his basic alphabets of sounds and forms. (p. 306)

The definition also cites areas in which inadequate ability constitutes a perceptual handicap, including auditory and visual discrimination, short and long term memory, sequential order of sounds and graphic forms, closure, temporal and spatial orientation, integrating intersensory information, and relating what is perceived to specific motor functions. In regard to etiology the authors state:

> Impairment of the processes involved in perception may result from accident, disease, or injury; from lags in development; or from environmental shortcomings. Impairment of perception may distort or disturb the cellular system and/or the normal function of one or more sensory systems. (p. 306)

This definition represents a sharpening and a refinement of the concept of learning disability. While it does not rule out the possible effects of "environmental shortcomings" (such as emotional, cultural, or educational deprivation) in producing a learning disability, that disability must be expressed through a perceptual or perceptual-motor handicap in order to be so labeled.

In clinical practice and in teaching, the expression "neurological inefficiency" is helpful to describe and embrace the array of difficulties dealt with in learning disabilities. This avoids the question of ultimate or original etiology, makes clear that it is a mental rather than emotional process, and covers all instances from the most mild to the most severe.

If the term learning disability is restricted to describing the nature of the behavior disturbance seen—that is, learning disturbances of a neurological character, without specifying etiology—we are then freer to consider the variety of etiological factors that could result in the behaviors noted. Here, as with mental retardation, we find Cattell's (1950) categories most useful and strikingly appropriate, for there is rapidly increasing evidence that learning disabilities can be related to biological determinants from all categories.

Genetic. Denckla (1973), Mattis et al. (1975), and Bannatyne (1971), among others, report high percentages of dyslexic children who have a history of the condition in the family. Bakwin (1973) reports on a study of 328 pairs of twins in which 97 cases of dyslexia were found among the 656 children, with 84% concordance occurring in monozygotic twins and 29% concordance in dizygotic twins.

Innate. Although there is no evidence that a specific genetic mutation causes learning disability, there is evidence that certain chromosomal disorders are associated with it. The case is clearest with Turner's syndrome, in which the individual has inherited one X chromosome but no other sex-determining chromosome. These individuals are always phenotypically female, and demonstrate a verbal-nonverbal IQ disparity (Shaffer, 1962; Money, 1964) in which they do well in language functions but poorly in tasks of perceptual organization, mathematics, right-left discrimination, and the like (Green & Perlman, 1971). Green and Perlman (1971) also report from their own work and from that of others (Money, 1964) some indications that men with Klinefelter's syndrome (in which there is an extra X chromosome) are more subject to language difficulties.

Congenital. Pregnancy and birth factors are perhaps the most commonly assumed causes of minimal brain dysfunction and subsequent learning disabilities. Bannatyne (1971) reviews these noting prematurity, anoxia, bleeding, drugs, X ray, excessive amounts of vitamins, faulty diet, fever, German measles, and difficult labor. Kawi and Pasamanick (1958) studied the hospital records of the birth of 205 boys with reading disorders, and 205 records of control subjects without reading disorders. Of those with reading disorders, 16.6% had been exposed to two or more maternal complications (mostly leading to fetal anoxia), as compared with 1.5% of the control group.

Constitutional. Postnatal factors such as head injury, meningitis, encephalitis, ingestion of poisons such as lead paint, and malnutrition are known to affect cognitive processes, depending on what structures and processes are compromised. The cognitive activities related to school learning are at least as vulnerable as any others.

As the concept of learning disability becomes more clearly delineated as a neurogenic disturbance, and the original cause of the neurological dysfunction linked to any one of a variety of hereditary or environmental events, there is more attention to the field of brain behavior. There is also a renewed interest in questions of neuroanatomy and neurophysiology as they may relate to basic academic skill acquisition. The interest in brain function is influenced not only by the continuing development of learning disability constructs but also by continuing developments in neurology and neuropsychology that allow for closer observation and a better understanding of brain-behavior relationships.

Neurological theoreticians are once again searching for connections between certain brain areas and related behaviors. This search had been abandoned for a long period, roughly between the two world wars, while a more holistic approach held sway (Sperry, 1975; Gardner, 1975). Besides the familiar notions that damaged cortical areas are related to specific learning deficits, there is, for example, a hypothesized attentional-deficit syndrome related to the reticular activating system of the mid-brain (Dykman, Ackerman, Clements, & Peters, 1971). A suggestion of Geschwind (1972) is that in some cases the disability is related to the small size of a particular region of the brain. In addition, new electronic, computerized techniques and equipment are being developed that provide data on brain activity not obtainable before, particularly in the area of hemispheric specialization. Biochemical theories dealing with the nature of the synaptic transmission of neuronal impulses are being researched (Bannatyne, 1971).

It will be many years before anyone can speak with certainty about the exact nature of structural and biochemical brain anomalies, and their effects on learning. However, it is not necessary to have this information in order to more carefully study the cognitive processes themselves. One of the most fruitful approaches to studying learning disabilities has been an information processing model. According to this model, the human adult or child is perceived as a selector of stimuli to which he attends, from which he derives meaning about his world, and on the basis of which he acts. Such a model accommodates the major concerns and trouble spots in children's learning, including attention, perception, discrimination, time and space orientation, memory, association, imagery, speech, and motor coordination. Bryan and Bryan (1975) have reviewed the research literature in three major areas of information processing applying to learning disabilities: visual processing, auditory processing, and cross-modal integration.

Most research in information processing is directed at some specific aspect (e.g., memory or discrimination), and consists of comparing different age groups or learning disabled children with normal controls. In clinical assessment, the instrument that most closely approximates the information processing model is the *Illinois Test of Psycholinguistic Abilities* (Kirk, McCarthy, & Kirk, 1968), generally known as the ITPA. The test was designed according to the communications model of Osgood (1957), but with some alterations. It is constructed to elucidate the quality of functioning in three major areas: (1) channels of communication, specifically visual-motor and auditory-vocal; (2) the psycholinguistic processes of reception, expression, and organization or integration; and (3) levels of organization (or levels of functioning), representative and automatic. One major difference between the ITPA communication model and the information processing model is the former's emphasis on language and psycholinguistic processes, somewhat to the exclusion of psychomotor functions. While the ITPA does include one subtest involving motor expression, the emphasis is on the use of movement to express an idea rather than on motor or perceptual-motor coordination. The difference between the ITPA model of learning disability and the Wepman et al. (1975) definition of learning disability, in which only perceptual and perceptual-motor handicaps are included, points up one of many as yet unsettled questions in this field.

Each of the three ITPA dimensions reflects a separate and significant dimension of learning disability. The first two dimensions combined are very similar to the Myklebust (1954) model of developmental aphasic disorders in children. The Myklebust model categorized children's language disorders on two dimensions: (1) whether the language disorder was receptive, expressive, or both; and (2) whether the stimuli presenting difficulties were auditory, visual, or both.

The third dimension of the ITPA, referred to by Kirk and his associates as the *level of organization* (1968) or *level of functioning* (1971), deals with the distinction between representational and automatic levels and constitutes a significant addition to the theory and clinical assessment of learning disabilities. Representational functioning involves mediating processes and, frequently, the conscious manipulation of symbols whose meanings must be understood and to which reasoning and judgment must be applied. Automatic functioning requires highly organized and integrated patterns of reception and response, less conscious and voluntary than representative level processing. Automatic level processing allows an automobile driver, for example, to carry on a conversation or plan the next day's activities while navigating through traffic, regulating speed to changing lights, or dodging pedestrians. If driving conditions are not routine, such as when one is first learning to drive or when unusually severe weather conditions arise, the driver will not be able to depend on automatic levels of functioning but will switch to more representational thinking, consciously analyzing conditions and planning responses.

This distinction between automatic and representational functioning is an especially useful one for analyzing learning difficulties. For one thing, automatic functioning is the foundation for all basic academic skills, including such skills as rote memory (for symbol-sound correspondence in reading and for number facts in arithmetic), visual memory and auditory sequence tracking (for reading and spelling), smooth and routinized movements (for handwriting and for arithmetic computation), and other neuropsychological functions that will be outlined and discussed in the following section. Another characteristic of automatic functioning is that it is relatively easy to assess in a child's academic performance, for it is largely immune to the effects of emotional disturbance and motivational problems.

Automatic level functioning is roughly synonymous with what Wepman et al. (1975) define as perceptual and perceptual-motor functioning. Whether or not the concept of learning disability should be confined to automatic level disturbances or should also include language and representational–conceptual problems may be determined more easily at some future time. Data are now being collected and analyzed with more scientific rigor than that which characterized research in the early stages of theoretical development.

An example of the kind of sophisticated research lately beginning to appear is presented in an article entitled "Dyslexia in Children and Young Adults: Three Independent Neuropsychological Syndromes," by Mattis, French, and Rapin (1975). It reports on a study of 82 poor readers (at least two grades below age level) "selected from a population of 252 children referred for evaluation of learning and behavior disorders by pediatric neurologists" (p. 151). The 113 selected met the criteria of verbal or performance IQ over 80, normal visual and auditory acuity, adequate academic exposure, and no evidence of psychosis or thought disorder. Of the 113, 84 were diagnosed as brain-damaged, and 82 as dyslexic (two or more grade levels below the level appropriate for age). Thus there emerged three groups: brain-damaged reader (N = 31), brain-damaged dyslexic (N = 53) and non-brain-damaged dyslexic (N = 29).

There are several distinguishing features in this study. One is its use of brain-damaged readers as controls, allowing deficits among the nonreaders to be more critically assessed rather than vaguely attributed to "brain damage." Another feature is its basic premise that dyslexia is not a specific clinical entity with a single causal defect or a single profile of abilities and deficiencies. The study isolated three syndromes accounting for 90% of the dyslexic children: language disorder, articulatory and grapho-motor dyscoordination, and visuo-spatial perception disorder. It will be noted that of these three syndromes, the first is language-related, and the second and third involve automatic level functions.

Neuropsychological Functions in Academic Skills

In clinical assessment, I have found the consideration of automatic level deficits to be very helpful. In contrast to Wepman et al. (1975), I do not consider automatic level, or perceptual and perceptual-motor deficits, to be the only deficits meriting the label of learning disability. There are a number of other difficulties related to verbal conceptualization or representational thinking that pose special learning problems for otherwise intellectually able children. A careful consideration of automatic level skills and deficits can significantly contribute to the clinician's understanding of the child's learning problem.

Clinical experience with several hundred children, examining their performances on standardized intelligence tests, achievement tests, learning disability instruments, and typical school tasks in reading, arithmetic, spelling, and writing, has resulted in the development of a list of processes or *neuropsychological functions* that are important in the acquisition of basic academic skills. (See Table 2.1.) These processes are akin to what Mykelbust has called the psychoneurology of learning (1968) and underlie much of the skill acquisition we expect of children in the primary grades.

Before considering in detail the categories and functions listed in the table, some introductory remarks are in order. The table contains virtually nothing new; only the table itself is original, that is, the particular compilation and distribution of items. The items are familiar variables frequently examined in traditional learning ability and disability tests such as the ITPA, Frostig, Wepman, and Detroit tests. The categories are also very familiar, although they are usually considered individually or perhaps in pairs. The two major receptive modes involved in information intake are visual and auditory. Language and movement are two major modes of expres-

Table 2.1 Neuropsychological Functions Important in the Acquisition of Basic Academic Skills

Visual	Auditory	Language	Motor
Perception	Perception	Articulation	Fine motor coordination
Discrimination	Discrimination	Fluency	
Memory	Memory	(Vocabulary)	Motor–spatial organization
Recognition	Recognition		
Revisualization	Reauditorization		Motor–temporal organization
Sequence	Sequence		

Intermodal Correspondence

sion. Table 2.1 provides a way of simultaneously looking at the automatic level processes most significant to learning and at the modal and input-output categories. Its usefulness is based on several premises: (1) that automatic level functioning is basic to the acquisition of basic academic skills; (2) that many learning disabilities are largely due to problems with automatic level functioning; (3) that there is no single cause or set of causes, and no single symptom picture or syndrome that can account for or describe learning disabilities; and (4) that learning disabilities occur in varying degrees from mild to severe, and are related to deficient functioning in one, few, or several specific neuropsychological functions.

The table also lists what to look at in assessing a child with a learning problem to determine whether or not a learning disability is a contributing factor. It is not a theoretical model of learning processes or learning disability.

In the following section, each of the items will be discussed and either explained or illustrated. When necessary, each item's relevance to academic skill acquisition and where it may be observed in the assessment will be pointed out.

Visual Processes

Visual Perception. This term is widely used and usually refers to a broad range of visual behavior. In the *Frostig Developmental Test of Visual Perception* (1964), for example, there are subtests of eye-hand coordination, right-left discrimination, and spatial orientation, among others. In using the term here, the objective is to keep it separate from visual discrimination and visual–motor activities, although at times that is difficult. In general, the term visual perception refers here to the person's *awareness* or *noticing* of the presence of some element or bit of visual information. The bit may be as small as a single letter or a period at the end of a sentence or as large as a full page of print or pictures. Perception in this sense involves recognizing that the visual percept has meaning, that it provides, either through content or structure, some information to the perceiver. An element's meaning does not have to be known or understood in order for it to be perceived. Thus, a youngster who can't tell a *b* from a *d* is having a problem in discrimination, and one who doesn't know the sound that *tion* makes is having a problem with symbol–sound correspondence; but neither is demonstrating a problem in visual perception. In both cases, the visual element is perceived or "noticed" as an information-bearing entity.

Some common problems of visual perception include: the failure among beginning readers to notice single letters that must be sounded in a word; the failure to notice linguistic markers such as prefixes, suffixes, a final *s, ed,* or *ing* in more competent readers; and the omission of small words. A more subtle problem is the difficulty experienced by some readers when they look at unfamiliar arrangements of material. Small children are sometimes visually distressed by seeing a full page of print, apparently because of their inability to see any inherent structure in the paragraphs, sentences, or words. Frequently, the same material copied in small doses onto sheets of paper can be read with relative ease. For example, a 5-year-old girl once experienced something similar when given a Stanford–Binet item at the 3½-year-old age-level consisting of twelve animal pictures on a card. She looked at it and said, "It hurts my eyes," and turned away. With coaxing and reassurance she looked again, and successfully matched all the pictures. One of the most common problems in reading is the failure to adequately perceive all or enough elements of the word. On the Spache (1972) word list, *cry* is often misread as *city,* although many of the children who make this error can read the word correctly when asked to look again carefully. It is the "noticing" of the *c* and the *y,* which they associate with the word *city,* and the nonawareness of the medial portion that causes the error.

A more common problem among older, more experienced learning-disabled readers is the inability to perceive an entire word instantly without breaking down and sounding out the parts. While the ability to sound out and reassemble words is a notable achievement in some young disabled readers, fluent, comfortable reading requires that they move beyond that stage to the point where they can automatically perceive the whole word.

Visual Discrimination. Difficulty in visual discrimination is most often noted in the misreading of a single letter that bears the same shape as another letter but owes its specific symbol value to its position in space. Thus, the letters *b*, *d*, *p*, and *q* may be confused, although as a rule it is the right-left dimension that is more confusing than the up-down one, so that *b* and *d* are more likely to be confused with one another than either of them would be with *p*. There are other discrimination problems having to do with small feature differences between letters—*h* and *n* are sometimes confused, so are *n* and *m*, and there are other common errors. This does not exhaust the possibilities of confusion, however, since some children have quite idiosyncratic "confusion pairs."

Visual Memory. There are two aspects of visual memory that are particularly important in academic skill acquisition: recognition and revisualization.

Visual recognition is the major technical skill required in fluent reading. The sight of the word should touch off immediate associations to its meaning without the need to sound out the word. In very young, beginning readers it is often visual recognition of the word that provides the only clue to meaning since whole word recognition often precedes knowledge of phonics and word attack skills. A deficit in visual recognition may be first noted in a child who fails to develop a sight-word vocabulary (sometimes called "look-say words"). In more proficient children with good phonic skills the deficit may be noted in their need to sound out many words letter by letter or syllable by syllable, rather than by simply "looking and saying." In essence, the problem seems to be that words seen previously do not leave a clear enough or strong enough memory trace, so that coming upon the word again is like seeing it for the first time.

Revisualization is largely synonymous with the more common term visual recall. The advantage of the former term is that it is somewhat more specific and descriptive of the process involved in remembering how to spell a word or set up a math problem in a certain way. When the memory does not come automatically, there is an effort to revisualize in the mind's eye what the word or problem looks like, in its gestalt and in its detailed features.

The most common academic problem associated with

revisualization deficits is in spelling. Most of us are familiar with the occasional experience of being unable to revisualize a word. We sometimes compensate by writing a test version to see if it "looks right" (for example, with one *l* or two, with an *i* or an *e*). In this way we turn a revisualization task into a less difficult recognition task, matching the written word and visual memory. The difference between normal revisualizers and those who have a deficit in this area is the number of words they cannot revisualize automatically. Many poor readers who eventually overcome their reading problems still have spelling problems. This suggests that while their visual memory has become adequate for recognition (matching a seen word on the page with a memory), it is not adequate for accurate revisualization.

Another area affected by revisualization deficits is arithmetic computation. Mental computation, totally without pencil and paper, requires the ability to create and retain a mental image of numbers in particular spatial relationships. Even with pencil and paper, the carrying over, borrowing, and recombining in all four basic operations (addition, subtraction, multiplication, and division) requires visualizing numeral images not seen.

Visual Sequence. Problems in visual sequencing appear most commonly in the perceptual task of reading and the memory task of spelling. In reading, it occasionally happens that a word is read with the sequence reversed, as in reading *saw* for *was* and *no* for *on*. It rarely if ever occurs that anything longer than a three letter word is read exactly reversed, and it seems safe to assume that even in the cases of exact reversals, the problem is essentially one of letters incorrectly ordered rather than one of reading backwards. In many instances the child seems to perceive all or most of the letters and to associate these too quickly with a known word with those sounds. Sometimes, children who have given up on expecting their reading to make sense produce a string of nonsense sounds. Depending on the child's experience and skills, he may sometimes be able to read the letters in the right sequence once his attention is called to the error and he makes an active effort to take them in sequence.

There are those, however, who cannot do this even when they concentrate on the attempt. A 42-year-old dyslexic man described his reading difficulty this way: "Some words, you have to cut them down and bring them out, and I can't do that." He has described his perception of a visual sequencing problem. Somehow, letters from the middle or end of the word appear at the beginning. A related problem is that of the middle of the word falling out. This frequently happens with multisyllable words in which there seem to be too many separate elements to handle at once. For example, a common error on the *Wide Range Achievement Test* (1965) reading subtest is the word *humidity* read as *humity*.

Visual sequence problems in spelling are seen in misspellings where all the required letters are present but not in the right order. Common errors are *girl* misspelled as *gril,* and *ie* and *ei* combinations confused when the rule is not known or not applied. These are common because phonetic sounding out does not give enough information. In some cases, in addition to visual sequence problems, there are also problems in auditory analysis. In such instances the child may remember to put in all the right letters but not remember their order. The child's inability to sound out the word while writing or accurately read what he has written prevents him from realizing that what he has written cannot be right. Usually, problems in visual-sequential memory are associated with more general problems in visual memory, but there are occasional individuals who well remember the elements but not the sequence or the general gestalt.

A related problem sometimes occurs in writing numbers, particularly the teens, where *16* will be written as *61*. The numbers 13 through 19 are particularly confusing for children with this problem. They hear the *six* before the *teen*, and since they do not have an accurate visual memory of the number, they tend to write the number according to the order in which the syllables are presented auditorily.

Auditory Processes

Auditory Perception. Problems in auditory perception are analogous to those in visual perception; children have difficulty sorting out part-whole relationships, and either fail to notice (perceive) specific parts or to integrate them into a recognizable whole. Thus, a child may not hear the single initial consonant sound of the letter *m* in the word *mother,* or the final consonant sound *t* in *cat,* or the *g* sound in the middle of the word *biggest.* Similarly, the child may not hear the rhyming recurrence of the sound element *all* in the words *ball, fall,* and *tall.* The converse situation is the problem of auditory blending, which requires that a child, after having decoded individual word elements from their graphic symbols to their sound equivalents, blend those separate sounds together and *perceive* the word they comprise. Children who may quite nicely break up the word *carpenter* into its three syllables, all of which they can pronounce, can run into difficulty in recognizing that they are speaking of a carpenter when they string the syllables together.

Auditory Discrimination. Auditory discrimination is needed to distinguish sounds, particularly phonemes that sound alike and may be easily confused in some contexts, such as d and t, b and p, f and v, and the short vowel sounds of i and e. A child who has trouble with auditory discrimination will have difficulty in knowing, for example, whether the word spelled *p-i-n* is to be understood as *pin* or *pen*. He might, as did one youngster I know, write on a greeting card, HAPPY BIRFDAY, DADDY.

Auditory Memory. While learning problems connected with visual memory are mostly ascribed to difficulties with long-term memory, the auditory mode presents difficulties in both short- and long-term memory.

Short-term auditory memory is used, for example, to remember a phone number you have said to yourself, after looking it up, long enough to go the telephone and dial it once. Unless you write the number down, most likely you will not remember it the next day. In fact, if there is no answer the first time you dial, and you are not concentrating on remembering the number while waiting for a connection, you will probably not remember it by the time you hang up. Short-term auditory memory (storage) deficits interfere with school work in a broad spectrum of activities. In early reading stages, children have to decode individual word elements and then run them together to perceive the whole word auditorily. To do this, they must remember all the sounds they decoded throughout the word until reaching the end. Since the sounds have no meaning in and of themselves there is no way to remember them except by rote (noncontextual or nonassociation) memory.

A child's school day is filled with instances of having to take in spoken information that cannot be instantly processed for meaning. It may take a few seconds before the child can turn his or her attention to it. In dictation, for example, if the listener is momentarily slowed down by having to erase or think about how to spell a certain word, and the teacher has continued dictating the list or instructions, the average student can store a certain amount of sounds for several seconds in their "raw" state until turning his or her full attention to them. A similar instance may occur if you are beginning to daydream during a lecture or conversation. If the speaker asks a question, and then calls your name, you are likely to be startled back to attention at the sound of your name. However, you will probably be able to recall some of the sounds you heard, run them through a second time to note their meaning, and perhaps even answer intelligently. It is short-term auditory memory that has automatically stored the incoming stimuli. A child with a deficit in short-term auditory memory may miss much of what is said in class. Some of these children may raise their hands and ask to have information repeated; but if they are told too often that they should have been listening, they will eventually get discouraged.

Problems in long-term auditory memory are analogous to those of visual memory; they are generally recognizable as being problems of recognition or reauditorization. Recognition of unfamiliar words, even when they are heard a second or third time, will be hindered if a child does not have a strong enough memory trace from previous experiences and cannot remember the context in which the words were used before. Reauditorization is involved in very early reading stages when the child has to associate a particular learned (and nonmeaningful) sound with a particular printed letter. Reauditorization is also necessary in order to learn any material by heart, to make use of spelling rules (e.g., *i* before *e* except after *c*), to learn the days of the week and the months of the year, to use relatively new words in one's native language or a foreign language, and so on.

Auditory Sequence. Auditory sequence is more dependent on memory than is visual sequencing. This is because visual sequences can be viewed while stationary in space whereas auditory sequences, by their nature temporal rather than spatial, cannot be perceived simultaneously or studied at leisure. Maintaining auditory sequence is necessary in stringing together the separate sounds that comprise a word in reading, and also in transducing the auditory elements of a spoken word into writing.

Language Processes

The language processes noted in this section do not bear as direct and mechanical a relationship to the acquisition of academic skills as do the processes in other categories. However, clinical and research evidence on the presence of language deficits in learning disabled children and the theoretical relationship between competency in spoken language and competency in the communication skills of reading, spelling, and writing make language processes important items for consideration.

Bannatyne (1971) noted, after reviewing literature on the presence of a genetic factor in language ability, that "language abilities in general and word fluency, spelling and grammatical abilities in particular are inherited to a considerable degree, as is their disability aspect, namely specific language disability or dyslexia" (p. 360). In addition to noting the frequency of an apparent genetic factor in this area, I have found as did Rabinovitch (1968) that some learning problems are characterized by a cluster of language area deficits and dysfluencies. Frequently noted difficulties are in the areas of articulation, speech fluency, and vocabulary.

Articulation. A number of authors have noted the association between reading disability and articulation problems, among them Mattis et al. (1975) and Bannatyne (1971). Although it is not necessary to accurately articulate in order to read and spell properly, there are a number of children with learning disabilities whose symptoms include poor articulation. In some cases the poor articulation appears to be part of a general language area deficiency; in others it appears more related to a cluster of fine motor problems. Some children with articulation difficulties also have an auditory discrimination problem. Thus, it seems that their difficulty in articulating some sounds stems from their problem in perceiving or discriminating those sounds in other people's speech. On the other hand, there are children with poor articulation whose auditory discrimination skills for all sounds is normal.

Speech Fluency. Speech fluency difficulties are recognized in hesitant speech, word-finding difficulties, mild anomias, and sequencing errors in which letter or word order is incorrect. Lack of normal speech fluency in learning disabled children has been noted by a number of researchers and clinicians. Denckla (1973) reported that 59% of her poor reader-speller group had difficulties with naming and word-finding, usually demonstrated through a slowness to respond and circumlocutions. On a naming test, Mattis et al. (1975) found a high error rate among their dyslexic subjects. Bannatyne (1971) cited a number of studies which indicate that disabled readers, as a group, have more dysfluency than normal readers. The deficits were in speed of association, accuracy of association, and verbal-label association.

Speech fluency involves a number of automatic level speech behaviors. Frequently, such problems as hesitation and word-finding difficulties fail to show up in everyday speech where the redundancies involved are so overlearned that errors are few and far between. In the more formal language of academic learning, where there is a need to use concepts that may be well understood but whose verbal label is less practiced, the problem may be more apparent. "It is the fact that *language must communicate the concept* that requires a search for verbal labels and these . . . have to be recalled in their own right. This can lead to tip-of-the-tongue, can't-think-of-the-word behavior, a common phenomenon with genetic dyslexics" (Bannatyne, 1971, p. 383).

A related problem is the inability of youngsters to correctly structure sentences though they have grown up in settings where the spoken language they hear is syntactically correct. Johnson and Myklebust (1967) discuss this problem in its most severe form, termed *formulation aphasia* or *syntactical aphasia* and described as follows:

> The children understand what they hear and can use single words and phrases but they cannot formulate and organize words according to correct language structure. They tend to omit words, distort the order of words, use incorrect verb tenses, and make other grammatical errors long after such skills are normally acquired. (p. 130)

Cases this severe are rarely seen by most psychologists in standard school or clinical settings, but similar problems are revealed in more subtle forms. Errors far less frequent and glaring are noted: clipped word endings, omitted words, confused idioms, the use of incorrect prepositions, the slight shuffling of word order, etc.

Vocabulary. In Table 2.1, the word *vocabulary* appears in parentheses because it is really a category of learned information rather than a neuropsychological process, and so it technically does not belong in the list. I have included it, however, because my experience and that of others (e.g., Bannatyne, 1971; Chassagny, 1966) has shown that in some learning disabled children vocabulary is notably weak or immature. This is sometimes revealed by the Wechsler or Binet vocabulary subtest, either in a low score relative to the general intellectual level reached, in the nature of the responses, or both.

Teachers are often more aware than anyone else, including parents and clinicians, that a child's vocabulary is not at the proper level, because they have a reference group, the rest of the class, as a standard of comparison. They also know the "vocabulary environment" offered in the classroom which the child is failing to assimilate. Like speech fluency, the problem is likely to be quite mild and subtle, unnoticed in everyday conversation but manifesting itself when school work requires the understanding and use of a more sophisticated vocabulary.

The problem in learning new words does not seem to lie in the difficulty or complexity of the concepts they represent, but rather in the rote memory required to remember which word stands for which concept. There is far less redundancy in the presentation and usuage of sophisticated words than there is with simpler, more commonly used words. For example, one 14½-year-old girl from an intellectually sophisticated family attending a highly challenging school could give good definitions for the words *migraine* and *migrate* but she could not say which definition went with which word.

Motor Processes

Although I agree with those who find some relationship between overall poor motor development and learning disabilities, such as Kephart and Ayres, there is a relatively limited group of motor skills that impinge directly on the academic skills concerned with here. Adequate gross motor skills need not precede fine motor development; we all know of many clumsy children whose academic learning skills are excellent. On the other hand, there are certain aspects of fine motor development that do directly affect the academic skills discussed throughout this book. These will be discussed here.

Fine Motor Coordination. The fine motor skills of most concern here have to do with handling the tools and conventions of writing. In the studies of deHirsch and her associates (deHirsch et al., 1966; Jansky & deHirsch, 1972), pencil use was a factor highly correlated with reading and writing difficulties. Pencil grasp and the ability to form letters smoothly and legibly, relative to age and general development, are basic skills easily observed.

Although the fine motor skills connected with writing have the most direct bearing on skill acquisition, there is some evidence that a wider range of fine motor problems tend to cluster in learning disabled children. Dencka (1973) found that 53% of her poor reader–speller group had fine motor anomalies, and Mattis et al. (1975) isolated an "articulatory and graphomotor dysco-ordination" syndrome characterized by problems in both articulation (though without apparent language deficit) and in copying figures (evidenced by gaps and overshoots of intersecting figures, irregularity of circles, and tremor).

> Most in this group were maladroit on tasks requiring rapid protrusion of the tongue and smooth repetition of buccal-lingual movements such as *ta, pa, ka*. Within this group were three children who could not protrude their tongues upon request and another four who could not raise their protruded tongue towards their nose without the aid of a mirror. (p. 154)

Motor-Spatial Organization. This term, like the one following (motor-temporal organization) is borrowed and adapted from Kephart, who has discussed the role of motor-spatial and motor-temporal systems in early, preacademic stages of development. (See Bryan & Bryan, 1975.) The term motor-spatial organization is preferred in this context to more commonly used terms, such as visual-motor integration, perceptual-motor coordination, or variations thereof, because it focuses the clinician's attention squarely on the problem of spatial awareness and organization. Three kinds of difficulties observed in this area are (1) maintaining proper space relationships while the major focus of attention is on the content of the written material or the process of writing it down; (2) a more serious problem with directionality, i.e., the child is uncertain about which direction to move the pencil in order to produce the desired symbol; and (3) copying from the blackboard.

The difficulty in maintaining proper space relationships is seen in the written language and in arithmetic. There are problems in keeping the size of the letters properly related to the lines on the paper and to other letters, in keeping a uniform space between words greater than that between letters, in setting off sentences from each other, and so on. In arithmetic, some children have difficulties in setting up the problems so that the columns are straight and the correct numbers can be added or subtracted from each other. As a rule, the children are aware of the need for proper spacing and correctly aligned numbers. However, the skill is not developed automatically and some children cannot focus enough attention on that aspect of the work when they are concentrating on forming letters or numbers, on spelling a word, or on the content.

The problem in directionality is *dysgraphia*, in the sense that a graphic symbol, which the child can recognize or revisualize mentally, cannot be automatically and accurately reproduced motorically. The most common difficulties are seen in younger children learning to write curvy and zig-zag letters and numbers (e.g., *s, z, n,* 5, 3, 2) and ball-and-stick pairs of letters (i.e., *b, d* and *p, q*). It is not clear to the child in which direction he must move his pencil so that the desired symbol will be left on the paper.

I have seen several learning disabled boys between the ages of 12 and 14; each now reads relatively easily but his handwriting still bears the signs of motor dysfluencies. By this time, all the boys have an automated set of symbols which they use consistently. (They all continue to print, insisting that cursive writing, or learning a new script, is too difficult.) However, their writing continues to be unsteady and they have developed some very idiosyncratic and jerky letters. One boy has great difficulty with smooth curved lines; his letter *c* is a 45 degree angle. Another has added a short wiggly line of varying lengths to the bottom of the letter *t*.

Copying from the blackboard requires maintaining an orientation to both the board and the paper so that one can look back and forth relatively smoothly; find the place; and, in older children, keeping writing almost all the while. Poor readers and spellers also have trouble copying because they must transcribe letter by letter rather than read words and phrases and then write from memory. However, it is not difficult to determine to what extent copying troubles relate to reading, spelling, and motor-spatial difficulties, once the child's reading and spelling are assessed.

Motor-Temporal Organization. Kephart specified rhythm, synchrony, and sequence as critical aspects of motor-temporal organization (Bryan & Bryan, 1975). This process affects the ability to write smoothly while maintaining sequence and synchrony with a temporal presentation of material. It is involved in the taking of dictation or the writing down of one's own thoughts.

An intelligent learning-disabled adult, for example, whose handwriting is still very rough, and whose spelling level is about 4th grade, wrote a short composition and spelled the word *problem* as *promblem, planet* as *plantet, Washington* as *Wastington,* and the phrase *that the sun* as *the the sun.* When the errors were called to his attention, he knew how to spell all the words he had missed. With many people the problem seems to be that the writing, the thinking, and the spelling require so much attention that synchrony is lost, although each operation may seem adequately handled in isolation.

Intermodal Correspondence

The four basic academic skills require the ability to perceive and appreciate the equivalence between visual and auditory symbolic representations. Thus, it is not enough that seeing the symbols *c-h-a-i-r* brings to mind the appropriate piece of furniture, or that hearing the word uttered does the same thing. It is also critical that the correspondence between the symbolic systems is perceived, consciously or not, and that there is easy transmission and integration between the visual and auditory perceptual systems.

An example will illustrate how critical this skill is and how complicated spelling can be when the process does not work automatically. A 21-year-old young man of average intelligence, who had completed a year of college, was asked to spell the word *equipment*. He wrote *equmen*. He was then asked to focus only on the very end of the word where a single sound was missing, and to see if he could say what was missing at the very end of the word. He could not. He was then asked to say the word aloud as he looked at what he had written and to try to find what was missing from the end of the written word. He still could not. He was then asked to listen to the examiner pronounce the word as he looked at what was written. This time he said he knew what was missing and added something to the *equmen*. The examiner looked, expecting to find a *t* added on, and found instead that the word was now *equmenment*. The same young man wrote *succest* for *success*, *pureach* for *purchase*, and *ordoor* for *order*. In each case, he seems to have substituted some rotely remembered visual unit; he was unable to coordinate, sound by sound, the appropriate sound and graphic elements.

In addition to the specific items in each of the four categories, there are two basic underlying skills affecting the accuracy and efficiency of automatic processing: speed and memory. There are a number of youngsters who, while able to deal with the information presented to them as well as most of their classmates, take longer to assimilate the material presented, associate it to other information, and produce an appropriate response. One pediatric neurologist, after examining a latency-aged boy with learning difficulties, gave the teacher the following advice: "Whenever you ask him a question in class, give him five seconds longer than you ordinarily would to answer you."

Some children have this kind of difficulty in learning basic arithmetic facts; they know the answer to "what is 5 × 7?" but it does not spring immediately to their lips when asked. They need a little time to think, to search perhaps for some visual or auditory image. They are several steps ahead of the child who must count to himself by five's, ticking off seven fingers until he reaches 35, or the child who remembers that three seven's is 21 and mentally adds on

14. Given time, rote drill, and adequate practice in applied situations, all of these children are likely to become more proficient in the speedy recall of arithmetic facts. The level of proficiency reached and the length of time it takes to reach that level will, of course, depend on motivation, general intellectual level, and various environmental circumstances, but it will also depend on the efficiency of neuropsychological functioning.

The same can be said for handwriting, spelling, and reading skills. However, it is worth noting that in reading and handwriting one can reach a level of technical efficiency relatively early which does not have to be improved upon in order to function adequately in any learning situation, whereas in spelling and arithmetic there is always more that could be mastered. The nature of these skills and the mastery of them will be discussed in more detail in chapter 8.

Before leaving this discussion of the neuropsychological processes involved in basic academic skill acquisition, it would be well to consider two other problem areas often noted in the literature as signaling learning disabilities. One of these is gross motor coordination difficulty, the other is difficulty in time orientation and organization. Time orientation and orgainzation refer to the ability to learn and refer to basic time constructs such as days of the week, months, and seasons. Very young children may have difficulty with the chronology within a day such as the order of mealtimes; and older children may lack a historical time sense in that they could not chronologically order, for example, the administration of Woodrow Wilson, the Middle Ages, the American Revolutionary War, and the birth of Christ.

While neither of these problem areas is directly involved in basic skill acquisition, they occasionally occur along with some other neuropsychological dysfunctioning more directly involved in learning. Specifically, disorientation in time often accompanies disorientation in space, and gross motor problems often accompany fine motor problems. In practice, these two problem areas may act as signals that other neuropsychological functions are compromised. On the other hand, problems of time orientation or gross motor coordination often occur isolated in children with no learning problem at all or in children whose learning problems are totally unrelated to difficulties in basic skill acquisition.

The Relationship of Learning Disabilities to Other Handicapping Conditions

Largely because early definitions of learning disability and minimal brain damage ruled out mental retardation and emotional disturbance as causal factors, it has been commonly held that only children who are not retarded, emotionally disturbed, or sensorily handicapped can be said to have learning disabilities. *The Task Force Report of the National Institute of Neurological Diseases and Blindness* (Clements, 1966) states: "The term 'minimal brain dysfunction syndrome' refers in this paper to children of near average, average or above average general intelligence . . . " (p. 9).

It seems clear by now, however, given the hereditary patterns and accidents of birth and early childhood that can result in learning disability, that children with emotional problems, low intelligence, or sensory deficits may also have learning disabilities. It is understandable that it was once necessary to rule out other reasons for learning failure in order to establish that some additional determinant does in fact exist. Having established that, however, it is critical that we consider the variety and interaction of determinants that may be operating within any one child. Awareness of the presence of a learning disability in a retarded, or emotionally disturbed, or culturally disadvantaged child can be critical in understanding the child's distress as he attempts to learn and in developing the most appropriate remedial measures and programs. Case examples of children with multiple handicapping conditions will be discussed in chapter 7.

Learning Disability as a Continuum Rather than a Present-or-Absent Condition

Learning disabilities can most profitably be seen as spanning a continuum from mild difficulties, or lack of talent in some particular area, to severe difficulties in which a number of neuropsychological processes are seriously affected resulting in a painfully debilitating learning handicap. When the handicap is severe, it is probably reasonable to label the child as learning disabled in the same way a youngster with severe emotional problems may usefully be thought of as an emotionally disturbed child. In less serious cases, we speak of a child "with emotional difficulties"; and an analogous designation for the mildly learning disabled would be appropriate. A child need not be labeled "emotionally disturbed" in some official or administrative way in order for one to consider how emotional problems might be interfering with his learning. In the same way, a child need not be perceived as a learning disabled child in order that one considers whether neuropsychological inefficiencies might be interfering with his learning. This specific issue will be illustrated with the case of Susan in chapter 7.

Crosby (1968) captured the sense in which neurological inefficiencies are as ubiquitous as psychological imperfections:

> It may be helpful . . . if we point out that no two people are neurologically the same or that no one is neurologically perfect. We all have eccentricities. We may have a poor sense of direction, or misjudge distances, or find mathematical computation difficult. We may be less than well coordinated so that we find tennis and golf and swimming more difficult to learn than other individuals. There are an infinite number of individual arrangements of neurological abilities. . . . As we grow up we become acquainted with our abilities and limitations. We plan our life and occupation around them.
>
> The dyslexic child is absolutely no different from the rest of mankind. Unfortunately, his neurological peculiarities happen to make it hard for him to read and write, and it is exceedingly difficult for him to plan his life around these limitations. (p. 7)

The severity of learning disability depends on the number of processes affected, and on the severity in each deficit area. The variation in combinations of affected processes is very great. Clinical experience and research (Bryan & Bryan, 1975) indicate that while there is some evidence for the existence of independent syndromes or symptom clusters in reading disability, there is still no general rule that a deficit in one area will be accompanied by other specific deficits. Thus, difficulty in some aspect of auditory processing, specifically auditory discrimination, does not mean that the same child will experience difficulty in auditory memory or in any other particular process.

Learning Disabilities as Deficits in Degree Rather than Kind

Most of the difficulties or errors in academic skill performance observed in the majority of learning disabled children are the same as those observed in nondisabled children. The difference is that the learning disabled tend to either perform as would younger normal children attempting to do the same task, or make the same but quantitatively more errors than their peers. Thus, their performances are in keeping with normal developmental progression and the difficulties are manifested as delayed mastery of a skill rather than anomalies. In their literature review, Bryan and Bryan (1975) noted that "when differences are found between good and poor readers at an early age, they are differences of amount, not type" (p. 230).

Any adult attempting to learn a foreign language, particularly one which uses a graphic alphabet different from the one the person knows, is likely to experience any or all of the difficulties I have discussed (when he or she tries to discriminate between vowel sounds, maintain visual sequence in attempting to read long and unfamiliar words, write smoothly and quickly, and so on). It appears then that the difficulties experienced by those with learning disabilities are nodal points in the development of communication skills in all human beings. The essential difference is that the learning disabled get stuck at those nodal points while the nondisabled manage to overcome them in an average period of time.

MATURATIONAL LAG

The concept of maturational lag carries with it the implication that some constitutional factor is influencing the rate of physical, mental, and/or behavioral development. The term is used in two different but related ways. One of these is highly specific and focuses on the concept of "embryonic plasticity" (Bender, 1958). The more common and relatively nonspecific use of the term is in the sense of "late blooming." It is often applied by educators and clinicians to children who are considered to be of at least average endowment and capability but who are slower than their age-mates in the acquisition of some physical or intellectual skill.

Maturational lag as a result of plasticity and slow differentiation is a concept used by Bender (1958, 1963) and further elaborated by deHirsch (1965; & Jansky, 1966). Their use of "maturational lag" differs from the more general meaning and use of the term. They point out specific aspects of cortical development, which have a wider range of maturational age than do other aspects of development and which result in lingering diffuseness and instability in body imagery, symbol recognition, the establishment of lateral dominance, and the performance of motor and linguistic tasks. They also take the extreme theoretical position that reading difficulties not otherwise accounted for by psychiatric disturbance, brain damage, global retardation, or environmental ill effects are due to this maturational lag. In other words, maturational lag is presented as the etiological explanation of learning disability. This position does not appear to be supported by others in the learning disability field, but there is fairly widespread acceptance of the idea that some instances of learning disability result from maturational lag (Wepman et al., 1975).

The more generalized use of the term is well illustrated by Ames (1968), who holds that the outstanding cause of school difficulty is immaturity. She argues that because grade placement is determined according to chronological rather than developmental age, immature children are pushed into performing tasks they cannot accomplish with success, although if given time to progress at their own rate they would do well.

While both the embryonic plasticity approach and the general approach to maturational lag are based on assumptions that no structural defect is present, they nonetheless differ in at least one important respect. Ames' general notion implies that the delay is within the range of normal development and requires a pressure-free attitude on the part of family and school. The Bender–deHirsh approach implies an atypical process and the need for intervention.

Knobloch and Pasamanick (1974) are critical of the use of maturational lag hypotheses, calling them tautologies rather than explanations, which do not help in understanding or ameliorating problems (pp. 238–239). It is my impression that the concept has often been used to protect children from more pejorative and discouraging diagnoses, particularly brain damage; thus it is frequently emphasized (e.g., Bender, 1958; Wepman, 1967) that the maturational lag involves no structural deficit. In more recent years, as learning disabilities terminology becomes more specific and refined, and more clearly differentiated from brain damage, there is less need to fall back on nonspecific explanations of maturational lag.

My clinical experience has been that while a number of children progress in some basic skills, at least enough to adequately handle their own grade-level school work, they continue to experience difficulty in other areas or in learning new skills which depend on psycholinguistic and psychomotor proficiency. For example, many delayed readers who have improved continue to have spelling problems, some continue to have handwriting difficulty, and many have trouble learning a foreign language.

It is my belief that, for many of these individuals, a neuropsychological deficit continues in the form of delayed learning rates. They become proficient enough in those areas in which they have had sufficient practice to achieve a level of competence equal to the task and to their peers. They catch up with their peers, not because their neurological systems have matured or improved in some basic way, but because their peers have previously reached a ceiling or adequate level of competence beyond which there is no need for greater skill. This is certainly the case with technical reading skill; beyond a certain level of perceptual ability, increased reading proficiency is a function of growing vocabulary and conceptual understanding rather than of improved decoding skills.

Clearly, longitudinal research and follow-up studies are needed in this area. One follow-up study touching upon this matter was conducted by Silver and Hagin (1966). Eighteen subjects had received remedial help and were followed up at ages 16 to 24. Of the 18, 10 had been assessed as having developmental rather than organic etiology. Among those in the developmental group, there was found to be a persisting failure to establish clear-cut laterality, although those subjects managed well in a number of other specific skill areas. In other words, the developmental or maturational lag group continued to demonstrate at least one deficit area.

To date, there is no way to distinguish between delay and deficit. That is, there is no way, according to the symptomatology or manifest behavior of the child, to know whether the problem will right itself in time so that the child will eventually catch up with his age-mates or whether he will need special intervention and remedial help in order to master the skills in which he is deficient. Even if one were able to distinguish between those who would eventually make it on their own and those who would not, there would still be the problem of what the child with maturational lag suffers because of failure experience and the resulting low self-esteem. Sympathetic teachers and open or ungraded classrooms are rarely adequate protection for the intelligent eight-year-old who sees six-year-olds surpassing him in daily classroom activities.

In practice, teachers tend to provide remedial help according to the degree of discrepancy between grade expectations and the child's ability rather than according to knowledge as to whether the discrepancy is a result of delay or deficit. For theoretical as well as practical reasons, that is probably the soundest approach, since it does appear that the greater the discrepancy and the slower the progress, the greater the likelihood that there exists a persistent deficit.

3

Psychological Determinants of Learning Problems

In this chapter, the psychological determinants of learning problems are looked at from three vantage points. First, there is a presentation of four broad categories for considering the relationship of psychological problems and learning problems. Next, a discussion of the interpersonal and the task-oriented aspects of learning follows. Finally, the psychological relationship between learning and the handling of aggression is discussed.

The discussion, here, is confined as closely as possible to *intrapsychic* emotional difficulties, with interpersonal and interactional issues considered in the following chapter. Undoubtedly the intrapsychic problems discussed here have their antecedents, and perhaps even their roots, in biological and sociocultural factors, and furthermore, are often supported and exacerbated by on-going family, cultural, and educational practices and relationships. Nonetheless, it is valuable to consider as carefully as possible the child's own personal involvement in his problems, what he brings to it, what he experiences, and what he finds gratifying and painful in his situation.

PSYCHOLOGICAL DISTURBANCE AND LEARNING PROBLEMS

The variety of psychological determinants of learning problems is legion. Almost any type of psychological disturbance, regardless of label, severity, or chronicity, may be accompanied by partial or general learning failure, or it may not. Thus, the ordinary categories of psychological disturbance—psychosis, neurosis, character disorder; obsessional, hysterical, mixed; oral, anal, phallic—will be of no help in cataloging psychological influences on learning problems. Neither will the severity of psychological disturbance be particularly helpful since some severely disturbed children do quite well at school while mildly disturbed children may have serious learning difficulties.

A useful way of cataloging the variety of psychological determinants of learning problems is according to the directness or intimacy of their relationship with the activities of school learning. Within this broad framework, it is often possible to note the role of specific psychiatric syndromes and to consider the relative effects of chronic versus acute, internalized versus reactive, and severe versus mild disturbance.

The following are four broad categories of relationships between psychological disturbance and learning problems, moving from the most distant and indirect relationship to the most intimate:

1. Psychological disturbance that is so encompassing or preoccupying that it prevents the child from cathecting or becoming involved in learning situations. In this category, the obstacle to learning has nothing to do with any aspect of school or learning.
2. Psychological disturbance that interferes with the child's ability to concentrate on school work for extended periods of time, or to tolerate the frustrations resulting from the ordinary demands of school life—time pressures, conformity to decisions made by the teacher or the peer group, occasional failure, or less than total success. The general problem here is inadequate ego controls, and the main difference from the first category, motivation. In this category, the child *is* motivated (to learn, belong, or be accepted in the school setting), and anticipates some pleasurable outcome from his involvement. However, the child has difficulty delaying gratification and tolerating any situation that fails to respond to, and deal with, his individual needs.
3. Psychological disturbance that appears in the form of neurotic reactions to specific circumstances, or as a more generalized character problem. This kind of psychological disturbance creates learning or behavior problems in selected circumstances that specifically touch on the child's particular problem. Unlike children with problems in the second category, children in this category do not suffer from a generalized intolerance of frustration, and can handle some difficult situations quite well.
4. Psychological disturbance that is focused specifically on some aspect or aspects of school, resulting in a distortion of the child's perspective and an inability to cope with them rationally and effectively. The difference between this category and the previous one is mainly one of degree, both in the extent to which the school issue has become central, and in the degree of distortion in perceptions of neutral or benign stimuli.

Before considering each category in more detail, some general remarks about this scheme are needed. The categories are not mutually exclusive in regard to a given child. A child may have periods of noncathexis of school, when he takes no part in what is going on around him, and other periods in which the child attempts to be part of the classroom situation or attempts to do a certain academic task and suffers from an inability to tolerate delay, frustration, disappointment, or failure. Another child may be quite involved in school life and present a specific kind of reaction to certain stress situations there, but under particularly trying circumstances that child may withdraw interest altogether or seem to fall apart over any small difficulty.

This scheme is applicable to seriously and moderately disturbed children, as well as psychologically healthy children during times of situational or developmental crisis. The category that best describes the child's situation will not be determined by the seriousness or chronicity of the disturbance, but, at the same time, these characteristics will be noted as the child's behavior *within* the category is described and discussed. In this way, a single categorizing scheme can be used for all cases without masking important information.

A major advantage of this scheme is its usefulness to teachers since it focuses on aspects of school that are relevant to the problem and may be amenable to intervention. This is in contrast to traditional classifications of psychological or social pathology, which while accurate in what they describe and perhaps even useful to mental health clinicians, do not relate themselves to the problem as it effects the child's school behavior, and do not provide information that might direct the teacher's approach. Teachers, and many astute clinicians, have long known the futility, for school purposes, of psychological reports pointing to "unmet oral needs" or "passive-aggressive personality."

A detailed discussion of each category, noting the kinds of behavior that each includes, some frequent reasons for such behavior, and various forms of school response or intervention, follows below.

Psychological Disturbance that Prevents Cathecting School

Referred to here are instances of almost total psychological withdrawal from school to the degree that both the demands and gratifications of the school situation are ignored in the interpersonal, as well as the task achievement, dimension. Children in such a state appear listless and withdrawn, and seem to daydream a great deal. They may or may not respond to the remarks of teachers and children. They may or may not do lessons, depending on which response, compliance or refusal, allows them the greatest freedom to remain shut up within themselves and cut off from their surroundings. These are not children who are stubborn, angry, discouraged, or hostile, who refuse to work or to relate out of fear of failure or a wish to retaliate. These are children who have no interest in school for reasons of their own which have nothing whatever to do with school, past, or present.

There are two groups of children within this category. One group comprises very seriously disturbed children (usually labeled autistic, schizophrenic, or psychotic) for whom lack of interest in school is a relatively consistent and long-standing condition. The other group includes those less disturbed, or otherwise well-adjusted children who undergo some severe situational crisis, such as death or divorce in the family, accident or illness, and as a result temporarily withdraw. The severely disturbed children will not be discussed here. They rarely attend school as we know it, and when they do, the problems that arise have to do with encouraging these children to relate to people and events in their simplest social contexts. They do not present learning problems in the sense in which the term is used in this volume. Those who eventually become invested in school often subsequently present the various kinds of learning problems discussed in later categories.

Children who temporarily withdraw their interest are seen far more frequently. A temporary or episodic withdrawal may be more a reaction to environmental events rather than a reflection of internal personality organization. However, the specific forms of behavior and the length and frequency of the periods of noninvolvement will certainly be functions of individual personality organization.

This group of children includes two types with which teachers are familiar. There is the well-adjusted child, generally attentive and successful in school, who withdraws in response to some life crisis and can be expected to return to his normal school behavior within some reasonable period of time. There is also the frequent daydreamer, who "tunes out" of classroom activity from time to time, distracted by chronic problems or compelling fantasies.

In the case of an ordinarily attentive and academically successful child whose emotional withdrawal is a reaction to a severe situational crisis, the teacher can assume that the withdrawal is only temporary and that the child will spontaneously, though perhaps gradually, return to his or her former level of school involvement. The teacher can help by being sympathetic and by trying to make school activities as tempting and gratifying as possible during the difficult period.

In the case of a child prone to withdraw from time to time, the teacher has a considerably more active role to play. This child retreats into a personal world at various times of the school day in the midst of learning or recreational activity, seemingly unprovoked and regardless of group size or the nature of the activity. The withdrawal cannot be linked to any particular kind of environmental provocation (e.g., task failure, peer rejection, conflict-arousing subject matter), but is apparently triggered almost entirely by inner mechanisms. One sees such behavior from time to time among the youngest children attending school, whose attention is still focused on home and mother and whose interest only sporadically turns to school. Patient, sympathetic, and sensitively active teachers know how to gently guide such children into various classroom activities that will catch their interest.

When older children demonstrate similar withdrawal behavior, the problems are usually more serious and entrenched. They are not simply solved by getting accustomed to a new class or teacher. For example, Roger, age 10, was prone to tuning out in class, although in other ways his behavior and skills had improved by the time he entered the fourth grade. He suffered serious emotional deprivation as a child due to his father's death shortly after Roger's first birthday and his mother's severe depressive reaction. His mother's depression, which continued for several years, caused her to neglect Roger, who, as a result, grew more and more withdrawn. Psychotherapy was helpful to both mother and son, and Roger began to come out of his cocoon, make friends, and develop interests in animals and nature.

The tendency to withdraw continued, however, in and out of school. Roger's classroom teacher found that she had to keep some fraction of her attention on him all the time in order to bring him back when he drifted off. It became an automatic habit for her, as she scanned the room, to see what he was doing, and to catch his eye or touch his shoulder when necessary. She liked him, enjoyed him, and didn't feel burdened. By contrast, Roger tended to have a difficult time with the specialty teachers for music, art, and gym, who had to relate to hundreds of children in the course of a week and found his inattentiveness irritating.

Unlike Roger, who was able to relate to other children and share common interests, some of these children are very much alone both in and out of school. In some instances they have developed obsessional, preoccupying interests in a particular topic or activity, which serve to fill their time and thoughts and can occasionally be used by a sensitive teacher to establish a trusting relationship. One 12-year-old boy had a passion for opera. He listened to at least one complete recording a day, read the opera magazines, and knew the personal and professional histories of many opera luminaries. He related to people mostly through talking about opera, felt personally accepted and liked by those who shared his interest, and rationalized that his nonacceptance by other children was due to his liking opera. By contrast, some children have no apparent interests and spend many hours a day watching television.

Many children who withdraw have a history of academic difficulties from the early grades, and are moderately or severely deficient in basic skills. It can be safely assumed that some level of primary learning deficit and a tendency towards withdrawal have interacted in these cases, worsening both problems. As these children grow older, they are less likely to be able to develop better social or academic skills if they are left to manage on their own in the regular classroom. However, some of these children do well enough to get by despite low levels of achievement and do not become candidates for special education intervention. Since their tendency is to withdraw quietly and not behave in a way that actively disturbs the classroom, they will be tolerated longer than children with equivalent achievement records who act out.

Psychological Disturbance
Due to Weak Ego Controls

Children in this category tend to be as interested in school as they are in any other aspect of their lives, and oftentimes more. There is interest in learning, peer acceptance, or parent and teacher approval, and there is pleasure in academic and social success. What is lacking is the emotional stamina to maintain these interests and to pursue these pleasures in the face of mild frustration, loneliness, boredom, rejection, and any other negative feelings that are part of daily life in school. In some children there are also problems with resisting internal as well as external stresses, leading to a distortion or personalization of the academic material. In general, the problem is one of weak ego controls which prevent adequate social and emotional equilibrium and sustained attention to school work.

Of all the four categories, these problems are most like those experienced by young children whose level of emotional maturity is not yet equal to that of the rest of their group. Thus, if the teacher has not smiled at him directly that day, a little boy may come home saying the teacher does not like him; if a little girl has not had her turn in the play corner, or if her name-tag pin is sticking her, she may be unhappy about school in general. When children are asked at circle time if anyone in the group has ever seen horses like those in the picture book, a child may launch into a rambling tale about his grandparents' farm, what they eat there for breakfast, and when the family is planning to visit again.

Such low frustration level and personalization difficulties, which teachers witness in small children and can usually help them overcome with time and patience, are of greater concern when they occur in older children and are further removed from the age-appropriate behavior of the class. The inability to sit and carry out an assignment within the child's intellectual capabilities; a continuous need for direct attention from the teacher or from classmates frequently achieved by calling out or poking or following the teacher about; displays of temper, tears, or despair when things do not go well—these are among the characteristic behaviors of children with weak ego controls.

David was 4 years old when he was observed in nursery school. Although he was at an age when one expects much immature behavior will be outgrown, David's situation seemed different. His behavior was far more like that of a 2-year-old than a 4-year-old, and was consistent with his history of several foster and adoptive placements between the ages of 2 and 3½, and the parents' description of his clinging to them. He never played with any of the children; he was always to be found next to the teacher. If the teacher had time to engage him in some task with her or alongside of her, he would generally cooperate; if she was busy, he would simply sit or stand beside her.

At one point during the observation, the teacher wanted David to work on zipping and unzipping his jacket, which he had not taken off that day. She covered her face with her hands and said to him, "Zip up your jacket and surprise me." He sat looking at her covered face. She continued to urge him to zip his jacket, which in fact he did in a desultory manner. However, he was clearly more concerned with seeing her face and finally got up and walked around to the other side of her, apparently in hopes of seeing her better from there. Like a toddler playing peekaboo, he was more concerned with the face behind the fingers than with any task or activity, whether that task was within his capacity or not.

An extreme example of personalization was noted in testing a 6-year-old child, Gila, on the original WISC, which includes the question, "From what animal do we get milk?" She answered, "A cat." Further probing indicated that she knew that milk comes from cows and that baby kittens are the ones who get milk from cats, but the primacy of her concerns about mothering had led to a loss of objectivity and a highly personalized and distorted handling of the question asked of her. If such is the case in a one-to-one testing situation, one can imagine the degree to which she is likely to give way to inner feelings and fantasies and lose adequate control over thought processes during classroom lessons.

Ned is a bright 9-year-old in the fourth grade. He scores well on intelligence and achievement tests, and his teacher has no concerns about his ability to understand the classroom material and discussions. However, for days or weeks at a time, he has great difficulty in sitting still in a discussion or doing a written assignment. He asks to go out for a drink or to the bathroom repeatedly during the course of the school day, he bothers other children with remarks and nudges, and he either barges into groups or hangs on the side afraid to venture in. Assessment indicated the presence of a painful conflict between Ned's wishes for closeness and a simultaneous fear of harm from those who were close. Ned's behavior in school symbolized this conflict and acted as a defense by maintaining a continual barrage of sound and action.

The three children, Gila, David, and Ned, have different kinds and varying degrees of emotional difficulty, widely differing family and cultural backgrounds, and intellectual capabilities ranging at the time of testing from low average to nearly superior. What they have in common is the general effect of their emotional problems upon school adjustment. Unlike the children described in the first group, they care about school, would prefer to be there than to stay at home, and look forward to something interesting or pleasurable occurring there. But they have difficulty tolerating the general demands of group life, the less than total attention from the teacher, and the need for sustained and focused attention to the task at hand. These demands are not highly specific to school, and as a rule these youngsters have the same kinds of difficulty outside of school as well.

If a teacher knows that the child's difficulty is related to a generally low level of emotional control and stability (rather than to some specific situational crisis or lack of investment in school or a particular aspect of school life), he or she may find it easier to anticipate the critical times and situations in the course of the day hardest for the child to tolerate. Poorly controlled children may have difficulty in adapting to long individual work sessions, too much time with a group, abrupt changes of activity, discussions about particularly stimulating or frightening subject matter, disruption of routine, an argument between other children, exciting trips or productions.

When the difficulty is largely in the area of behavior controls, the teacher is most easily made aware of it, whether the reaction takes the form of withdrawal or disruptiveness. Affective disturbance, in the form of temper tantrums, tears, or a scowling face, is also fairly easily noted. However, there are some youngsters whose sadness, worry, or anger does not take any specific overt or dramatic form and requires closer observation. Thought distortion, overpersonalization, and general loss of objectivity in relation to subject matter will be apparent when the child is communicating his or her thoughts through class discussions or written assignments. Even then, interpreting the responses as emotionally based rather than as simple nonsense or wrong information requires some sensitivity and sophistication, as well as the time to find out what the child actually knows about the subject. In spite of the difficulties in recognizing and responding to the range of ego failures, some awareness of a child's vulnerability to stress, of situations the child finds most difficult, and of the forms the poor functioning is likely to take should help teachers in responding to the child promptly and supportively.

Psychological Disturbance Related to Specific Aspects of School

The majority of school and learning problems with significant psychological determinants belong to this category. The children tend to have problems that are somewhat encapsulated and that mainly create difficulties with aspects of school life that impinge on these problems. The situation is like having a sore arm or leg muscle that hurts only when certain movements are made. Then, the arm or leg hurts a great deal, often resulting in expressions of pain and the development of protective and compensatory maneuvers.

In some cases the problem is perceived as existing only at school, although this is usually because the behavior involved is consonant with family interactions and expectations and therefore not experienced by the parents as disturbing to themselves or the child. Further exploration almost always results in the revelation of similar behavior and reactions at home or in the neighborhood, although some parents may not acknowledge "problems" in these areas even after specific incidents, reactions, or relationships have been cited.

The children almost invariably have certain social, psychological, and academic strengths. A child who will not produce any homework will participate actively and constructively in class discussions; one who becomes distressed when presented with new and difficult work is able to tolerate long periods of complicated and tedious work without complaint, provided it is in some way familiar; one who whines and clings to the teacher is a stable leader in the peer group.

Before presenting some representative problems of children in this category, it would be useful to consider some of the characteristic demands—academic, social, and emotional—that school places on children. There are demands to concentrate, learn the material required by the curriculum, produce acceptable work, and show progress over time. There are the ongoing demands to accept the authority of the teacher as the arbiter of acceptable work and behavior, and to accept one's role as part of a group. There are times when one must work independently of teacher or group assistance, and other times when one must work under teacher direction or as part of a group. Sometimes one must perform individually without the protection of the whole group, and at other times one must conform to group wishes and procedures. There are occasions when one must confront new and difficult challenges in work, and occasions when one must memorize facts and repeatedly practice tedious drills and exercises. Insight and quick understanding are rewarded at one time, and careful, neat, exacting, and complete work are required at another.

A note of caution is in order regarding the following case studies. Each is presented to highlight specific learning problems, and in no sense can they convey the richness, complexity, and multifaceted nature of the child's character, life circumstances, or even the child's problems. A persistent effort has been made in relating the following material to avoid oversimplification and overgeneralization in interpreting the connections between the psychological problems and the learning problems. However, it is easy for both the writer and reader to begin to feel that a single explanation or interpretation explains all. No single issue can explain any long-standing serious difficulty, in learning or in anything else. On the other hand, partial and tentative explanations are invaluable in their own right, and contribute to a fuller and more comprehensive picture. They often provide a first handle for understanding and intervention at school, usually in the form of a different attitude and set of expectations on the teacher's part, and occasionally generate new procedures that may involve the family as well as the child and the school.

Teddy was 7 years old and in the second grade when he was referred for psychological evaluation by his pediatrician because of learning problems. The major difficulty was in reading, which Teddy accomplished very slowly. He was a small, attractive, appealing boy; he was very bright, and well liked by other children as a friendly and sensitive companion. He rarely assumed a leadership role in the group. He had a good fund of information, participated actively and willingly in discussions, and was doing well in arithmetic. He was in a multigraded classroom of kindergarten and first and second grade children; there was easy access to outside play space; and the programs were sufficiently individualized so that at any given time one was likely to find children in various places, both inside and outside the classroom.

Teddy was getting extra reading help and both his classroom and reading teachers described the same process: he would plod through the reading, going slowly but managing to read fairly accurately; after a short page or two he would begin to sigh, he would furrow his forehead and read more and more slowly. Teddy rarely complained openly. The teachers were reluctant to press him since he seemed to be suffering so much and they were afraid this would only intensify his discomfort and dislike of reading. So, they tended to interrupt the lessons early and suggest he go out in the yard and play, or find some other activity in the room.

Teddy's parents had recently divorced and he and his older brother and sister lived with their mother. Interviews and testing indicated that regressive wishes and concerns were very strong in Teddy, aided by his father's absence and his mother's general feeling of helplessness in controlling the children. Teddy never misbehaved in any open or assertive way; a major issue was his refusal to get his hair cut, to wash up and bathe on schedule, and to wear anything other than jeans and a dirty old gray sweater to school every day.

It was Teddy's response to the question, "Which animal would you most like to be if you could be any animal in the world?" that provided a major clue to the resolution he had found for his conflicts and to the connection between this resolution and his learning problem. His answer was striking, both in the vivid graphic image it presented and in the rarity of its occurrence. He wanted to be "an ant," a response this writer had never heard or read about in the protocols of several hundred children, although it is occasionally mentioned as the animal one would "most not" want to be. In response to the question, "Why?" Teddy explained, "Because an ant is so tiny, and you know those little holes in the sidewalk? Well, if some big scary thing or person came along, I could just scrunch myself down into one of those little holes, and then it would step over me and I wouldn't get squished." By this explanation, Teddy was telling us that he wanted to be small, nonassertive, and noncombatant in the face of adversity; to pull away, duck down, and wait for the threat to go away or slide by over his head. That is what he did with reading lessons, the only part of the school day which held some difficulty for him. Rather than struggle to overcome the problem, Teddy would "scrunch" lower and lower in his seat until the teachers would stop the lesson and send him out to play.

A few additional facts and comments about Teddy will round out the picture. His reading difficulty was partly due to a problem with immediate word recognition, so Teddy had to sound out many words that most children of his intelligence and language skill simply look at and know. Without the motivational difficulty he would probably have overcome the mild delay in recognition without any special attention. Without the recognition problem Teddy's motivational difficulties might have remained undiscovered for several more years, or as long as the curriculum presented only areas of study which he could understand and master with little more than good intelligence and a good fund of knowledge.

The assessment led to some specific remediation suggestions for both Teddy's mother and his teachers. First of all, Teddy's response to the question of which animal he would "most not" want to be was "a pig" because they are "dirty and smelly." This suggested that he might be ready to give up his regression into unkemptness if he had enough strong support from his mother. His mother was encouraged to take a firmer stand about what constituted appropriate grooming and attire, and she reported that Teddy had responded positively and even enthusiastically to the new demands. There were a number of indications that Teddy was ready and willing to respond to difficulties in a more hardworking, assertive way if asked to do so and if supported through his efforts.

Two specific suggestions were made to his teachers. One suggestion was to assign Teddy an expected amount of reading at each lesson, either by pages or by time, and to encourage him when he flagged by reminding him that though it was hard he could do it. In order to enhance Teddy's general self-image as a successful worker, it was suggested that he be given homework assignments which would be due the teacher the following morning. They were to consist of work he could do on his own, and although his mother might check his work if he wished, he was to do it by himself. He was given handwriting practice, which he needed, and a few arithmetic problems—all of these tasks he could do independently.

In Teddy's case, the suggestions were followed and they worked, at least in the short term. He responded very positively to the homework and clean-up campaigns, accepted the reading contract without a sigh or a frown, and began to read with more energy and to accomplish more. However, while it was felt that the learning difficulty was essentially overcome, at least for the present, it was not assumed that success in this area would work well enough to have a significant effect on the general family situation and Teddy's role in it. Therefore, he and his mother were referred for psychotherapy.

Katy was also 7 years old and in the second grade when she came to the attention of the school psychologist at midyear. It was discovered that the problems she presented had been continuing since the beginning of the year, but they had become extreme at the time of referral. The problems had worsened when her teacher was about to leave to have a baby and the replacement teacher had begun working a week or two earlier in order to provide a sense of continuity for the students. Katy's problems were mostly behavioral and associated with being asked to do work. She would scowl, turn her back on the teacher, occasionally crumple her paper and throw it on the floor, or gash holes in it with her pencil. When offered help with a paper, Katy refused or became stony faced. The first teacher had been able to cajole her into doing most of her work, and the relationship between them was manageable. The replacement teacher, however, became the object of Katy's anger over her teacher's leaving. Katy's behavior became more and more regressive to the point where she crawled on the floor in imitation of a cat; and on one occasion, while making clawing gestures at the new teacher, scratched her arm hard enough to draw blood.

Actual learning problems seemed to be centered on arithmetic, in which she was most unsure of herself, was not sufficiently familiar with the number facts, and was most prone to ripping up papers. She was very good in language areas, particularly in writing original stories. Katy got along well with the class as a whole. However, she had what the teacher termed "love–hate" relationships with particular girlfriends, in which her feelings alternated from intensely positive to negative.

When the parents came to school for a meeting, they were

bewildered at the reported behavior and said that Katy had no problems of any kind at home. Katy's father suggested that perhaps the teachers had no rapport with her, which proved to be a rather astounding projection on his part. It was eventually reported that Katy had had a similar negative reaction two years earlier, while in kindergarten in another city, when her teacher went on maternity leave in midyear. This knowledge was useful and somewhat reassuring to the new teacher as an explanation of the violent reaction directed towards her, but it did not help in understanding Katy's resistance to doing work or getting help.

As the conference continued, more information emerged when, again, the father suggested that the school was failing somehow, this time in teaching arithmetic. Since she was behind he was working with her at home, drilling her and going over homework papers. The mother described the sessions as shouting matches which father eventually won; and the father smiled as if pleased with her description and said, "Well, she has to know her math, doesn't she?" The teacher then turned to the mother and asked if she ever saw the stony face and turned shoulder, and what she did about it. The mother replied that indeed she saw it whenever she tried to help Katy with her violin practicing, and she dealt with it by leaving her alone.

The parent conference suggested that Katy's experience with being taught at home had been generalized to school. Being taught was a battle and to her it meant a constant risk of being shown up as stupid. Her solution to that, unlike Teddy's, was to fight back with stubborn resistance and sporadic physical acting out. It seems likely, too, that every new teacher had to prove to Katy that she did not teach like her father, after which Katy could relax and relate to the teacher as an individual. This supposition would help explain Katy's intense negative reaction to the midyear change. Testing made it clear that there was a significant element of guilt as well as intense anger and fear in Katy's reaction at school. There was an intense rivalry with mother as well as mixed feelings about father, and the teacher caught the negative sides of Katy's fear of her authoritarian father and her rivalry with mother. Noted also was Katy's tendency to make a good mother–bad mother split, which might further explain her animosity toward the new teacher.

Some limited intervention was possible in this instance. Achievement testing in arithmetic indicated that Katy was, in fact, beyond her own grade level in understanding arithmetic processes and concepts. This proved to be enough to convince father that he need not work with her any longer. The classroom situation eased once the new teacher had established her own relationship with

Katy. In addition, the reassurance about Katy's arithmetic ability and the interpretation of what the child might be experiencing in their relationship made it easier for the teacher to work out her own way of handling crises as they arose.

Adolescent issues frequently find expression in school learning and behavior problems. The fear of growing up, whether newly developed or carried over from earlier years, may complicate the struggle for independence with regressive explosions and withdrawals, and conflicts displaced to the teacher. Conversely, the need to reject parental and school goals in an effort to establish a sense of individual identity and independence may result in a self-defeating flaunting of conventional educational routes. For example, an impulsive decision to quit school and get a job, less than a year before graduation, accompanied by feelings of being self-sufficient and having broken with the past, is a common occurrence. Understanding on the part of the adults often allows the adolescent to reconsider what is best and make an independent decision to complete school.

Victor was a young adolescent presenting more complex and overdetermined school problems. He was completing eighth grade when his mother sought psychiatric consultation about him. Victor had had a reading problem as a small boy; he now read well but had continuing difficulties in handwriting and spelling and was clumsy and poorly coordinated. Victor scored 30 points lower on the Performance Scale of the WISC than on the Verbal Scale on two different administrations, five years apart, each time scoring a Verbal IQ of about 130. Thus far he represents a type of learning disabled youngster that most school psychologists easily recognize.

In the present context of intrapsychic conflicts expressed through learning problems, what is interesting is not the learning disability itself but the use to which it was put, albeit unconsciously, in the service of a neurotic conflict with authority, which overlay serious concerns about identity and self-esteem. His father was disappointed in him and did not hide his feelings. His mother, who was largely responsible for his upbringing, expressed mixed messages about his academic talents and credentials. On the one hand, she supported him in his criticism and rejection of school teachers and their requirements, and on the other, she warned him that if he did not do more work and more reading he would grow up to be like the college students she taught who were unable to write a decent paper. Victor's dilemma at school centered around his specialness: was he specially handicapped or specially talented, and in either case did he warrant special consideration?

Victor had an exaggeratedly low opinion of his competence in his weak areas and, perhaps in compensation, a somewhat overblown sense of his talents in his stronger areas. He was strong in verbal reasoning, had a good vocabulary, and a good fund of general information. When he spoke, however, he tended to go on at length, employing empty phrases and weak rationalizations, attempting to impress both himself and the listener with his erudition. By contrast, when he dealt with something about which he felt less confidence, Victor tended to give up even before he had begun. When once asked to copy a series of geometric forms, he began by doing them all, even the simplest, in an overly casual, desultory way, until the examiner asked him to please take them seriously and draw them as accurately as possible. Victor responded to this, and did so well on a few of them that he surprised himself and openly expressed his pleasure.

A typical problem for Victor arose when an outline for a term paper was assigned to his class. Although so verbally skilled that he could talk at length on almost any topic, Victor had difficulty organizing his thoughts and ideas into a coherent work and, in addition to this, his handwriting was painfully slow and his spelling several years below his vocabulary level. Victor did make some attempt to do the outline but gave up fairly early. By the time he arrived at school on the day it was due, he had worked himself around to the other side of the coin, the side he more often presented to his teachers. He told his teacher that he wasn't handing in the outline because it was only assigned to help students before they wrote the final paper; and since he knew just what he was going to do with that paper and how it would be organized, he didn't need any further help from the teacher.

Victor's tenuous rationalizing and reverse reasoning is apparent here, since he knew that the outline was required and not optional. He was baiting the teacher, challenging his authority by acting as if a requirement were not a requirement, and thus renewing with him the battle they had been carrying on all year. Victor's school history revealed that in every year since the fourth grade, he had found one teacher with whom to carry on such a battle.

It was recommended that Victor's work be planned and supervised as much as possible with his school counselor, rather than his mother; that the counselor help Victor and his teachers set realistic assignments; and that Victor meet regularly with the counselor to discuss how he was getting along with teachers and assignments in each class. It was further suggested that if resources and motivation were available, some remedial spelling and handwriting work could be helpful.

It is important to recognize in Victor's case, as in many other situations, the side-by-side presence of neurogenic and psychogenic difficulties. It would be easy to argue, on the neurogenic side, that the problems with assignments and teachers are but a natural outgrowth of real difficulty with visual memory and visual–motor skills. It would be similarly easy, on the psychogenic side, to argue that weak skills are an excuse that can be used to cover and to fuel an ongoing interaction with authority that attempts to resolve questions of personal identity and value. It seems quite clear that both neurogenic and psychogenic determinants are creating problems, and that failure to recognize this and attempt to deal with both is likely to result in a poor outcome.

Psychological Disturbance in which School or Learning Are Intimately Connected with Basic Issues

As noted earlier, the major difference between problems in this category and the previous category is one of degree; the degree to which the problem pervades all aspects of school and learning and to which there is an illusion that school or learning is not simply difficult or painful but actually dangerous. The clearest example of this is *school phobia*, in which school is avoided altogether as if going to school placed the child in some danger. As Eisenberg (1958) has pointed out, the fear in school phobia is not of school but of leaving mother or, occasionally, father. However, school serves as a metaphor for the danger or the frightening aspect around which the central psychological problem revolves.

The fantasied danger may be conscious or unconscious. In the case of school phobia, it is the conscious fantasy of going to school that becomes the nub of the crisis for child and family. In other situations, where learning rather than attending school is feared and therefore avoided, the fantasied dangers attributed to learning are more likely to be unconscious.

There are some recurring attitudes attached to learning. One that occurs more often among younger children is the idea that learning means growing up and having to assume responsibilities for which they feel unprepared. Parents sometimes unwittingly encourage frightening fantasies of the future when they urge their small children to work hard so they can earn good grades, attend a good college, earn a degree, find a good job, and adequately support their future family. Kessler (1966) reports on a second grader who was being pushed into a premature and anxiety-provoking concern about responsibilities which he clearly could not visualize in any realistic sense. Yet he experienced this concern as though adult burdens were soon to be placed on his seven-year-old shoulders. He conveyed some of this feeling when he said to his therapist, "I don't even know who I'm going to marry yet!" (p. 218).

Several authors note that an inhibition of curiosity about family secrets may spread to an inhibition of learning in general (Brodie & Winterbottom, 1967; Kessler, 1966; Sperry, Ulrich, & Staver, 1958). The secrets are not only about the usual objects of early childhood curiosity, such as sex differences and how babies are born, but also about, for example, a serious illness in parents or siblings, extramarital relationships of a parent, or some family skeleton. The anxiety and tension the secret generates and the parental denials that there is either a secret or tension results in communication to the child that probing and investigating beyond what one is specifically told is not valued and even bad or dangerous, that one's own feelings and perceptions lack validity, and that fears and threats of possible loss or suffering are to be denied. One might as well say, "Don't look and listen, don't explore, don't ask, don't draw conclusions. Then, when information leaks through to you in spite of all these injunctions, don't believe it and don't worry." Children who totally adopt these attitudes not only fail to engage in the intellectual give-and-take of school but may also deny the seriousness of their situation when the teacher tries to confront them with the lack of academic achievement.

Another aspect of learning is the sense of competition it stirs up in some children. Although there is much about school that is realistically competitive, there are fantasied extensions of the sense of competition that symbolize, in the metaphor of school, an intrapsychic conflict within the child. Often the fantasied competition is with father, and in some cases the underlying wish is to fail so as not to run into difficulty with the father (fear of success), and in other cases the predominating concern seems to be the fear of exposure, ridicule, and humiliation that would come with failure (fear of failure).

Kessler (1966) cites the case of a bright youngster who was answering questions beyond his age level and was being encouraged to continue with the difficult items by being told that these test items were for older children. The child thereupon announced he was finished, saying, "Don't ask me any more questions. Only a father knows things like that" (p. 220). While it is not clear from this brief quote whether the child might ultimately be more upset by success or failure, it is striking that he has spontaneously brought the image of his father into a setting where he has just been complimented on doing well. Sperry, Staver, Reiner, and Ulrich (1958) have reported on passive boys with learning problems who resolve their conflicts by renouncing success so as not to cause any disapproval or dissension in the family.

Older children, girls in particular, are subject to feeling that academic success, with its competitive and aggressive implications, will cost them personal acceptance among their peers, and therefore may dampen their efforts to excel. This topic is discussed at greater length in a later section of this chapter; at this point the intent is to note another fear that can be attached to learning. My experience has been, however, that this is unlikely to lead to severe learning problems or failure, but rather to an inhibition of full involvement in learning and an avoidance of excellence.

INTERPERSONAL AND TASK ORIENTATIONS IN LEARNING

In the title of their collection of essays, *From Learning for Love to Love of Learning,* Ekstein and Motto (1969) point to a significant developmental process that should transpire when children are asked to turn their interest and energies to school work. They will be rewarded by love and admiration from parents and teachers if they learn their lessons. With the assistance of several psychological mechanisms, including identification with the interests of the loved ones and association of their own loved and loving feelings with the work (as the salivation of a well-known dog became associated with a bell), children become attached to learning with its assorted tasks for its own sake, and not simply for the praise and material rewards it may bring.

Of course, learning and task orientation do not first begin at school. From early in their lives, through doggedly persistent efforts to stand up and to walk, long hours spent working at block construction, tricycle riding, and the like, most children have amply demonstrated curiosity, persistence, and pleasure and pride in accomplishment, much of it unrelated to parental appreciation. School does present a new set of demands, however, in the nature and scheduling of the tasks set before children. The materials are those chosen by institutional personnel, mostly symbolic and verbal and less intrinsically appealing to most small children; and there are requirements as to the timing, amount, and quality of the work.

Good teachers can be very gentle and persuasive in initiating small children into the housekeeping, academic, and social routines of the early grades. However, for most children the charms of the first grade teacher are not sufficient to blur the boundary between work and play; for some the need to do work, or to do the work the teacher gives rather than the work liked best, is an imposition at best grudgingly accepted. In less formally structured classrooms, interpersonal aspects of learning are increasingly extended to the peer group. Cooperative study and project groups are a regular part of such classrooms, and they require some flexibility in leader–follower roles, generation and sharing of ideas, accepting and constructively challenging the ideas of others, and so on. While the teacher's role of authority may be somewhat weakened in such settings, it never disappears and continues to be a factor for each child to deal with.

While a major goal of education is to encourage children to become independent, enthusiastic learners, with the curiosity and confidence to probe into deeper and broader realms of knowledge and inquiry, the teacher always remains a critical figure in the learning process. The teacher's role changes as students get older; there is diminishing need for direct instruction and guidance and for extensive dependence on the teacher's knowledge, judgment, and authority. Yet no matter how far particular students may develop intellectually or how far they may outstrip their teachers, the students never become entirely independent of them, nor of the work and opinions of others. All scholars, despite how advanced or isolated they may become, maintain some relationship with their mentors, colleagues, and critics, even if only through fantasy, conscious or unconscious. The manner in which the scholar accepts or rejects the work of others and the expectations as to how his own ideas will be received by others influence the content, form, volume, and quality of the scholar's learning and of that which he passes along to others.

In other words, the interpersonal orientation of learning is never outgrown or absent. Its character changes as the learner grows and develops, and everyone works out his own particular equation. In general, one must find an appropriate balance between respect for and independence of the authority of his or her teachers. What constitutes an appropriate balance will depend on such factors as age, intelligence, and experience. The failure to establish an appropriate balance reflects a variety of learning difficulties.

When children are awed by and unduly accepting of the

authority of the teacher, they are afraid to voice their own opinions and to express discontent or disagreement with a teacher's opinion or decision. Kessler (1966) tells of Henry, a 10-year-old youngster whose teacher repeatedly mispronounced his name, but who could not bring himself to correct the teacher and was shocked when the idea was suggested.

By contrast, there are some children, most frequently boys, who like Victor feel driven to an ongoing battle with the teacher. Most often, some aspect of required school work is the issue. There are many times when, in fact, the anxiety or guilt around a difficult or incomplete assignment does trigger the renewal of hostilities. Quite separate from the question of the assignment or the child's ability to do it, however, is the need to react in some forceful, vocal, actively resistant way against the authority inherent in the teacher's role, irrespective of the actual style or character of the teacher as a person. Teachers' ideas and suggestions, as well as instructions, are rejected arbitrarily, and criticism cannot be perceived as constructive.

It has been noted that youngsters who handle their aggression problems in an overly active and aggressive manner test higher on IQ tests (Harris, 1961). These youngsters seem to be in a more favorable position for eventual success in school (Sperry, Ulrich, & Staver, 1958) than those like Henry who submit and withdraw in fear. It is reasonable to assume that their freer access to aggressive energies would indeed allow them to invest more of themselves in their school work. On the other hand, their difficulty in handling the teacher–student interpersonal aspect of learning has detrimental effects. The adult, authoritative activity of the teacher is perceived not as helpful and supportive but as an arbitrary wielding of power. With that perspective, cooperation becomes submission, and submission is what must be avoided at all costs. For a few youngsters in this position, superior intelligence and a value system in which learning and academic achievement rank high may be combined with the continuing struggle against teachers. The combination motivates students to excel and to prove to their teachers that they are better and smarter than the teachers, and do not need their ideas or support in order to succeed. For most, however, the alienation from teachers is accompanied by alienation from school and learning in general.

When children are overly anxious to win teacher interest, involvement, and attention, they may consciously or unconsciously suppress their capabilities for independent work in order to attain a closer and more intimate relationship with the teacher. This is a particularly notable phenomenon in little girls, and not uncommon into the fourth and fifth grades. There are probably many small boys who would also enjoy the closeness, occasional cuddling, and general passive dependency provided in such relationships, but our culture does not encourage boys to seek this affection from their teachers. Although there are some instances in which the child's wish to relate to the teacher in an infantile, dependent manner is essentially a way of warding off the frightening aspects of difficult work and the teacher as an authority, there are also instances in which the wish is for real love and affection, rather than comfort and protection. In some cases the wish for a loving relationship with the teacher becomes a preoccupying concern, and the more independent, task-oriented aspects of learning, while not actively disliked or avoided or rejected, play a secondary role.

Let us look more directly at task orientation in learning. As already noted, children arrive at school with ample experience in task accomplishment and pleasure in achievement. An important new element, which for many children is introduced for the first time upon school entry, is the idea of *doing work*. This is distinct in the child's mind from play, even if some teachers avoid the use of the term and present reading and number work as fun and games. Although there is value in maintaining the distinction between work and fun (which is not to say that work is not sometimes fun), it is important that children learn relatively early in their school career, if they have not learned it earlier, that there can be pleasure associated with work. When teachers and parents only praise right answers, clear successes, and high grades, children may fail to value, or even recognize the feelings of pleasure, effectiveness, and competence (White, 1959) that accompany simply working on school assignments.

When children are in the earlier school years, assignments are relatively short and the gratifications of completion and praise are forthcoming with regularity and frequency. It is not expected that they enjoy struggling with hard problems before they have developed enough confidence in their ability to work problems out. However, children can be helped to know that their "working" and not just the result of their work is important and valued. Older students working on longer projects, in which completion and rewards are further delayed, can enjoy the process more if their schooling has led them to experience the pleasures of full and effective functioning and of total absorption in a problem (Bruner, 1960, p. 50). As Peller (1956) writes, "the pleasure hinges not only on the goal—the acting, the doing, the functioning as such is gratifying and hence the joyful, often lavish expenditure of energy and effort" (p. 439).

An important part of learning, which contributes to task orientation, is interest in the subject matter. As with deriving pleasure from intellectual activity and problem solving, there is an increase in this over time as the student depends less on the teacher to choose what is to be learned or to entertain the class with materials. There is little subject matter requiring mastery in the early grades. The emphasis is on the acquisition of basic learning skills (reading, arithmetic, writing, and spelling), and subject matter is largely a vehicle for that acquisition. As interests in particular subjects and disciplines develop over time, it is possible to see here, too, a change in the teacher's role; there is a decreasing need to help maintain interest in school by setting forth specific requirements and offering short term rewards. Instead, interest in the subject matter becomes its own reward and supports task orientation.

School work will not always be pleasurable, no matter how interested a student has become in his studies or how successful at achieving academic goals and enjoying the processes of effective cognitive functioning and competence. There will always be some aspects of learning that are drudgery, and some that provoke such anxiety about one's own competence and the potential success or failure of the effort that the process is painful. There will always be the competing attractions of other activities which offer greater pleasure and less pain.

Part of the process of developing task orientation—the interest in learning for its own sake with gratification from its intrinsic pleasures which include effective functioning, discovery, understanding, and production—is closely tied to the growing and changing relationship of the learner and the teacher. Pearson (1954) has dealt at length with the teacher-child relationship noting the series of identifications children make with their teachers. The desired outcome of these serial identifications is their incorporation into the student's ego ideal, after which the student works largely to satisfy himself rather than any particular teacher. Both Pearson and Peller (1956) note that the importance of the teacher tends to diminish as students grow older, and the motivation and approval increasingly emanate from an incorporated ego ideal.

It is clear, then, that interpersonal orientation and task orientation in learning are highly interdependent. To some extent, task orientation grows out of positive identifications with the values, interests, and disciplinary characteristics of a series of teachers (and other significant adults), and it never becomes entirely independent of some continuing approval and appreciation from others. On the other hand, learning based exclusively or disproportionately on identifications with teachers and the need for approval fails to promote the independent gratifications that accrue from more task-oriented involvements. This kind of learning is likely to be overly sterile and mechanistic, failing to tap and incorporate the dynamic, richer, and more instinctual interests and motivations of the student. This issue will be discussed in somewhat more detail in the following section which deals with a variety of relationships between learning and aggression. In concluding this section, let us simply note that it is useful, in assessing a child's learning problems, to raise the question: How does the child handle the interpersonal and the task-oriented aspects of learning?

LEARNING AND AGGRESSION

In many different ways, learning is dependent on the constructive channeling of aggression. Strong positive feelings for people are also a large part of learning, but they rarely create problems. Problems arise only when the feelings are so pressing that they distract the student from more independent, task-oriented aspects of learning or when they are used to defend against intrapsychic and interpersonal aggressive conflicts. Because of the ubiquitous nature of aggression in learning, and because its influences are disruptive in such varied ways, it is important to consider the relationship between aggression and learning.

School learning can be divided into three sectors in which the handling of aggressive impulse is at play: the interpersonal relationship with the teacher, the cognitive and manipulative processes of learning, and the subject matter. Learning inhibition and failure tend to revolve around the first two sectors, and are seen in the student's inability to invest energy in intellectual productivity or to comply with academic requirements.

Jon is a good example of a youngster who had difficulty in both of these sectors. He was considered a good, compliant, pleasant, 12-year-old boy, and he was also a fine student until it came to putting pencil to paper. Other than this, Jon participated actively and intelligently in discussions, helped other students in the foreign language class where he excelled, and was the first to volunteer for any job. Yet, he found it extraordinarily difficult to do any written work, to commit himself in a performance that would be judged.

He also never got angry at anyone, and tended to stay on the fringe of spontaneously organized groups. If a group of his friends collected outside his house, it was not uncommon for him to go inside and leave his younger brother playing with the group outside. Testing indicated that intense anxiety about being evaluated effectively immobilized him for any sustained organized activity, and that he could use only the most subtle and indirect methods of expressing any aggressive impulse. His anxiety about production made the TAT an unbelievably long and agonizing project in which it took nearly an hour to produce five stories. Nevertheless, the stories were rich in creative fantasy, and one story in particular neatly condenses the double issues of adequate production and passive aggression. Synopsized here is a story which took Jon 15 minutes to tell:

> A young man labors endlessly over the production of a bench, and finally, after many trials and failures, does produce a perfect bench. He takes it to the man who ordered it, but warns him not to use it yet for it needs a cushion. The man sits on it anyway, and it breaks.

We note that the man (father, teacher) is aggressed against, but very mildly and indirectly. The question of who is to blame is made ambiguous, and the issue of perfection is entangled with the production of something adequate and serviceable.

Girls who have problems in working effectively and independently tend to have fewer difficulties with actually presenting the work to the teacher, for they find it far easier than the boys to ask for help. This is probably because they can play a dependent, passive role without loss of self-esteem. On the contrary, they often seem to be enjoying themselves, and in getting help feel they have enhanced their image in the eyes of the other children.

Aggression problems involving subject matter do occur from time to time in connection with, for example, dissecting animals, studying warring cultures, and the like. However these occurrences seem to be relatively isolated in a given student's career and appear to be unrelated to any general pattern of learning disorder or failure.

Problems with aggression in learning do not always surface as learning failure. The student may be intelligent and conscientious enough to meet school requirements, even though his difficulty with managing aggression is interfering with the quality of his work and his feelings about it. This was the case with a group of high school girls studied by the author (Sanders, 1964), all of whom were seniors and high achievers. Through a questionnaire they had been characterized by their teachers as anxious to please, worried about doing well, and needing teacher reassurance. Simultaneously, they had ranked low in intellectual curiosity and in initiative in presenting their own ideas, and tended not to question teacher or textbook authority. They were labeled the "Compliant" group, and were compared with a matched group of girls who were high achievers and who were oppositely characterized by the questionnaire. The second group was referred to as the "Involved" group. There were seven students in each group; all had higher than B averages and were registered in at least one advanced placement course in their senior year in high school. The groups did not differ in IQ scores, nor in parents' education and occupation, religious affiliation, number of siblings, or birth order. Each student was seen individually in two sessions, totaling about 3 hours, for a structured interview and tests, including a nine-card TAT.

The study was originally undertaken to investigate differences in attitude about authority between the two groups and to explore possible differences in the kinds of gratification each group experienced from academic achievement. The results showed other, more dramatic differences between the groups. Conscious attitudes towards teacher and general adult authority did not differ between the two groups. There were, however, statistically significant differences between the groups in the extent to which they experienced school as pressure and to which the outside world was generally perceived as unfriendly and hostile, rather than friendly or neutral.

They all felt very busy, but the Compliant group tended to find school a painful, oppressive burden, whereas the Involved group wished for more time to do all the things they found interesting. The Compliant group unconsciously perceived a far more unpleasant and frankly aggressive quality in the people and circumstances encountered in daily living (according to interview and TAT analysis), and their way of dealing with the perceived hostility was to succumb with guilt or submission rather than to resist or avoid it. Both groups described themselves as sensitive, but the Compliant valued sensitivity less. They seemed to experience it as vulnerability rather than as perceptiveness and openness to the pleasures of new insights and understanding.

The Compliant group saw itself as more inhibited, shy, and likable; the Involved group as more aggressive, assertive, competitive, confident, dominating, poised, and self-reliant. The Compliant group saw itself as generally vulnerable in a hostile world, but while perceiving more aggression in the TAT than did the Involved group, there was also a manifestation of the need to aggress. They frequently had to deny or defend against this; and one way of doing so was to displace aggressive impulses onto male figures, even when this required the distortion of TAT figures whose sex identification was not ambiguous. A major difference between the aggressive fantasies of the Compliant and Involved groups was the primitive, unsocialized, physical character of the Compliant group's fantasies, as distinguished from the Involved group's more socialized, emotional verbal expression.

In learning and achievement issues, again there were significant differences. The Involved group demonstrated far more achievement motivation, not in the sense of getting high grades, but in the psychological sense defined by Stein (1955): "To work at something important with energy and persistence. To strive to accomplish something creditable. Ambition manifested in action" (p. 50). While both groups consisted of educational achievers in the sense that they did well on exams and earned good grades, and while both groups valued intellectuality, the Compliant group experienced the academic demands of school as pressure and coercion by authority, and the Involved group was stirred by wishes to involve themselves in meeting the challenges, mastering them, and producing something of value.

The Compliant group lacked active involvement in learning, which by its very nature requires self-exposure, a willingness to take chances and risk being wrong or criticized (cf. Bruner, 1960, p. 65). The different attitudes about taking risks are nicely illustrated in the following two interview excerpts. The first is from one of the girls in the Involved group. She is talking about why she liked a teacher whom many students felt was much too critical.

> Oh, I know she's critical, but that's what I like.
> I don't care what they say, as long as I can . . .
> I want to master and correct my mistakes.

The second is from one of the Compliant girls. The excerpt is about why she wanted a coeducational school.

> In a coed school, in classes, boys are more apt to raise, volunteer information than girls. I found that here. Boys are much, you know, get into fights, or something, about different issues right in class, they don't—it doesn't faze them.

The intense feeling of vulnerability which characterizes the Compliant group effectively prevented them from getting involved in their work, for in protecting themselves from being hurt they closed off avenues of involvement. Not only did they fail to respond to challenges for mastery of a challenging academic task; they also, because of their need to deny and repress many of the issues with which they were struggling, failed to bring to their academic studies the dynamic and motivating energy of personal issues. Since they could therefore not find anything in their academic work having intrinsic meaning or import for them, it is even more understandable that school requirements were experienced as the pressure and coercion of authority rather than as stimulation in areas that concerned them deeply.

By contrast, an Involved student who was struggling with the adolescent issue of separation from family and family influence, and the question of whether her idealism was a matter of her free will or of their influence upon her, became very involved in her term paper about Woodrow Wilson's policy in Mexico. She saw Wilson as very idealistic and as perhaps wanting only to bring democracy to Mexico. Yet, on the other hand, she thought he might also have been influenced, perhaps unconsciously, by economic questions. She explained during her interview:

> And I haven't been able to figure out whether people's ideas come from their position in society, whether they're due to economic factors, you know, factors that people have no control over, or whether it's just the exercising of the mind, and that somehow they see things that appeal to them and formulate their ideals from that.

Compliant students, struggling in their school work to satisfy others rather than for self-expression, cannot bring these personal issues to their work. As a consequence, they lose out in two ways: they miss opportunities to work through adolescent growth issues, and they learn less that can be truly integrated and made relevant. It is apparent, then, that their difficulties with aggression influence the three sectors of academic learning noted earlier, if not by causing failure then by hampering potential growth and pleasure. They cannot relate themselves to subject matter, they cannot enjoy struggle and mastery in academic tasks, and they cannot develop a happier, more mature relationship with their teachers.

In their projection and displacement of aggressive impulse

onto boys, and in their image of themselves as inhibited, likable people, the compliant girls suggest an explanation of the consistent high ratios of boys to girls in school underachievement. It seems that both the compliant girls and the underachieving boys have problems around aggression. The girls, however, although their learning may not be as gratifying or as integrated as one might wish, are nevertheless successful in school by the standard terms of academic achievement. They accept the pressure and submit to the authority; and one could argue that they are able and willing to do this because such behavior is syntonic with their feminine self-image which includes acquiescence and perhaps suffering and masochism as well. The boys, on the other hand, cannot be acquiescent to school demand; for them, acquiescence and submission are not ego syntonic and the threat to their masculine identity is too great. It is not possible to say who ultimately learns more under these circumstances, but it is clear that the girls' resolution conforms more to society's demands.

It is worth noting that this study was originally planned to include both boys and girls. However, it was not possible to identify even one achieving male high school senior who consistently demonstrated the pattern of compliance found among the girls. Some came close to it, but they always managed to act up in at least one class. There were either no boys handling aggression problems with the kind of compliance the girls demonstrate, or boys who did so were not able to maintain enough free, aggressive energy to qualify as high achievers in terms of grades.

This chapter has treated the intrapsychic influences on learning and learning problems. The focus has remained as much as possible on the child's attitudes and feelings about learning, without attempting to relate these to the family or cultural variables which invariably contribute to them. What will now be considered are those environmental variables which most directly relate to learning: family, culture, and school.

4

Social Determinants of Learning Problems

This chapter surveys the ways in which three major societal institutions—the family, the culture, and the school—influence school learning and contribute to the development or perpetuation of learning problems. The specific issues and dynamic relationships that prevail within each of these institutions are considered as well as some problematic aspects of the relationships between them.

THE FAMILY

Once again, I shall risk seeming to oversimplify or offer one-dimensional explanations, this time as we look at particular dyadic and family relationships and certain structural family characteristics. We shall be considering mother-child, father-child, and other family relationships, and the ways in which certain sex and birth order sequences may contribute to family interactional patterns. None of the situations or relationships discussed here need result in a learning problem, and it is quite likely that none of them would in isolation. In many instances these variables result in psychological problems that are not in the area of learning at all. Nevertheless, they are potential sources of trouble with learning; and whether or not they do in fact contribute to a learning problem will depend on the strength of the specific variable, and how it combines with other social, biological, and psychological determinants.

Mother–Child Relationships

An understanding of the possible deleterious effects of mother-child relationships on learning has come from clinical practice, clinical research, and child development research. The critical issue is that of independence, of the mother's promotion or allowance of enough separation between herself and the child. Buxbaum (1964) presents the case of a boy with a severe learning problem who demonstrates the effects of very close ties to his mother. As long as the mother continues to do everything for the child, he learns neither of his own abilities nor of his realistic limitations. He fails to learn the pleasures of mastery, but at the same time is encouraged to perpetuate omnipotent fantasies since the mother so frequently gratifies his needs and wishes even before they are expressed. Brodie and Winterbottom (1967) offer another perspective on the same issue. In a controlled experiment with boys who had learning problems, they used a series of hypothetical stories involving a mother and son. In each story, the mother has received some information that is potentially anxiety arousing and which either concerns the son or about which he has some hint or partial information. The mothers of the boys with learning problems and those of the control boys having no learning problems were presented with eight such hypothetical situations, and each was asked to tell how she would handle such a situation with her son. For example:

> You and your husband have been arguing about his working on weekends, and it isn't settled yet. One evening, during a fight, your 7-year-old boy appears at the doorway to ask what the noise is all about. What would happen next? (Brodie & Winterbottom, 1967, p. 705)

The mothers' responses were scored according to whether they communicated reality, withheld information, or distorted and modified the truth in their explanation. The mothers of the boys with learning problems were significantly more secretive, some consciously withholding information and others distorting elements beyond recognition. In denying the child information, the mother is in fact controlling what the child will think about, thus denying opportunities for learning about the difficult realities in life and how to cope with them. Attempts to limit independent thinking and judgment deny the child practice in cognitive understanding and mastery, in much the same way that indulgence and overprotection deny practice in mastering physical and more concrete tasks.

Winterbottom (1958) found that elementary school children demonstrating stronger achievement orientation tended to have mothers who had demanded and rewarded independence and mastery in their early childhood years. As Kessler (1966) points out, these attitudes reflect the mother's willingness to allow her child to grow, which in turn encourages the child to seek gratification in mastery and independence and relinquish more dependent and infantile forms of pleasure.

The reasons why mothers fail to foster independence are, of course, varied. Some are responding out of a long-standing intrapsychic disturbance generally related to early childhood experiences with their own mothers. Others are reacting or overreacting at least partly to some realistic and more current situational variable. Brodie and Winterbottom (1967) report that the mothers of two boys in their learning problem group presented themselves as ambulatory schizophrenics.

Buxbaum (1964) notes that the older brother of one of the boys she studied had died by drowning, and one of the mother's difficulties was in letting her younger boy out of her sight, although he was a competent 9-year-old. Among other things, he was not allowed to go to his therapy appointments alone. The fact that the clinic was located near a lake was, of course, significant.

Another frequent cause of maternal overprotection is illness or a physical or mental handicap in the child. It is a natural reaction for mothers to attempt to spare their children the abnormal amounts of pain, frustration, and unhappiness that are unavoidable when certain activities, toys, foods, or other pleasures are beyond the child's ability or endurance. To compensate the children, and to spare themselves the daily anguish of passively witnessing their children's distress, the mothers (and fathers too, though generally to a lesser extent) tend to overindulge the children in areas they can enjoy, do things for them that they could do for themselves, and fail to encourage development towards independence, mastery, and self-control.

Tammy, a 7-year-old brain-injured child, who had been unable to locomote herself at all until she was about 5, had, according to her mother, never heard the injunction "No!" As the mother pointed out, since she was not in danger of running into the street or touching a hot stove, there was no occasion to learn that. All other demands tended to be immediately gratified. At age 7, one of Tammy's problems was that she was unable to tolerate the sight of someone else using her things without immediately wanting the same thing; and so in order for Tammy's friends to come and play with her, her mother had to keep a double set of all toys and play materials.

In another family, the effect on school and work adjustment is more directly apparent. There were four sons and a daughter, and two of the boys had inherited a disease affecting muscle development. They each required two or three operations and several long hospitalizations before age 10. Afterward, they were each left with a limp but could engage in all activities. The mother had indulged them during the hospitalizations and in addition to this she would argue with the father when he tried to discipline the two boys in the same way that he disciplined his other children. Both boys had difficulties (one quite severe) with completing school, although intellectually they were as capable as the other three children in the family who handled school with little difficulty. Their father died before either boy had reached the age of twenty. At thirty, each was still living at home, unmarried, and one of them was only sporadically employed. Although the mother was by then anxious to move into a small apartment herself and occasionally threatened to do so, she could not abandon them. From time to time one or the other of the boys left home, or made plans to do so, but in every case the plans fell through and the boy was back with his mother within the month.

In contrast, there is Dalia, also born with a genetic disease affecting muscle growth and development, although hers was much more serious. Almost all motor development, which occurs spontaneously in normal children, had to be learned by Dalia painfully and slowly, including sitting, standing, crawling, and walking. She accomplished sitting unsupported after her third birthday; and walking after her sixth. She is being included in the present discussion because though her mother had all the natural protective reactions of mothers of handicapped children, she avoided major pitfalls with the help of excellent counseling and a unique community setting.

Dalia had the good fortune to be born in an Israeli kibbutz, which can, if all goes well, offer an almost ideal set of circumstances for raising a handicapped child. The children are partly raised in a children's house, and the entire community numbers only several hundred people. These facts ensure that the handicapped child will not be isolated in the parents' home (as often occurs in a city), and that a good deal of the child rearing will be carried on by child care workers who know and love the child but do not have the same vulnerability that parents have. Dalia was also fortunate to have been seen early by a gifted psychiatrist–neurologist who diagnosed her rare condition and then spent hours sitting with her parents and the children's house staff to discuss how to work with her.

She was to be raised with her peer group, rather than in some special setting or at home. This meant that she would sleep in the children's house, play and eat most meals there, and be with her parents daily from about 3:00 P.M. until bedtime. Kibbutz parents participate in some of the routine care of their children, both at the children's house, where they may handle bedtime undressing and toileting, and at home, where there is toileting and occasional light meals or snacks. Contrary to a popular belief, family life on a kibbutz is about as intense as that anywhere; children's personalities are largely shaped by their family relationships, and the usual problems of separation, autonomy, sibling rivalry, Oedipal struggle, and the like occur just as they do elsewhere. Thus, mother-child attachments are as we know them, and so are the special anxieties and wishes to protect which develop in mothers having a handicapped child.

Dalia spent as much time in the children's house as her peers. Special arrangements were needed so that Dalia could sit at the table when they ate, and for several years she needed to be fed by someone until she gained adequate control to grasp food and bring it to her mouth. There was always the behavior of 4 or 5 (and later 12 or 15) other children to imitate and try to catch up with, and play activities to try to join in whatever way possible. She balked at times; dressing herself and getting herself onto the toilet could take an interminably long time. The staff always had to think about where and how to compromise. She couldn't do up her buttons, but she might if they sewed extra large, knobby ones on her clothes. For years she had to crawl to get anywhere, and the asphalt paths of the kibbutz quickly wore out her overalls and the toes of her shoes. Parents, house staff, and kibbutz tailors worked together with various combinations of corduroy, vinyl, padding and leather, and eventually devised a kind of overall with quilted padding from shin to thigh. It was so successful that it was adopted in other kibbutzim for other handicapped children. The community's investment in promoting this child's development and independence added to the parents' sense that they were not struggling alone. It was gratifying to know that their collaborators were not only doctors and physical therapists but neighbors.

When Dalia first started going outside on her own, she crawled from her parents' house to her grandparents' house, a hundred or so yards away. Later she could manage greater distances, but she tired easily and needed to rest. Once, another kibbutz member came to the mother saying that Dalia was on the path from the children's house and that the mother should go after her. The mother had to explain and reassure her neighbor that the child could manage; it was a refreshing change from her frequent role of being the anxious one. Dalia's father set the highest standard for independent movement—not so much to build Dalia's character as to ensure that she had the requisite amounts of exercise needed to develop her muscles. When she began walking, he would urge her to try to go a little farther by herself before taking his hand. One day while she was walking with her grandfather she asked for his hand, and he gave it to her. A few moments later he heard her rehearsing to herself "If we meet Daddy on the path, I'll just tell him I got tired. People *do* get tired."

The reason for this rather long digression has been to show that what a kibbutz upbringing offers a handicapped child (as a result of child-rearing practices which developed from socialist philosophy) can also have practical applications in our standard nuclear family living style. Community and school intervention programs that acknowledge special needs and thereby join the mother in her concern for the child, without the special emotional ties that create anxiety and lead to overprotection, present the child with a wider world in which he can operate, feel safe, and develop independence and mastery. While the kibbutz way of living offers the mother shared responsibility and concern as a matter of course, our programs' staffs will have to assume more initiative in making their presence known and offering their services.

It is worth pointing out the contrast between Dalia's and Tammy's mother. In many ways these two mothers were similar; both were attractive, intelligent, psychologically healthy Israeli young women. Both had seriously handicapped children. Yet, Tammy's mother had been told her child would never walk or talk and had been advised to institutionalize her at birth. Instead, however, she devoted herself to raising and training her child and began to study special education. Dalia's mother also studied special education, but the question of raising and training her child had been shared with sympathetic professionals and friends from birth onwards. Both Tammy and her mother had been isolated at home with their problems, not only geographically but also emotionally; they were deprived of community and neighborhood support and of the responses and feedback of concerned adults and other children. Thus, the contrast in these two instances is not in the handicapping conditions of the children, or in the reactions or capacities of their mothers, but in the interaction between family and community.

Father–Child Relationships

The literature on father-son relationships in learning problems consistently points to two particular characteristics in fathers that contribute to learning inhibition or resistance to learning: the father's failure to provide the boy with an achiever role model with which the boy can identify, and the father's rivalry and competition with the boy at either pre-Oedipal or Oedipal levels (Buxbaum, 1964; Friedman, 1973; Grunebaum, Hurwitz, Prentice, & Sperry, 1962; Harris, 1961; Kessler, 1966). The rivalry appears to be present in most instances, at one level or the other, while the father's self-image as achiever is not necessarily an issue. Grunebaum et al. (1962) note that many of the 18 fathers in their study were in fact quite successful in terms of their educational and occupational attainments, but nonetheless they tended to derogate themselves and their accomplishments and to feel helplessly stuck where they were. Kessler (1966) points out that the father's image of achievement is not disturbed when reality circumstances have interfered with goal achievement. There are, for example, the many immigrant parents who could not achieve what they may have wanted for themselves due to lack of money and formal education, but were able to support their children emotionally and financially through advanced schooling and to enjoy their successes.

While it is appreciated that the father is able to negatively influence his son's self-esteem by failing to provide an adequate role model and by maintaining a rivalry that continually extinguishes any spark of initiative the boy may have generated, experience has shown that the neurotic inhibition of learning cannot by itself account for the number of children who fail to learn. Since the investigations of neurotic learning inhibition preceded the awareness of learning disabilities among psychodynamically oriented clinicians, it is quite likely that a number of the children they tested and studied had some neurogenic learning problem in addition to a psychogenic learning inhibition. The fact that their reports frequently note that learning problems persisted after significant therapeutic gains had been made, and that a number of the parents of the children treated had also had learning problems as children, strengthens the impression that clinicians were often dealing with neurogenic learning difficulties.

The inhibition of *production*, however, is frequently a more clear-cut result of father-son rivalry and neurotic conflict. As Strickler (1969) has pointed out, a dictatorial parent attitude is frequently projected by the student onto the teacher. An example was Nick, who was referred for therapy by his pediatrician because of severe constipation problems (ten days to two weeks between bowel movements) which had not been alleviated by various physical treatments such as laxatives and diet management. The factors that were quite clear early on in assessment were: the Oedipal rivalry; a stubborn, obsessional, intellectualizing, and somewhat pompous father given to blasts of temper; a very intelligent mother who presented herself as quite helpless; the boy's close attachment to his mother and very strong identification with his father; and the boy's withholding pattern. It soon emerged that there were some severe conflicts at school between Nick and his teacher. Nick often argued about whether or not he had to do something and made the teacher angry. The arguments were exactly like those between Nick and his father at home, except that Nick was far more tentative in challenging the father and was often protected and defended by his mother.

Of particular interest is the poignant demonstration of the rivalry between father and son. Nick's father was named Samuel; Nick's real name was Samuel, Jr., and from his birth until about age 4 he was called Sammy. Then one day he came in the house after playing outdoors and announced that he wanted to be called Nick—there was a tougher, slightly older boy in the neighborhood named Nick—and so Sammy was called Nick from then on. One day, when he was about 6 years old he announced that he no longer wanted to be Nick, he wanted to be Sammy again. His father replied, "Okay, but if you aren't going to be Nick anymore, I'm going to be Nick." At that, Nick decided that he would not give up the name after all, and Nick he remained. There are several possible interpretations of this story, but none of them are positive. What is particularly striking in view of the constipation and production problems is the competition which the father introduced in the name issue and Nick's withholding reaction. Something he had been about to discard is suddenly deemed valuable because of the father's interest in taking it for himself, and so Nick chooses to hang onto it. In holding onto that name, he gives up his intent to once again share his father's name. The father appears unwilling to share, setting the condition, "If you take my name, I'll take yours." Added to all the interpretation is the unsympathetic, teasing response of a father to a sensitive issue.

Grunebaum et al. (1962) offer a more straightforward illustration of rivalry:

> The extent to which rivalry permeates the father–son relationship can be illustrated by an incident in which one of our fathers was playing with his son. He insisted that he should have the larger toy gun and gave his son the smaller, broken one.

Family Interaction

The combination within a family of a mother who cannot allow independence in her child and a father who is competitive with his son or resigned to a self-image of nonachievement will be particularly difficult for a male child. Grunebaum et al. (1962) describe a group of families where this is indeed the case. The infantile and neurotic needs of the parents dictate the family interactional pattern in such a way that the children's needs can be neither recognized nor met. Fortunately, there appear to be a number of families in which one parent is sufficiently free of conflict to support the child in the developmental aspects which the other parent cannot sponsor. Fathers can support independence and mastery when mothers cling to their children. Mothers can encourage and reward achievement, and be partial role models themselves, without necessarily creating a conflict whereby achievement is associated solely with women and the father seriously and permanently derogated in the child's eyes. It is harder for the child to succeed this way, and a great deal depends on other factors, including the availability of other male role models, such as relatives, teachers, tutors, or counselors.

There are other family interactional patterns, besides the traditional ones noted in the psychoanalytic literature, that support the development of learning difficulties. Either or both parents may have unrealistically high expectations of a child, and their disappointment with what is produced discourages the child from trying at all. A frequent and more subtle problem arises from parents' demanding too little, not because they underestimate the child's intellectual ability but because the child has some specific learning or emotional difficulty, and they believe that he cannot be expected to learn or make progress until the problem has been resolved. However, while the parents ostensibly have low expectations, they often communicate to the child their disappointment and disapproval, as Friedman (1973) has shown.

Friedman uses a structured interview for assessing school learning disorders, in which both the parents and the child participate. In summarizing 53 such family interviews he found that in 19 cases the communication between parent and child regarding parental expectations, child performance, or disappointments with performance were characterized by ambiguity or dishonesty. In 18 cases "permission was given by the parents to the child to fail, continue immature behavior in school, underachieve, avoid stress, act out resistance to the educational process, or passively resist school learning" (p. 93). (Parents should not be too hastily blamed, however, for their mixed and confusing messages, considering the mixed and confusing explanations they often receive from school and mental health professionals about what their child can do and what to expect of him or her.)

There are also parents who express lack of concern with what a child is doing at school, usually because they are preoccupied with some other issue, often another one of their children who is especially talented or presents some special physical or emotional problem. One youngster had an exceptionally talented older brother who was both an excellent student and a fine artist. When the younger brother got only mediocre grades, the parents reminded themselves that after all they did not expect of him what they did of the older boy, although the younger one was in fact more capable than they assumed. When the older brother was killed at the age of 19 in a freak accident, the younger boy displayed his perception of the parents' lack of emotional investment in him when he confided to relatives that he himself should have been the one to die for the parents would then not have experienced such a total and inconsolable loss.

Bell and Vogel (1960) have conceptualized and described the process of family scapegoating, by which a particular child becomes the focus and bears the brunt of family conflicts that actually stem from stresses in the parents' relationship with each other or with the community. A child who is having some mild or temporary difficulty in school may have the problem exacerbated if his parents, instead of being helpful and supportive, use his problem as a displacement of their own worries and to avoid a conflict with each other. For example, Katy, who was discussed in the previous chapter, was having battlelike tutoring sessions with her father over second grade arithmetic. It was later learned that during this period the father was unemployed; that he was having great difficulty not only in finding work but in looking for work; and that there was considerable strain stemming from this issue between the parents. While the father tutored Katy and the mother tried to help her with music lessons, Katy's incompetence and lack of achievement (which were more imagined than real) became the focus of attention, and the question of the father's ability to support his family did not have to be confronted.

In some instances, an intellectually limited youngster becomes the depository of a parent's displaced secret worries about his own or his spouse's intellectual ability. A parent may explain to the teacher, "Nobody else in the family has problems like that; we both did well in school and none of our other children has given us any trouble with school." Thus, instead of the child's receiving supportive acceptance and encouragement from his parents, he is used by them to localize and separate from themselves any anxiety about intellectual competence. This assists them in maintaining a satisfactory family or personal self-image vis-à-vis the community. In one family with many children, two of the adolescents were having serious learning and behavior problems at school and were repeatedly truant. The parents had essentially given up any effort to control them and were focusing all their anger and dissatisfaction on a second grade boy who was having difficulty with reading. One of the family secrets was the mother's illiteracy.

Sex and Birth Order

In clinical practice, some sibling sex and birth order positions appear more susceptible than others to being drawn into a family interactional system that may negatively influence the way the child relates to learning, to work, and to teachers. Two groupings stand out: (1) only and youngest children, and (2) sibling pairs, either in two-child families or in larger families where two same-sex children are very close in age.

Only and Youngest Children. Only children are more susceptible than others to prolonged overprotection and indulgence. Psychologically sophisticated families may try to avoid the concrete aspects of doing and giving too much, conscientiously teaching habits and skills expected at a certain age and restraining themselves when purchasing toys and equipment. There remains, however, the more subtle and potentially damaging quality of single-minded concern and focal attention, which leads to an immediate, and at times, reflexlike response by the parent at the first sign of difficulty, impatience, or frustration. Intense concern and involvement are characteristic parental responses to any first child. When other children come along, however, the first born is forced to make some adjustment to the transfer or, at best, sharing of concern, and then learns more tolerance for frustration and anxiety. Only children (or youngest children who are born ten or more years after their siblings) may never have ample opportunity to learn delay and frustration tolerance until school entry. There, the problem is apparent in the child's inability to struggle for a few moments with a difficult problem, or to wait his turn for the teacher's attention and help.

There is an opposite problem with only children and youngest (by many years) children, more frequent in the latter group. In these instances, the parents are inadequately focused on their child because the bulk of their interests lies elsewhere. Those who have already raised a family are familiar enough with the stages of early development not to be entranced with them; and they are older, more tired, and into another stage of their own lives. We have seen two children in this position; a boy of 7 and a girl of 9, each with a mild learning disability that made school more of an effort than it otherwise would have been. In each case, the absence of built-in coping skills and the parents' difficulty in turning their attention to the needs of the child had intensified the problem. Their households were no longer child oriented; dinner table conversation centered on their retirement plans or the activities of their college-aged and married children. Both children had an aimless, distracted quality about them.

Youngest children may be in a similar position of expecting help without having to struggle too hard if their experience at home has taught them to expect that parents and older siblings will take care of the hard jobs and finish their uncompleted chores. Even in families that give their youngest some responsibilities, it is often easier for a parent to finish off the youngest's task than the oldest's. This is because the task itself is simpler and the parent has come to depend on the older children for help and feels more personally let down if they don't follow through. One often finds a sense of entitlement in youngest children, an expectation that one way or another the world will come around and give to them without exacting some quid pro quo. Parents frequently describe the charming quality in these children, and their ability to "wait you out" or "wear you down" as they fail to do household chores or get their homework done. As the children get older this quality is less acceptable. Since in many instances the general family relationships are quite solid, some direct confrontations with parents and children can lead to redefining and restructuring expectations and responsibilities.

The opposite side of the coin is the youngest child in whom inability to do what older siblings do is experienced as a liability more than an asset. Rather than exploiting and enjoying his "baby" position, the youngest more often feels the dismay of not being able to do what they do, and develops a self-image that is incompetent and unqualified. In these instances, too, the carry-over to school is likely to effect task orientation, with the underlying attitude being, "I can't," rather than, "I don't really have to."

Sibling Pairs. A sibling pair is any two children in a family who are regularly perceived as a group or in some way separate from the other children. If there are only two children in a family they are a pair, twins are a pair, same-sex children very close in age compared to the ages of the rest of the siblings are often pairs. Although the two children may have some strong spontaneous attachment to each other, being a pair depends largely on the parents' tendency to compare the two, focus and comment on differences, and thus evoke behavior consonant with those differences.

The two children are considerably limited by this inflexible reference set, for the same characteristics tend to be commented upon and each child regularly perceived as high or low, more or less, good or bad on those dimensions. Were the reference set larger, even if it included only one more child, each child's weak points would not always look so weak and, in addition, other characteristics would get some attention. The same holds true for the child's developing perception of himself. If the child consistently sees himself in relation to only one other child, he has less flexibility in the assessments he makes of himself and in the roles he can try out. It is true that youngest and oldest children are always in those particular positions vis-à-vis all other siblings. Yet, even their roles alter depending on the age and sex and general personality of the particular sibling with whom they are playing, arguing, plotting, or cooperating. If a child is consistently paired with the same sibling, the chances are greater that he will be more rigidly typecast by others and by himself and will have less flexibility in relating to various people and situations.

Pairing appears to have potential importance for learning in two particular patterns: an older boy and a younger girl in a two-child family and a pair of same-sex children close in age. As suggested earlier, the presence of one of these pairs does not in itself create difficulty, but in some families it serves to evoke certain recognizable, even stereotypic parental reactions and family patterns.

The two-child family with an older boy and a younger girl is a provocative arrangement for traditional sex typing of the children. The daughter, being both the youngest and the only girl, is at some risk for being consistently responded to as a cute, sweet, doll-like child, who plays a somewhat dependent, helpless role to her big brother. This scenario can provide enough gratification to all four participants for several years, but at some point in the daughter's elementary school years someone may begin to feel discomfort—parents, teacher, or the child herself. The teacher sees a sweet, ingratiating child with little real interest in the subject matter or mastery aspects of school. The parents talk of her immaturity, easily hurt feelings, naivete, or lack of interest in work, and compare her to her talented, successful older brother. The daughter feels picked on, and complains of being teased.

Perhaps the change in attitude and expectation is due to the ordinary demands of school; perhaps to a change in the culture which has recently come to expect as well as allow more independence, self-assertion, a sense of competence, and mastery in its women; or perhaps to a change in the parental and family interaction partly influenced by cultural shifts. What is clear is that the family raised a little girl with one set of expectations to fulfill in a mutually gratifying interactional pattern; then in midstream the specifications and expectations for success and pleasure were changed. While she is running true to form she no longer satisfies expectations and as a result can no longer be satisfied with herself. In the families I have seen in this situation, the fact that the girls' strivings for competence and mastery are not entirely submerged is encouraging. The family has tended to discount and devalue the daughter's efforts because compared with those of her older brother, who is viewed as especially intelligent, they are lacking. One girl wrote a composition which her parents felt to be inadequate. When they told her, she became upset and insisted on leaving it her way. They sent her older brother to her to reason with her and explain why she was wrong. In fact, the composition was fine according to the teacher's evaluation. Another set of parents, during a discussion about their daughter's sole interest in play and her refusal to take responsibility, was asked if she liked to help out in the kitchen, making salads or desserts. The parents looked startled, and the mother said, "You know, she does sometimes come and ask if she can do something, but it's easier to do it without her."

Unless these girls have some specific learning problem stemming from other determinants, they are not likely to become learning failures. Instead, unless their energies are rechanneled, they will probably be compliant students, willing enough to please so that they will do their work but unable to invest much of themselves in it.

Same-sex pairs seem especially vulnerable to a *splitting* tendency in the same-sex parent, in which the parent tends to split qualities consciously and unconsciously perceived within himself or herself, and to project one set of qualities onto each child. The split is generally between positive and negative characteristics labeled according to the parent's value systems. Thus, there does develop a sense of the "good child" and the "bad child" with the good one frequently held up as an example of what is expected and valued.

There are some characteristic splits that mothers and fathers make. Each has some implications for learning styles and problems, and, as usual, the effects on the boys are likely to be more handicapping. The problems, again, have to do with aggression, but the dilemmas are different for each sex. The woman's question has tended to be, "Am I a good, lovable person?" while the man's has been, "Am I a strong, successful person?"

Mothers who find their own aggressive impulses unacceptable

may have one good, quiet, compliant, and responsible daughter, and one who is more argumentative, defiant, and assertive and more likely to act out and act up. While the first daughter is likely to do better in school when it comes to studying for exams, handing papers in on time, and earning good grades, a lack of self-discipline in the second daughter may be sufficiently compensated by her ability to get involved in the academic material. If she is also fortunate enough to have teachers who enjoy her and who don't become caught up in the authority struggle, she might also earn satisfactory grades.

With fathers and sons, the aggression problem is more likely to be expressed through achievement issues and the boys' varying competencies in school, athletics, and industriousness in after-school jobs and helping out at home. One son is encouraged and supported in his strivings for accomplishment, even when he is not successful. The father finds it easier to identify with him, appreciate his achievements and new interests, instruct him with patience, and even let his son teach him. The other son is cast as the rival; his successes are inadequate or trivial, his failures humiliating, his interests childish or harebrained. If he tries to explain something, he may be accused of disrespect. In school one would expect to find discouragement and apathy, a withdrawn passive-aggressive reaction, or openly hostile resistance and behavior.

It should be noted that the projection of these various attitudes onto children can take place in any family constellation. While pairing may invite and highlight problems, it is not a necessary condition for this sort of scapegoating.

THE CULTURE

This section deals with problems generated or perpetuated by a mismatch or conflict between the cultural or subcultural background of the child and the expectations and demands of school. The school is perhaps the most unequivocal representative of the dominant, majority culture. In this section, family attitudes about school and education will be looked at as well as the differences in the experience, training, and expectations with which children arrive at school.

Family Attitudes about School and Education

Given that schools generally reflect the dominant middle-class beliefs and values of the culture, conflict may develop between school attitudes and practices and those of various subcultural groups who in one way or another do not fit the middle-class mold. The conflict is expressed in two important and different ways, both of which may contribute to learning difficulties. In one case, those who belong to the subculture may accept and value the traditional goals of the dominant culture, but believe themselves (often quite realistically) unable to attain them. In the other case, the subculture group is critical and rejecting of the dominant cultural standards of belief and behavior as represented by school personnel, structure, and curriculum. In both cases, some degree of distance, alienation, or antagonism between family and school exists which may adversely influence academic achievement. In both cases, authority and control issues are critical.

The subcultural groups most vulnerable to feeling alienated from the dominant culture and its schools are those who are in some way disadvantaged—socially, economically, or by minority status. There is every indication that the disadvantaged share the "dominant-culture concern with status, material possessions, ingroup morality, Judeo-Christian ethics, competition, etc." (Gordon, 1970, p. 254). However, for many parents perceptions of their disadvantaged status and of the realistic possibilities of achieving their goals heighten the feeling of distance and sometimes alienation from the school. Instead of seeing the school as a benign or even neutral community institution, many families regard it as a monolithic, authoritarian agency, no more inviting (and perhaps less so) than the local police station. Frostig and Maslow (1973) point out how the teacher may encourage such an attitude: "She feels that she has achieved her position because she has upheld white middle-class ideals regardless of her race or class origin. She presents a clean, conventional, courteous front (the three *c*'s of the middle class)" (pp. 36-37). As a rule, if school administrators and teachers do not take some initiative in reaching out to families and inviting them into the school for meetings, parties, discussions, after-school activity groups, and the like, the parents' perception of the school as an alien institution is not likely to change.

When dealing with an awesome authority, the tendency is to tell only what you believe the authority would like to hear, and keep quiet about the rest. The tendency is also to assume that the authority can handle anything it wishes, that the authority has no internal problems or difficulties, and that acceptance by the authority constitutes a solution of your problem. Kathleen was 8 years old and moderately retarded, receiving special help in a resource room at the local public school and attending a regular second grade class for part of the day. When her mother decided, for unknown reasons, to transfer her to a neighborhood parochial school the following fall, she registered her for third grade without giving any indication to the new principal that Kathleen might need special attention. The parochial school had no diagnostic services and no special educational facilities other than a few tutoring hours available to it. Within the first weeks of school, her teachers learned that Kathleen could do almost none of the class work.

By chance, a local university's graduate psychology program was looking for school children with learning problems who might benefit from evaluations by graduate students, and the headmistress gratefully suggested Kathleen. Kathleen, her parents, and her teacher were seen; the old records were sent for; the school was apprised of the nature and degree of her learning difficulties; and the parents were helped to acknowledge and accept both the realities of Kathleen's problems and the limitations of the parochial school in helping her.

Kathleen's wasted, and perhaps destructive third-grade year demonstrates one of the great liabilities of an authoritarian relationship between school and family: the family has no opportunity to know and evaluate the school (either because the family sees no need, or the school does not invite such acquaintance, or both) and to decide if it meets their philosophical and educational requirements. Decisions are made according to some fantasied, generalized idea of what school is and what it does. In Kathleen's case, there was already a clear and known problem which was exacerbated by the lack of communication between family and school. In Billy's case, which follows, there was no learning problem prior to school entry, but the family's attitudes about school and learning in contrast to the school's, and the lack of communication between them, contributed to the creation of one.

Billy was a black 6-year-old from an urban ghetto whose family was very concerned that he get the best education possible in the best school available. They enrolled him in a private, progressive school in a neighboring academic community. Having heard it was "the best" they felt no need to visit and find out what that constituted. In this instance, the family apparently assumed the best of the dominant-culture mold, while the school's staff in fact worked hard to stay out of that mold. Billy presented some behavior problems when he entered and was failing to complete all his work sheets. The teachers, however, were not very concerned and were working at getting him to be able to spend increasingly longer periods of time on school work. Unbeknownst to them, his family was very concerned about the incomplete papers and had begun forcing him to finish the work at home, which sometimes involved tying him into a chair. Billy's behavior at school became increasingly unsettled. It was only after his grandmother began coming to school to sit in the back of the room and make sure he behaved that the discrepancy in educational approaches emerged clearly. The conflicting educational philosophies, and the failure to recognize and discuss them, were creating an ideal breeding ground for learning problems.

The converse of those families who strive to make their children acceptable in the eyes of the school are families who do not accept the school philosophy and the dominant culture standards it represents. These parents carry on either an overt or covert struggle with the school through their children—occasionally at their children's expense. The argument with the school tends to be intellectually based, with parents criticizing choices of subject matter, types of assignments, teacher competence, or classroom organization. Rather than being awed by the school's authority, they deny and sometimes defy it. If the family has strong counterculture feelings they may take their children out of school altogether. In one case, a mother was militantly antischool and decided to establish a free school for her children. This turned out to be more difficult than she imagined. For two years, when her youngest would have been in first and second grade, the free school was an off-and-on affair. When he entered public school in the third grade, he was not only seriously behind academically but he also had great difficulty in adjusting to any school routine. His mother continued to be critical of the community public schools. Although she sent him to the local school, she tacitly supported his nonconforming, nonadjusting behavior. Her ongoing criticism of the school also allowed her to ignore his increasing deficits in academic skills.

Highly educated academic and professional families may not approve of the schools available to their children, but they are unlikely to take them out altogether, since they want the children to have an education that will lead to college entry. While leaving the children in school, they may express their disapproval and disagreement very openly through arguments with school personnel, or they may confine themselves to comments at home about busy-work homework assignments, old-fashioned exams, poor curricula, and the like. Children who are doing well at school can handle a certain amount of dissonance between home and school opinions. However, those who are having academic or behavior problems may use the parental attitudes to reinforce or justify a decision to flout school requirements. Parents are likely to be delivering mixed messages such as, "Yes, you have to do that homework, but I wouldn't blame you if you didn't."

Differences among Children Starting School

In addition to individual differences among school children, there are culturally determined group differences which, while not applying to every child, are sufficiently widespread to require serious attention as a group phenomenon. The research on disadvantaged children continues to generate professional and public debate on hereditary-environmental-interactional determinants and on the methods and efficacy of intervention programs. However, there is general agreement that disadvantaged children, as a group, arrive at school less prepared for the schooling they will receive than their advantaged classmates (Deutsch, 1967; Gordon, 1970).

Gordon's (1970) term, *differential characteristics in disadvantaged populations*, is an apt one for the differences relevant to learning problems. We will consider two categories of characteristics, intellective and nonintellective. The intellective differential characteristics are language, perception, and concept development; the nonintellective are motivation, rapport, and practice. The latter three characteristics were grouped and researched by Haggard (1954) and further discussed by Riessman (1962).

Intellective Differential Characteristics

Language. There are a number of ways in which the language style and experience of disadvantaged groups may hinder academic progress. The child's mother tongue may be something other than English or it may be a nonstandard form of English, such as black English or some other dialect. The problems of the non-English-speaking child are obvious. Children who do speak English, but who have spent their early childhood years in settings where well-articulated and semantically correct standard English was not regularly spoken, may have less obvious problems. These difficulties are not limited to socially and economically disadvantaged children.

Robert, for example, was born in Italy and came to the United States at the age of 3 months with his Italian mother and American father. Both parents were physicians completing their medical residence, and they lived on the hospital grounds where Robert was cared for by his maternal aunt. The language spoken at home was

Italian so when he entered nursery school he had trouble with English. When Robert was 10, his examining psychologist noted that Robert's expressive language did not flow easily, whether oral or written, and that in speaking he made occasional small errors in phrasing and mixed up pronouns when there were several in one phrase.

Studies by Quay (1971) and Eisenberg, Berlin, Dill, and Frank (1968) indicate that children speaking nonstandard English do not have difficulty comprehending standard spoken English. However, as both Achenbach (1974) and Torrey (1970) point out, their inability to speak standard English may adversely affect their teachers' evaluations of them. Furthermore, since reading depends to a considerable extent on language experience and what one anticipates finding on the printed page, nonstandard English speakers are likely to read less fluently and accurately than otherwise comparable standard English speakers.

Bernstein (1961) studied the language of lower class youth and reported it to be "restricted," in contrast to the "elaborated" language of middle and upper class youth. Restricted language tends to be stereotypic, with a highly predictable lexicon and organizational structure. It is also quite dependent on nonverbal aspects of communication, such as gestures and intonation, for more individualized expression. Elaborated language includes more complexity in syntax, wider and more subtle vocabulary ranges, and consequently more power in communicating subtleties of ideas and relationships through words. Restricted language operates more as a signaling system, with particular words or phrases conjuring up, for the in-group, a host of unverbalized associations and concepts. Elaborated language is more dependent on the extended use of words, complexly organized, to reflect the subtleties of a specific situation. In addition to developing a restricted vocabulary and syntax, children accustomed to recognizing nonverbalized meaning from cue phrases will not listen in the same way for the verbal meaning of words.

For example, Cazden (1973) reports on the experience of Laura Lein, an anthropology student who was studying selected aspects of language among black migrant children. These children's families migrate from Florida to upstate New York every summer as farm laborers. While living among them in New York, Lein became interested in how the children responded to commands. The following is an extract from Cazden's report:

> Responses to parents are of two kinds. "Reasonable" commands, such as, "You can't go outside now, it's dark," are immediately

obeyed. But commands without obvious justification, like, "Wipe that smile off your face," or "Come stand over here by me," are treated differently. The children understand the latter quite correctly as invitations to engage in a routinized verbal game in which the children resist, the adults repeat, with escalating insistence until the adults appeal to higher status members of the family or community to enforce the command. The game often lasts fifteen to twenty minutes, and everyone understands it as such. One can easily imagine what Lein found in school. The children thought that the situation for this game was defined by the content of the commands and did not understand that it was defined also by the setting (home but not school). Thus, they resisted playfully when their teachers gave the meaningless commands which teachers are apt to give, were labeled "defiant" by the teachers, and never understood the source of the problem. (p. 142)

An additional illustration of the same issue, i.e., using the teacher's message as a cue to playful behavior rather than attending to the semantic meaning of the message is offered by Mattick and Murphy (1973). In describing a group of young inner-city children from poor and disorganized families they write, ". . . when crossing the street a child would be sure to imitate the teacher's words of caution, but neither that child nor the others who would join enthusiastically in shouting, 'Watch for cars, kids' made any attempt to actually look for cars" (pp. 451–452).

Another aspect of language usage is illustrated in the study by Beem, Van Egeren, Straissfuth, Nymen, and Leckie (1969) demonstrating that middle-class mothers tend to use language with their young children to teach, guide, encourage, and praise correct solutions, while lower-class mothers are more likely to use words when disapproving and controlling. There are at least two kinds of learning limitations that may result from language usage that involves a restricted code or that conveys more disapproval than explanation and encouragement. First of all, as already noted, the children may tend to listen for nonverbal meanings rather than noting the semantic content of the utterances they hear. Secondly, with the steady use of short, grammatically simple phrases, the children do not hear the repeated use of longer and more complex verbal messages, which are an essential part of school learning. It is the redundant use of longer and more complicated expression in middle-class families that contributes so much to preparing their children for the language of formal learning.

Perceptual and Conceptual Development. Unlike language structures, one cannot hear or see the perceptual and conceptual structures that disadvantaged groups may be using. When they score lower on various tasks than middle-class children, questions always arise as to the interference of motivational and practice variables. There is no indication or suggestion that different and competing perceptual and conceptual structures are developing that are per se less conducive to learning (as is the case with language). M. Deutsch (1967) suggests a number of cognitive areas in which preschool environment may limit experience and practice. Among these areas are past-present sequences and time judgments; concepts of relativity and comparability; auditory discrimination, enunciation, grammar; and knowledge of the physical, geographical, and geometric world around him. C. Deutsch (1968) notes the circumstances that can lead to limited experience and practice:

> The slum child is more likely than the middle-class child to live in a crowded cluttered home—but not cluttered with objects which can be playthings for him. There is likely to be less variety of stimuli in the home, and less continuity between home and school objects. Where money for food and basic clothing is a problem, there is little for children's playthings, for furniture in which to store the family possessions, and for decorative objects in the home. Where parents are poorly educated, there is likely to be less verbal interaction with the child, and less labeling of objects (or the distinctive properties of stimuli) for the child. There is less stress on encouraging the production of labels by the child, and on teaching him the more subtle differentiations between stimuli (for example, knowing color names and identifying them). Thus, . . . the slum child has both less redundancy and less education of his attention to the relevant properties of stimuli. As a result, he could be expected to come to school with poorer discrimination performance than his middle-class counterpart. (p. 79)

One need not subscribe to a critical period hypothesis to anticipate the potential learning difficulties inherent in children's arrival at school when they are less cognitively ready than their middle-class counterparts. While there is good evidence to support the belief that the lag can be made up at school with appropriate lessons and practice, schools rarely plan that way. With lockstep entry and nationally rated grade level achievement tests, the system places the burden on the child to prove that he can do what is expected of average first graders. In addition to the discouragement and lowered self-esteem resulting from early difficulties and failure to keep up, there may be a continuing and perhaps progressively worsening problem of cognitive development, as Whiteman and Deutsch (1968) point out. Assuming that intelligence develops as Piaget (1947/1960) has described, with a successive series of assimilations and accommodations forming cognitive schemata or structures, the failure of the school curriculum to match the current internal structure acquisitons of the child will increase the gap. Not only does the child fail to learn the presented material; he is also deprived of opportunities for optimal, continued cognitive development. This is because the child is not receiving the kind of task that he could assimilate and that would therefore foster accommodation and mental development.

Nonintellective Differential Characteristics

Practice. Disadvantaged groups are likely to lack practice in the physical and mental manipulation of certain materials as well as in the testing and learning situations that are so much a part of school. There is research evidence that the lack of practice is detrimental to performance. Furthermore, there is evidence that when practice is provided, the deficit decreases or disappears.

Practice does not necessarily mean formal training; in the examples that follow, practice involved only prior experience. Covington (1967) found that lower-SES children performed poorly compared to middle-SES children on a task of discriminating between abstract visual forms. Experimental and control groups were formed for each SES sample, with the experimental groups having a daily exposure to the test forms and the control groups an equal amount of exposure to animal pictures. All the children were simply told to look at the pictures. On the posttest of the discrimination test, both experimental groups improved in comparison to their control groups. However, the lower-SES experimental group gained almost twice as much as the middle-SES experimental group, and the final achievements were similar in both groups. The control groups, on the other hand, continued to demonstrate the difference in discrimination ability.

In their study, Zigler, Abelson, and Seitz (1973) proceeded from the hypothesis that disadvantaged children often test poorly because of motivational factors, due particularly to their wariness in interactions with strange adults rather than because of cognitive deficits. They tested economically disadvantaged and nondisadvantaged children twice in a one-week period with the *Peabody Picture Vocabulary Test* (Dunn, 1965), and they found that the mean increase in IQ score among the disadvantaged children was ten points, compared to three points for the nondisadvantaged group. A follow-up study found similar results. It also established that the increase was not related to familiarity with the examiner, since in the follow-up study some children were tested by the same examiner in both administrations and some by different examiners each time, with no evidence of effect due to changing examiners.

Rapport. In his book *The Culturally Deprived Child*, Frank Riessman relates the following story:

> A few years ago a birthday party for a member of the staff at a well-known psychological clinic played a novel role in the test performance of a Negro child. Prior to the party, this boy, whom we shall call James, had been described on the psychological record as "sullen, surly, slow, unresponsive, apathetic, unimaginative, lacking in inner life." This description was based on his behavior in the clinic interviews and on his performance on a number of psychological measures including an intelligence test and a personality test. His was not an unusual record; many culturally deprived children are similarly portrayed.
> On the day of the birthday party, James was seated in an adjoining room waiting to go into the clinician's office. It was just after the lunch hour, and James had the first afternoon appointment. The conclusion of the lunch break on this particular day was used by the staff to present a surprise birthday cake to one of the clinicians who happened to be a Negro. The beautifully decorated cake was brought in and handed to the recipient by James' clinician who was white, as were all the other members of the staff. The Negro woman was deeply moved by the cake—and the entire surprise. In a moment of great feeling, she warmly embraced the giver of the cake. James inadvertently perceived all this from his vantage point in the outer office. That afternoon he showed amazing alacrity in taking the tests and responding in the interview. He was no longer sullen and dull. On the contrary, he seemed alive, enthusiastic, and he answered questions readily. His psychologist was astonished at the change and in the course of the next few weeks retested James on the tests on which he had done so poorly. He now showed marked improvement, and she quickly revised not only the test appraisal of him on the clinical record card, but her general personality description of him as well.
> The high point of their new, positive relationship came some months later when he confided to her that she had gotten off on the wrong foot with him on the first day in the first three

minutes of contact. She was taken aback and said, "What do you mean? I was very friendly, I told you my name and asked you yours." He responded, "Yeh, and I said James Watson and right away you called me Jimmy and you bin callin' me Jimmy ever since. My name is James, 'cept to my very good friends maybe. Even my mother calls me James." Then he went on to tell her how he had changed his opinion of her on the day of the birthday party because of the close relationship he had seen between her and the Negro psychologist.

This little story illustrates a number of things: First, it shows that *the test is a social situation.* The testing situation, whether it be a psychological test or any other kind of test, for that matter, reflects a relationship between people, a relationship that is often remarkably subtle. And when anything hampers this relationship, the result is likely to show in the test score itself. This can occur on an individual test as well as a group test, an I.Q. test as well as a personality test, a subject matter examination as well as a psychological measure.

It also shows how the behavior evidenced in the clinical situation tends to be seen by the psychologist as indicative of the basic personality of the child. This is frequently done with little awareness of how much this behavior is a product of the particular relationship of the psychologist to the child, and of the testing situation as such. Children from different cultural backgrounds respond very differently to clinical situations and to the idea of being tested or evaluated.

The anecdote also points up the fact that a well-meaning, clinically trained, unprejudiced psychologist can have poor rapport with a deprived child, not because of deficient psychological technique, but because of limited knowledge about certain cultural attitudes. In this case, the attitude in question is the feeling held by many Negro people that the informality intended by shortened nicknames signifies a lack of respect when it takes place across cultural lines. This does not suggest that the child himself was aware of this reasoning, but that, rather, he was simply reflecting his parents' wish that he be called by his full name.[1]

The story has implications for learning as well as testing settings. One of the critical issues it highlights is the ease with which experienced and accepting professionals from different cultural backgrounds can unknowingly create an interpersonal climate that vitiates involvement and motivation. Everyone makes mistakes, and

[1] From *The Culturally Deprived Child* by Frank Reissman. Copyright © 1962 by Frank Reissman. Reprinted by permission of Harper & Row, Publishers.

in most cases that teacher's general attitude will come through sooner or later. However, if the subcultural experience has encouraged a general distrust and wariness of the dominant culture adults, and the mismatch in cultural mores heightens these feelings, the establishment of rapport becomes a more sensitive and salient concern.

Another way in which particular subculture experience may interfere with the establishment of rapport is suggested by the wariness that Zigler et al. (1973) noted in the children they tested. This characteristic is further amplified by Mattick and Murphy (1973) as they describe the relationships of the children of poor and highly disorganized families:

> In coping with an unpredictable, capricious and often dangerous environment they had learned to operate with a facade of bland smile, responding in a surface manner to the perceived or actual demands of others but remaining uninvolved, unmotivated to actively explore and manage themselves in their environment. (p. 453)

> At first look most of them appeared highly responsive to people and it was observed that on the street their ingratiating maneuvers yielded these children an uncommonly rich supply of candy, pennies, affection and more or less tangible "gifts" . . . . The social behavior described . . . turned out to be the entire social repertoire and defined the extent of a relationship between these children and other people, i.e., attention seeking, superficial manipulative contact, without continuity or any back and forth sequence. . . . Such children's longing for attention, expressed by constant focus on the teacher's whereabouts, while at the same time showing distrust, suspicion and wariness, is an important obstacle to their ability to accept guidance and to learn from people in a teacher role. (p. 451)[2]

This group of children illustrates a different and more entrenched rapport problem than does James. They do not openly indicate by expression or surface behavior that there is any lack of rapport with the adult, and the problem cannot be resolved by any single demonstration of understanding or respect.

---

[2] From "Cognitive Disturbance in Young Children" by I. Mattick and L. B. Murphy in *Children with Learning Problems*, edited by S. G. Sapir and A. C. Nitzburg. Copyright © 1973 by Bruner/Mazel. Reprinted by permission of the publisher.

Motivation. One of the differential characteristics indicated by a number of studies is the failure of some disadavantaged groups of children to strive for academic success for its own sake. Douvan (1956) tested disadvantaged and middle-class children, first with no comment about the importance of the test or any reward. The middle-class children performed considerably better. When the test was rerun, this time with a reward promised, the performances of the disadvantaged children improved much more than that of the middle-class group. As Riessman (1962) has noted, middle-class youth are motivated to perform closer to their optimum level of performance when immediate rewards are absent. Deprived youth respond more fully when promised rewards that are direct, immediate, practical, and meaningful. Gordon (1970) notes that the findings of several investigators, as do Douvan's, support the idea that depressed motivation tends to occur in disadvantaged children, and he explains it as follows:

> The degree of motivation and the direction which it takes among many of these children are often inconsistent with both the demands and the goals of formal education. But although the quality of aspiration is often depressed, it is usually consistent with the child's perceptions of the opportunities and rewards available to him. Symbolic rewards and postponements of gratifications appear to have little value as positive motivators of achievement. For these children goals tend to be self-centered, immediate, and utilitarian, as are the goals of the dominant culture. However, children growing up under more privileged circumstances have available many sources of immediate satisfaction and immediate feedback as well as many more evidences of the utilitarian value of academic effort. The differences between the privileged and the disadvantaged in this area are not so much differences in values as differences in the circumstances under which the values are called into play. (p. 254)

Gordon suggests that disadvantaged children lack sources of immediate gratification and immediate feedback. Beem et al. (1969) and Mattick and Murphy (1973) are among the many investigators who have noted that parents of disadvantaged children tend not to praise their children's successes or give them encouraging feedback on their efforts. To the extent that this is true in any family, there is the likelihood that achievement for its own sake does not become incorporated in the child's ego ideal. Mattick and

Murphy (1973) present the striking example of Sally, who could not learn numbers in sequence or one-to-one correspondence, but:

> . . . one day revealed that she possessed a wealth of knowledge about numbers as related to pawning various articles. She talked not only about the fact that you get more money in the pawnshop for a steam iron than for another kind of iron, but subtracted the amount and explained what you could and could not buy in the way of food for each. What was impressive here was not only that she had memorized these figures, whereas she could not seem to memorize the so-called more "simple" or "basic" ones, but that she could actually deal with these complex numerical concepts on an abstract level, in response to other children's questions of a clearly hypothetical nature, such as, "How much d'you get for my new sweater, for a dog, a car, a candy bar, my baby's bottle?" etc. (p. 448)[3]

In considering the impact of nonintellective factors on children's measurable achievement, one can only wonder how many children are assumed to have "cognitive deficits" that cause them to test low or seemingly not learn, when in fact they are intellectually far more capable than we can find out by standardized measures. Zigler et al. (1973) found this out because they tested the children twice; James's psychologist found out because by chance James witnessed a staff birthday party; and Sally's teachers found out because in her special preschool program there were uncommon opportunities for teachers to promote and listen to free discussion among the children. In regular school settings the information that would allow for revised judgments is rarely available. In the following section, we shall consider some of what is available in regular school settings.

THE SCHOOL

By its nature as a community instrument, designated to transmit cultural beliefs and standards as well as the more universal academic areas of science and the humanities, the school tends to be a fairly monolithic, slow-changing institution that reflects the dominant social and political culture of the community. The "community" may be the nation as a whole, a particular school district, or an individual school. Whether rules and standards are deter-

[3] Ibid.

mined by national laws and customs, by the individual classroom teacher, or by any other social or governing body, they are always based on the group's expectations and goals. Thus, they will always be inappropriate to the special needs of some individual children. At times they will also be inappropriate to the needs of identifiable groups of children. Standards and an awareness of normative behavior are essential in education. When their use contributes to the development or exacerbation of learning problems, it is because maintenance of the standard, as the educator understands it, has in some way taken precedence over helping individual children to achieve it.

To a large degree, schools are what society asks and allows them to be. In many instances, schools are presented with overwhelming problems and allotted totally inadequate resources for dealing with them. Nevertheless, there are also the smaller-scale failures to meet the individual needs of children, failures that are within the abilities of individual teachers and administrators to avoid. These are usually attributable to either policies, methods, or materials of the curriculum, or to teacher-pupil interactions. In the material that follows, some of the small ways in which schools fail to meet the individual needs of children are considered. These failures, which contribute to the development and perpetuation of learning problems, occur in two areas: curriculum and teacher-pupil interaction.

Curriculum

When teachers fail to adapt their classroom lessons to the individual needs of children, it is usually because they believe they can not or should not do so. Some teachers see the curriculum as fixed, with an obligation on the part of the teacher to teach a particular set of materials and concepts. If it is altered, the child is not given first (or fifth or ninth) grade work, and the teacher sees that as unfair to the student, his classmates, future teachers, and the system. Teachers feel that the placement of a problem child in their class is unjust. They may blame previous teachers and the family for not having sent the child to their class prepared for what they have to offer. They may blame the school administration for not providing special classes or homogeneous grouping. In any event, the child's inability to do grade-level work becomes the reason for not trying to teach him.

One conscientious third-grade teacher complained bitterly and repeatedly about a child in her class who could not do any of the assigned work and was a constant behavior problem. "He can't even write his name!" she complained. When someone suggested that she teach him to do that, she was stunned and answered, "But suppose he learns that, what will I do next?" Her reaction made it clear that it was easier for her to regard the child as a total failure and not her responsibility than to try to teach him at his own level. Once she assumed any teaching responsibility for him, she would feel obligated to work with him towards the achievement of grade level skills (a realistically impossible task), and the thought of trying to do this while teaching the rest of her class was overwhelming. She was then reassured that whatever she might accomplish would be worthwhile, and not to worry about what came next. In fact, the outcome was very rewarding to everyone concerned: the child was so pleased at being able to do something consistently and well that he pleaded to be taught more things. The teacher was also pleased with her success in teaching and with his remarkable change in behavior and attitude. Finding a few minutes to work with him became a pleasurable and high-priority item in her mental agenda rather than a burdensome and guilt-provoking responsibility.

This is not a total success story, however. Other children in the teacher's class failed to get needed special attention, and neither the boy's good behavior nor learning progress continued smoothly through his school career or even that school year. The teacher did not undergo a personality change, and the prescribed curriculum continued to be the dictator in the classroom. Still, the incident demonstrates what can happen when a child feels that he is learning and a teacher feels she is teaching.

In contrast to the teacher who believes that the curriculum must be presented to everyone is the teacher who feels that a child having academic or behavior difficulties should not be pressed to perform. Rather, the child should be allowed to play, run errands, or go to another activity until he feels ready. Although such teachers may feel real concern for the child and place his interests above that of some theoretical curriculum demand, their benign neglect too often constitutes an abdication of responsibility. Thus, young children are sometimes seen wandering aimlessly in classrooms, unable to approach a group of children or settle down to work. In open-structured classrooms a child may avoid a certain subject or skill area for months. The collusion between the child's anxiety and the teacher's laissez-faire educational philosophy results in an ever-increasing deficit.

In one extreme case, a fourth-grade boy with superior intelligence and generally high motivation was unable to write his own name. The school philosophy was that children can learn when they are ready and that there are no learning problems except for those created at school when children are forced to do what they are not ready to do. The philosophy dictated curriculum as rigidly as in any old-fashioned, conservative, lockstep, formal classroom. As a result, the boy's learning disability, which involved poor reading and spelling as well, was not noted until his mother stopped depending on the school staff's judgment and took him for a clinical evaluation.

Teacher-Pupil Interaction

Social psychology literature offers information on two specific classroom phenomena that directly affect the development of learning problems. One of these is the tendency of middle-class teachers, both black and white, to reject lower-class and particularly black lower-class children. Deutsch (1967) notes that while there is great sensitivity in middle-class schools to the home and school pressures that might be affecting a child, the problems in lower-class schools are so massive that teacher sensitivity becomes blunted. Clark (1973) believes that the insensitivity results from the fact that the social and economic predicaments of the children remind some teachers of their own heritage, and they react punitively or negatively. One of the most disturbing findings by his HARYOU (Harlem Youth Opportunities Unlimited) staff was that, "When we examined the attitude of Negro teachers toward Negro students in the Harlem schools we found the teachers on the average quite as rejecting, quite as full of stereotype, as white teachers" (p. 463).

The second phenomenon was most clearly highlighted in Rosenthal and Jacobson's *Pygmalion in the Classroom* (1968). While controversial as to methodology and data analysis (Elashoff & Snow, 1970), the text illustrated what others, including Reissman (1962), had noted: the teacher's expectations regarding pupils' performance can serve as an educational self-fulfilling prophecy. In the Rosenthal and Jacobson study teachers were given the names of children in their classrooms (20% of the class enrollment), names chosen at random, who would show unusual intellectual gains during the coming academic year. According to Rosenthal and Jacobson, those children did score higher on subsequent IQ testing than did their controls. In addition, the teacher ratings on these children were more favorable than they were on those individual control children who also made intellectual gains. Thus, the tendency among middle-class teachers to have negative expectations of lower-class children is even more ominous in what it suggests about the effect such expectations have on the children's intellectual development. As Clark (1973) states, " . . . these children will learn if they are taught and they will not learn if they are approached as if they cannot learn" (p. 467).

Disadvantaged children, and children who for one reason or another are emotionally rejected by their teachers are not the only ones whose intellectual growth may be hampered by teacher attitudes. In some instances, the sympathy and too-ready assistance of the teacher encourages a passive, dependent orientation towards learning. The motivating force then usually becomes some combination of longing for teacher affection and poorly channeled aggressive energies. In the previous chapter this behavior pattern in girls was discussed. When a teacher is too responsive to that behavior, he or she reinforces it and simultaneously fails to search out and nurture any seeds of more active, independent strivings.

Analogous to the teachers who get caught up in children's dependency patterns are those who are caught up in authority struggles with students. It would probably rarely, if ever, occur that the teacher actually created the learning problem in either of these situations. Yet, there is little doubt that teachers can encourage and fuel such problems in children who bring them to class.

5

Clinical Assessment: Interviews

In the clinical assessment an attempt is made to identify and evaluate the various biological, psychological, and social determinants discussed earlier. Although the assessment may include a number of measures identified as specifically biological, psychological, or social in character (e.g., the E.E.G., intelligence testing, and the parent interview, respectively), it should not be assumed that each source provides only one category of information. In fact, one of the continuing demands on the examining clinician is to remain alert and sensitive to the varieties of information about the child that come from all sources. Teachers report on achievement but also provide vivid descriptions of the child's interaction with children and adults at school. Parents are often an excellent source of information about the child's progress through various stages of motor, language, and social development. They offer detailed anecdotal material that is very meaningful in assessing a learning problem, though it might not have been recorded in the pediatric record. Conversely, the pediatrician can often report on significant aspects of family dynamics, seen in the course of treating the child over time, that might not come to light in the psychologist's interviews with the parents or the family.

The assessment program presented in this chapter is in many respects similar to the familiar child guidance clinic evaluation consisting of social, medical, psychological, and, frequently, school information. One interviews the relevant family and school people; checks out the medical and health factors; tests, talks, and perhaps plays with the child. In the end, the clinical assessor collates the information, reaches diagnostic conclusions, and plans the indicated intervention program. In content as well as form there are similarities. In both instances one looks at family dynamics, the personality and behavior characteristics of the child, the child's relationships with peers and adults, and his intellectual functioning. The differences are in focus and in goals, in the kinds of specific information sought, and the uses made of it.

While the differences are mainly of degree, there is at least one fundamental difference in kind. In child guidance practice the presenting complaint—be it a disturbance in thought, affect, or behavior—is seen as a symptom of some central, overall disturbance in the child's psychological functioning. Were it not considered so, he would be referred to some other service, usually medical or social, to deal with what is regarded as a basic disturbance in the child's physical condition or environmental setting.

When a major presenting problem is a learning disorder, I find it more useful to regard it as a central problem in its own right, rather than only as a symptom of something else. For the child, school is his occupation, and the major focus of his life outside of his family. The child's academic achievement and behavior are matters of crucial importance in his personal development, in the way in which he is regarded by others, and in his own self-perception. This is not to deny that in some cases a learning problem is symptomatic of other problems; it is rather to assert that the learning difficulty is deserving and in need of comprehensive assessment in its own right. Only after such an assessment can one determine the extent to which it should be viewed as symptomatic of some other underlying condition. The child guidance evaluation model is a useful guide in learning problem assessment, stressing as it does the need for clinical sensitivity, multiple contributing factors, and the overdetermination of behavior. However, it can be hazardous if it leads the clinician to consider presenting problems of learning disorders as he or she presents fire setting, nightmares, or school phobia; that is, as symptoms which will be alleviated or disappear with the application of appropriate psychotherapeutic treatment.

A useful analogy to this approach is vocational counseling, in which the major goal is successful performance in the work sphere. In the service of that goal the counselor makes use of a variety of data concerning the client's personality, interests, abilities, aspirations, interpersonal relationships, physical skills, limitations, and so on. The counselor is interested in the client's general personality functioning to the extent that it affects occupational success. Should the counselor find that the psychological disturbance is so great as to require attention in its own right, the vocational matters, even if they move from center stage, will still require specialized professional assessment and planning. The psychologist has the same responsibility to the child with learning problems; no matter how seriously disturbed or handicapped the child is in other areas, the child's learning situation demands and deserves full attention in its own right. In short, one might say that the present approach is a modified child guidance approach; the modification is in making learning problems the central focus, much as vocational counseling focuses on work problems.

The learning assessment may be carried out in a psychiatric setting such as a child guidance clinic or private psychiatric or psychological practice; it may be done within the child's school system and under that auspices; it may be done in either a public or private setting devoted specifically to the diagnosis and remediation of learning problems. Depending on the facility, the orientation of the professionals, and the presenting problems, the learning problems may be assessed separately or in conjunction with a general psychological evaluation. Depending on the availability of professional workers and their backgrounds, it may be carried out by one person, or by a group representing various disciplines. In the following material I refer to the assessing person as the clinician or psychologist for purposes of simplification, but there are many parts of the assessment that might be carried out by some other professional person—a social worker, a remedial specialist, a guidance counselor, or a psychiatrist, depending on the area involved. In every case, a learning assessment includes interviews with parents and teachers, intellectual assessment, and assessment of basic academic skills. In some cases, there will also be a need for special learning abilities or disabilities testing, personality testing, or medical or paramedical evaluation (e.g., neurological, audiological, ophthalmological).

The remainder of this chapter deals with interview material, and in the following chapter, testing and referral are discussed.

PARENT INTERVIEWS

The parent interviews of the standard child guidance diagnostic study are a useful model for collecting factual information and for developing clinical impressions about the causes, nature, and effects of the child's learning problem. Interviews in a learning problem assessment differ mainly in their emphasis on certain aspects of the history, attitudes, and feelings related to learning. The emphasis is designed to assess the possible effects of the biological, psychological, and social determinants that so often influence success or failure in learning. As in any diagnostic study, it is very important to be thorough and exacting in the collection and recording of information. It is also important to simultaneously maintain sensitivity and flexibility in listening for and pursuing clinically rich material. Outlined below is a standard interview schedule. Noted in the discussion of each item are the issues to be stressed in a learning problem assessment.

Referral

It should be established whether the parents themselves requested the assessment. If so, it should be noted whether they have done so on their own or after consultation, advice, or urging from someone else (perhaps a teacher, doctor, friend, or relative). If the assessment is being done at the initiative of the school or some other agent, then the parents' interest, willingness, resistance, resentment, and so forth, should be clarified. In many cases the parents are in considerable disagreement with each other about the desirability of an assessment. This is a fact that may be stated immediately by one of them or that may go unmentioned if expression is not encouraged. A parent's resistance to assessment may stem from many things. A typical attitude is that too much fuss is being made and the child will grow out of it or come around if left alone. Some parents feel that the assessment is a painful and punitive thing to do to the child and that it constitutes blaming him. A converse attitude is that to look for deep psychological reasons is to indulge the child who ought to simply be disciplined more severely and made to tow the line. Such parental attitudes, whether shared by both parents or not, are likely to influence the entire interview. Eliciting these feelings early on, through a direct question as to how the parents happened to come for the assessment, is helpful in understanding and directing the ensuing discussion.

It is very important to know what has precipitated the referral at this time. In many cases it is some pending school decision. This is frequently so in the spring, when plans for the coming year are being made and questions are raised about repeating a grade or transferring to another school or program. Either the parents or the school may seek an assessment then, sometimes anxiously or defensively hoping to "prove" that the child should or should not stay with his own class. Yet often enough, there is good will on both sides and relatively unbiased interest in trying to determine what will be best for the child. As state and federal governments become more active in mandating special education and in establishing regulations about what school systems must provide for their educationally handicapped children, political and financial pressures are likely to influence school administrators and parents to seek particular kinds of assessment results. For example, parents may be searching for a label of "severe learning disability," which could justify their demand that the municipality pay for private learning disability schooling. Or, a school may be seeking documentation of emotional problems to back its claim that the public school remediation program is adequate and that parents and child must turn to psychotherapy rather than private schooling for the solution of their problems.

If there is a particular, perhaps hidden agenda prompting the assessment referral, the clinician must know about it. While assessment can be comprehensive and even exhaustive, it can never be total in the sense of scrutinizing and reporting on every aspect of learning. It could not provide an answer to any and every question that might ever be addressed to it. The questions must be known ahead of time, so that the clinician may determine whether the assessment procedures can be expected to answer them, and if so, which questions, tests, and interviews (or other procedures) are most likely to yield the necessary information.

Hereditary, Health, and Medical Background

Parents should be asked if anyone else in the family has had learning problems, particularly the parents themselves, the child's siblings, and the parent's siblings. Here, one must distinguish between two kinds of learning problems. The first concerns some almost legendary family member, such as the mentally retarded aunt or the school dropout cousin, who is clearly seen as a failure by the family, and may often be held up, explicitly or otherwise, as a prediction of what will become of the child if he does not do better. The family member is likely to become a strong identification object for the child. The other kind of learning problem to be noted is more subtle, often a thing of the past, seen in the present as having been overcome or compensated for. In particular, clinicians should know about early reading difficulties, or reading that is now competent but slow, and past or persisting difficulties in spelling or foreign language learning. It is not uncommon when such a question is raised to hear one parent, usually the father, say that he was late in learning to read or that he still cannot read as fast as he would like. Wives are often surprised at this piece of information, and the fathers themselves have generally not associated their child's problems with their own struggles of some thirty years ago. In these instances the parents may become more empathetic with the child's distress. Of course, there are also some parents who refer to their school problems and subsequent successes as reasons not to be so anxious, concerned, or protective of the child. The clinician should also note any speech or language problems observed in either parent such as stammering, poor articulation of some sounds, and difficulty in expressing ideas in cursive speech.

Beale Ong (1968) summarizes the major pregnancy and perinatal factors that may indicate brain insult or cerebral anoxia and about which parents should be questioned: maternal history of a prolonged period of infertility or several miscarriages, premature birth, difficult or prolonged labor, overmedication of the mother, infection immediately preceding delivery, difficulty in establishing respiration, jaundice, exchange transfusions, infection in the neonate, and administration of oxygen. Dr. Ong also notes that since the following illnesses or injuries may have neurological significance, they should be reviewed: measles with possible encephalitis, dehydration severe enough to warrant hospitalization, convulsive episodes with or without high fever, and head injuries, particularly those resulting in loss of consciousness or followed by behavior changes.

Parents should be asked explicitly if there have been any signs or complaints from the child of difficulty or discomfort in hearing or vision. Possible problems include slowness in responding when spoken to, a tendency to mishear, headaches, and eyestrain. It is a good practice to establish whether the child is known to be in good general health and, if not, whether he is being treated or followed by a physician.

Developmental History

The clinician will want to know whether there was either a general delay in development, or a lag in language or motor development. Parents' memory for milestone dates is often unreliable, but they will generally remember having believed some aspect of development to be slow, if such was the case. Sometimes the child's doctor has such information in his records. It is useful to ask about any problems or delays in accomplishing some of the common tasks of childhood, such as naming colors, tying shoes, or riding a bicycle. Color naming is one of the first signs that automatic learning of abstract symbols has taken place, and difficulty with this may signal later symbolization problems in reading. Difficulty with shoe tying and bicycle riding may signal perceptual-motor problems. Knowledge of the child's preferences in games and sports and of any activities that he regularly avoids, may add useful information about specific perceptual-motor or language problems. Difficulty with coloring within the lines, putting together jigsaw puzzles, block building, or catching a ball (compared with the abilities of classmates and siblings) suggests the possibility of perceptual or perceptual-motor inefficiency or lag, if not deficit.

The Learning Problem and the Child's Scholastic Strengths and Weaknesses

Parents vary in their ability to describe and specify the nature and extent of the child's learning problem. They often know more about the problem than they are aware of knowing until they are asked to speak about it. Even if they do not specifically know what the child lacks in information or skills, they do maintain some more or less conscious image of his capabilities and difficulties. The image is based not only on what they hear about school work, but also on what they observe during family dinner-table discussions, trips, arguments, and other routine aspects of daily living. Parents can easily observe the child's memory skills; interest in and comprehension of political issues; sensitivity to other people's viewpoints and feelings; reactions to intellectual games, puzzles, and riddles; and ability to read and understand road signs, billboards, directions, and menus. They have frequently worked with the child at home and can often describe quite vividly what that is like. For both assessment and remedial or therapeutic intervention it is important that the parents spell out their perceptions of the child's intellectual and academic strengths and weaknesses. Even minimally cooperative parents can portray a revealing and sensitive picture. They may point out strengths which are not seen at school, particular skills, or a capacity for intense concentration and perseverance that comes to light through a project or hobby. In the same way, parents may be able to report on the child's efforts to deal with homework. Does the child struggle and get nowhere, appeal to parents or siblings or friends for help, or try to avoid doing it altogether? It is helpful to inquire how the parents respond to the homework issues; whether they are in touch with the teacher; whether they accept the teacher's judgment and handling of the problems; and how they feel in general about the child's current school placement. What are their feelings about the school, class, subjects, teachers, classmates, special help, the lack of special help, and the like? Some parents can report on how the child feels about the problem; they know if he is actively distressed about it, how he expresses this, and whether he tends to deny it or pass it off as unimportant. Has the child been told about the assessment, and what is his reaction?

Parents are sometimes the best informants as to how the child feels about school in general, irrespective of the learning problems. They often can tell whether the child likes going to school, looks forward to anything about it, or finds it hard to face the prospect of going each morning. Even if they cannot speak about how he feels, they can say whether there are any problems with getting up, dressing, washing, breakfasting, and leaving for school. It should be noted how the child gets to and from school, and with whom he goes. Peer difficulties, anxiety about missed buses, a parent who daily delivers the child to school when one would expect he got there on his own—information such as this is enlightening and may come up when the question of transportation is raised.

School History

In the course of the assessment, parents and teachers are asked to report on the child's yearly school history. These reports are complementary both in the information they provide and in the occasional omissions and contradictions they highlight. Parents may feel that the problem lasted for several years while the school did not properly attend to it. They may claim they knew nothing of any serious difficulty while the school staff reports that they have been appealing to the parents for a long time to get some outside help.

Parents are more likely than the current teacher to be able to report on how the child has responded to school since he first began attending. They can talk about his "good year" with an understanding, pleasant, or talented teacher; and they know about his difficult times with an inexperienced or unsympathetic teacher, a new school, frequent illnesses and absences, family crises, and so on. Here again, in the process of reviewing and reciting the hsitory, parents often become newly aware of a pattern or series of difficulties with which the child has been struggling for a number of years.

The parents should also be asked about any special help the child has received in or out of school, the extent to which they feel it helped, and how the child himself responded to the help. Occasionally a child has received help that the school is unaware of. Attempts to help may result in intensified discouragement and despair if the child continues to have difficulty. The help may have failed because it was inappropriate to the problem. Yet, parents are rarely in a position to evaluate the suitability of professional help; they only know that the child failed to improve. The child's sense of personal failure and lack of worth is increased, and parents may cite lack of progress to indicate the futility of further efforts to assess or remediate the problem. A familiar statement is, "We've done all we can, he just won't (or can't) learn." Similar statements are occasionally heard from frustrated, discouraged teachers. The child is thus both abandoned and blamed. In other, similar cases the child is equally given up on, but the adult attitude is not so much despairing and blaming as it is patiently sympathetic and "understanding." In these cases the general sentiment is that one ought to stop bothering the child by expecting anything of him. The resulting self-image is equally laden with feelings of failure and lack of worth.

Family Interaction

Bearing in mind the frequent effects of sex and birth order on the family expectations and attitudes about the importance of learning and academic success for its various members (as discussed in chapter 4), it is important for the psychologist to have a clear picture of the age, sex, and academic status of the child's siblings. Knowing the child's position in the family will help the clinician generate hunches; he or she can then direct questions to elicit material that can confirm, elaborate, or refute those hunches.

Some variant examples not previously noted follow. An oldest son, whose academic difficulties have been a particularly sharp disappointment to his father, may be helped or hindered by his status as oldest in coping with his problem. A younger son whose older brother's academic success defies competition may be thereby induced to look to other realms for achievement. The "baby" of the family, whose cuteness or naughtiness is enjoyed by the rest, and from whom very little is demanded or expected, may not have had opportunities to learn to accept and enjoy responsibilities. An only child, a physically ill child, or one who, for other reasons, has been overprotected and sheltered by his family, may not have been given opportunities to confront difficulties and learn to cope with them.

In considering family interaction, it is helpful to note whether the parents differ in their individual reactions to the child's problems. In some instances, one parent is particularly anxious while the other takes a more objective approach in trying to allay everyone's anxiety. One parent may blame the child, while the other tries to protect him from blame and anger. Siblings may support a child with learning problems by helping with schoolwork or defending the child against other children; or they may regularly turn against him, teasing and competing. One way to get at this information is to ask if the child is particularly close to any of his siblings, or if the child has special problems with any of them. There may be other family or household members (aunts, grandparents, household help, etc.) who are significantly involved. Often the response to a question about whether the child has any household chores or responsibilities in taking care of family pets will reveal a good deal about who does what for whom within the family.

Some clinicians (e.g., Friedman, 1973) prefer family interviewing to parent interviewing in order to observe family interaction at first hand. While the family interview provokes interaction and provides material that is not likely to be elicited when interviewing parents alone, the clinician must also find some time for collecting factual information from parents which only they are likely to know. This information is often left unnoted when the drama and emotional involvement characteristic of many family interviews is underway. Since assessment time is limited, each clinician will have to decide on a format or combination of interviews that will most economically render the data he needs.

Play and Social Activities

Some understanding of the child's life outside of the school and his immediate family allows a broader perspective on his general adjustment. It is important to know whether and to what extent the learning problems may create social difficulties, making the child unable to play some games, to be a competent team member in group sport, or to get along easily with others his age. If he cannot read the instructions or rules in certain games, or if he is uncoordinated and clumsy at sports, questions arise as to how he manages and how the other children react to him. Children whose learning disorders are a relatively discrete and isolated phenomenon often demonstrate impressive ego strength and social skills in their peer relationships. They sometimes cover their learning deficits and sometimes ask and accept, without embarrassment, the help of their friends. It is important to ask about the child's friends—whether he has one or a few close friends, gets along in school and neighborhood groups, tends to spend time with younger children, is generally led by other children, or can hold his own in initiating and directing. If he participates in organized groups, such as scouts or church groups, it is important to know if it is with enthusiastic involvement, moderate interest, or mainly in order to satisfy his own or his parents' wish that he "belong" to something. If the child has no friends, this generally indicates serious personality problems. However, learning problems can add to such a child's social difficulties, depriving him of useful socializing skills and further weakening his self-esteem.

Parental Hopes, Aspirations, and Projections

The older the child or the more serious the problem, the more likely that parents have been actively concerned about how long his schooling will continue, whether he can manage high school or college, and what he will do afterwards. Parents with teenage or seriously handicapped children should be asked what they would like to see their child achieve from his schooling, and what they would like to see him doing once he leaves school. Have they discussed this with the child; does he have anything in particular in mind for himself? (The psychologist will most likely wish to discuss this with the youngster himself as well.) In some cases, it turns out that the parents have quite specific ideas and plans for the child (e.g., "He'll always have a place in my business."), which may or may not be realistic in terms of the child's abilities and interests. In any case, questions on the subject evoke useful material regarding parental expectations and estimates of the child's abilities and current standing. While some parents tend to deny difficulties, there are others who underrate their children. For example, the 16-year-old daughter of a very talented and successful father was having minor difficulties in one or two subjects and showed some resistance to homework, although in other areas she demonstrated real talent and was consistently regarded at school as a serious and capable student. In the parent interview, the father suddenly remarked that he wondered if she would be accepted into a college, a worry that in this situation was totally unexpected and equally unrealistic. The mother was shocked to hear that her husband felt that way, and clearly saw it as evidence of his depreciating their daughter. The dynamic issues involved, between the parents themselves and in their daughter's perception of herself, were in this way highlighted, eventually contributing to a better understanding of the girl's learning difficulties.

Parents and the Remedial Program

A psychological diagnostic study includes an estimate of the parents' ability to participate in and benefit from a recommended psychotherapeutic program. In the same way, parent interviews in a learning assessment should contribute to estimating their ability to actively participate in a remedial program. Despite whether or not parents are to be involved in some form of psychotherapy in connection with their child's problems, an active decision must be made at the end of the assessment as to what role they will play in the learning program. Whether they should be encouraged to provide direct help to the child (e.g., with homework or reading), provide ancillary help (such as looking into summer programs or after-school groups), or to depend as much as possible on others to do the programming and tutoring will partly depend on the clinician's assessment of them, as well as of the child's specific needs. Some parents are quite capable of helping their children without being either indulgent or punitive. Some cannot provide direct help without becoming very anxious and impatient and taking it out on the child, though they need to feel that they can actively help and contribute to the child's academic welfare. Other parents need to be relieved of the whole business entirely, for the child's sake as well as their own. With the benefit of a sensitive and comprehensive clinical assessment, there is no need for such global dicta as, "Children should never be helped by their parents, it just makes them feel more pressured and anxious; let the teachers take care of the teaching," or "All parents need to have some active part in helping their children so that they feel less anxious and guilty about what they regard as their failure."

TEACHER INTERVIEWS[1]

Teacher interviews is used here as a general rubric which includes interviews with other school personnel (principal, guidance counselor, school social worker, remedial teachers, school nurse) whenever relevant. The term is also meant to include the collection of recorded information such as standardized test scores, school history, special help, and so on.

Classroom teachers know a great deal about the children they teach, based on informal observation over long periods of time. They have seen a much fuller range of performance and behavior than the clinician sees in his or her limited number of office visits. They are witness to the child's reactions to success and failure and to his experience with varieties of stress. Teachers know, from firsthand experience, how the child deals with other children and how they respond to him. A teacher's report provides a useful check on the psychologist's clinical hunches, often confirming and elaborating them. At times the teacher's perspective will be in conflict with the psychologist's, thereby demanding efforts to explain the differences. These efforts generally lead both psychologist and

---

[1]Some of the material in this section was previously published in a different form in M. Sanders, *Guidelines for the Educational, Social and Psychological Assessment of Children in Special Educational Need* (Cambridge, Mass.: Research Institute for Educational Problems, 1973). Permission to reproduce this material is gratefully acknowledged.

teacher to a more differentiated and articulate understanding of the child's situation, even if the differences are not fully resolved.

The extent and richness of teachers' information, observations, and impressions are often untapped because of the clinician's failure to involve teachers in the assessment. In some cases, teachers are not consulted at all; in others, they are asked to fill out behavior checklists, or contacted only as a matter of form. Clinicians frequently suffer from stereotyped, prejudged expectations of teacher attitudes and abilities; they tend to anticipate an insensitive, unconcerned, rejecting, or openly hostile response both to the child and to the clinician's interest in him. My experience has been that most teachers are only too glad to be asked for their help and, in turn, contribute a great deal. Unfortunately a great number of teachers seem to be in awe of medical and mental health professionals and are reluctant to initiate the contact themselves; thus, for the most part, if the clinician does not request a meeting, there will not be one. I have also found that teachers who are neither psychologically minded, sympathetically concerned about the child, nor glad to meet with the clinician can nevertheless give a most useful and fairly objective picture of the child's classroom achievement and behavior. If the clinician finds the teacher to be harsh, punitive, and quite unable to understand or accept the child, this is, of course, important information to have. When the psychologist and the teacher show a sympathetic concern for the child and mutual respect for each other's professional contribution to the child's development, a working relationship can develop which extends beyond the original assessment. This relationship can continue to benefit the child during the remedial treatment and can allow teacher and clinician to learn a great deal together and from each other.

Just as the psychologist should have a fairly clear idea of the kind of information required from the parents, he or she should also know the type of information required from the teacher. While the teacher has the advantage of long periods of observation and a good sense of how the child compares with other children, it is not likely that he or she is trained to know what kinds of information are relevant nor how to interpret what is seen. Therefore, the psychologist should be prepared to pointedly inquire about certain areas, rather than to simply open a discussion with, "Tell me how he does in school," and expect the teacher to expound on pertinent issues.

The kinds of information that teachers can provide can be classified as follows: (1) school history; (2) school behavior; (3) current levels of academic performance; and (4) home-school relationships.

School History

A year by year chronology of the child's school history is basic demographic data for a learning assessment. Some school systems routinely maintain a running record indicating for each year the following kinds of information about each child: city, school, grade, teacher, and any special services requested and received (such as speech therapy, special class placement, remedial reading, and psychological testing). This bland statistical information may reveal important and otherwise unmentioned information, such as periods of school attendance in a foreign country or missed altogether, frequent moves, or numerous attempts at remediation through a variety of special services. Sometimes the history simply provides useful factual material; at other times it serves as a prelude to deeper and emotionally meaningful interviews with the parents or the child. The history may also provide new information for the current teacher, or if the history was known, it may not have been heretofore regarded in relationship to current problems. An example will illustrate. Robin was at the beginning of third grade when she was referred to the school psychologist because of reading problems and some adjustment difficulties. When routine testing indicated high intelligence and no sign of specific learning disability, the psychologist ruled that the reading problem must be due to emotional problems. He did not know that Robin had spent her first grade year in Italy, where she had learned to speak and read first-grade-level Italian. Later, an analysis of Robin's reading indicated that her major problem was with the vowels, which she tended to read according to Italian phonetic principles (whereby "like" would be pronounced *lee-keh*). She would thus produce a non-English word, which she might then correct by guessing according to the context, but of course she could not understand why what she originally read did not match what she was supposed to say. She only knew that she was not reading right, and she felt that she was stupid.

If the psychologist had known about Robin's year in Italy, he would have made a different assessment. More importantly, work with Robin would have included explaining the Italian problem to her and working with her directly on the vowel sounds as they are written in English. Robin did have other problems in addition to her Italian–English vowel confusion, many of them related to the loss of her mother in infancy, but while attention to those problems might have aided in her general family and school adjustment, it constituted a distraction from her reading problem.

While collecting material from school records, the psychologist should also record whatever test scores are available from group intelligence and achievement test administrations. For tests comprised of many parts or subtests, such as the Differential Aptitude Tests and tests of primary abilities, it is important to record all subtest scores as well, in whatever forms they appear—percentile ranks, grade equivalents, stanine scores, standard scores, etc. These scores will be evaluated in light of the psychologist's own current testing results.

School Behavior

In considering school behavior, the child's academic and social behavior in the classroom is of primary concern. However, there are often significant aspects of school outside of the classroom—on the playground, in the cafeteria and auditorium, in the corridors between classes, on class trips, during extracurricular sports and cultural activities. Much of what the clinician routinely considers in relation to family dynamics—role, interaction, models, sources of gratification, rivalries, male-female and adult-child attitudes and relationships—can be directly applied to the child's school life. The more the psychologist knows about the people and activities in the child's class and in the school as a whole, the better he or she will understand what the child contends with and responds to there. Moreover, the psychologist can be more helpful in planning a remedial program that will take greatest possible advantage of the school's resources.

Behavior During Lesson and Nonlesson Periods. Routine information about the child's school day and material pertaining to intrapsychic and interpersonal issues are both important. A series of questions (see Appendix I) concerning (1) the activities and setting in which the child does function at his best; (2) those in which he has the most difficulty; (3) topics of special interest; (4) skills or problems during nonlesson periods; and (5) his ability to handle responsibility will help elicit a picture of the child's school life. These questions provide assessment data and lay the groundwork for later remedial planning which must be based on adequate knowledge of the normal school environment.

Ability to Work in Various Groupings. A child's ability to work independently by himself or in the midst of a group, and his ability to work cooperatively with large and small groups, are significant factors in his manageability, relationships with other children, learning, and the satisfactions derived from his own work and from his involvement with others. It is important to know whether the child can maintain himself personally and socially within the established style and framework of the classroom (with time scheduled or open, work assigned or freely chosen, discipline tight or relaxed) or whether he needs special arrangements to accommodate his problems. If the child needs special arrangements, it should be determined whether he has been getting them and how effective they have been. Appendix I lists some specific questions that may be useful in eliciting this information.

Relationships with Children and Adults in School. There is considerable variation among classrooms and schools as to how much opportunity a teacher has to observe the development and the nature of friendships among his or her pupils. As a rule, the smaller the group and more informal the style, the greater the opportunities for children to openly demonstrate their interest in each other and for teachers to observe the interaction. Besides describing their observations, teachers can indicate the extent to which they believe their classrooms offer opportunities for contact with other children. In some instances, teachers have a more accurate perspective on a child's friendships than do his parents. Teachers are more objective, and have better opportunities for observing such things as whether a child's relationships with other children are real friendships or based on something else such as caretaking, protection, or fear.

Some children develop special relationships with adults at school. While some are generally eager to ingratiate themselves with any adult, others form special attachments, for example, to a particular teacher, secretary, the building custodian, or athletic coach. Some children develop intense antipathies toward certain teachers, or to certain types of teachers. Some, like Victor who was discussed in chapter 3, carry on a fight with at least one teacher every year. Specific questions will be found in Appendix I.

An invaluable supplement to interviewing teachers is the psychologist's own observation of the child in school. Many aspects of the child's behavior in various social and academic situations can be observed by the psychologist at first hand with rewarding results. If the psychologist observes what teachers or parents have described, his or her confirmation of their impressions will not only provide welcome corroboration but will also offer possibilities for a more elaborated and comprehensive understanding of the observed behavior. In addition, direct observation frequently yields information not otherwise available. Children observed on the playground, in the corridors, at lunch, or in gym as well as in formal classroom settings may behave in a manner that speaks clearly to a trained and single-minded observer but that has not been noted or reported by others.

School psychologists who are regularly at the school and can observe a child over a period of time are in a better position for reliable observations than an outside clinician who comes into the school once or twice to learn about one child. The dangers of overgeneralizing from limited observation are obvious, and it is incumbent on the observing psychologist to check his or her impressions with the teacher, and sometimes the parents, to see if the observed behavior is characteristic and if the clinician's interpretation is warranted. Even if no one has been aware of the specific behavior before, an accurate interpretation of it should resonate with other behavior of which people have been aware.

Current Level of Academic Functioning

At this point in the assessment what is asked for is a description, rather than an analysis, of the child's classroom achievements in various subject areas. This description is given in terms of the child's position in relation to the rest of the class. With young children the concern is with basic skills; with older children, basic skills and such subjects as foreign language, social studies, literature, science, and mathematics are of concern. The clinician needs to secure from the school that information which only the school can provide. What does the child's class do in the course of the school day; what are the various academic activities? Where does the child manage well, where does he regularly fail, and where does he manage only with special help or under altered conditions? It is often helpful to ask the teacher to describe the typical school day by covering each subject, explaining at what level and with what materials the children are currently working, and comparing the child's performance in each subject to the general class standard. Here, as with interviewing on the subject of behavior, asking for specific detailed information may stimulate the development of a more differentiated perception of the child on the part of the teacher. It may also spark a renewed interest in closer observations and experimental approaches. Another series of questions in Appendix I, divided according to subject areas is designed to develop a detailed picture of the child's academic skills.

Reading. It is useful to distinguish between reading technique and comprehension. The first refers to the child's ability to decode the written language and know what it says, in the sense that he can call out each word. Comprehension generally comes after technique, in that it is only after the child has recognized the words that he can deal with their meaning. However, many children can very well comprehend a paragraph in which they are unable to decode, or to decode accurately, many of the words. The teacher should be asked to distinguish between the child's technical reading skill and his reading comprehension, and to report on each as they manifest themselves in class. Teachers in the early grades are usually aware of the child's technical skill from his reading aloud at various times. Children in the older grades may have technical reading difficulties which go unnoticed.

Spelling. If a child is having difficulty with spelling, questions arise as to where in the schoolwork the problems are seen, what kind of spelling instruction has been available to him, and to what extent the problem is a hindrance in other academic areas. Some children spell phonetically and reasonably, but have failed to intuit, or to learn (if they were taught) the conventions and rules of spelling. Some do well on a weekly spelling test, but poorly in writing assignments. Some can find and correct their own mistakes if asked to do so; others cannot see that anything is wrong. Schools and teachers vary greatly in the extent to which they emphasize and teach correct spelling; many who have encouraged free expressive writing have intentionally not insisted upon correct spelling. They have also failed to include it elsewhere in the curriculum. Once children can spell phonetically, they learn to spell through a combination of phonic analysis and visual memory. Most of the words they write have not been taught but have been learned through experience—that is, by reading. Thus, children who do not read, either because they cannot or do not like to, or children who were late in reading are especially prone to have spelling difficulties.

Handwriting. Handwriting is the basic skill most quickly abandoned as a separate area of instruction, after which it is used only as an instrument in other learning areas. Thus, as a rule, only the very youngest children get any regular help or instruction in how to form letters correctly, maintain proper spacing and proportion, hold the pencil, and sit properly. All of these factors affect the child's ability to write legibly, comfortably, and smoothly.

Most aspects of handwriting will be observed directly by the clinician when he or she sees the child, but not all. Some questions for the teacher are in Appendix I; and it is also suggested that the clinician ask for some handwriting samples from daily classwork or homework, including samples of the best and worst writing, according to the teacher's judgment.

Arithmetic. It is helpful to consider three areas of mathematical ability in asking the teacher to describe a child's difficulties in the subject. These are:

> *Content* (or concepts)—the basic symbols and processes such as counting, correspondence, conservation, and form discrimination. Problems in this area are most likely to occur with younger children. However, these problems can appear at higher levels, for example, with difficulty grasping such concepts as the square root, logarithm, and cosine.
>
> *Operations* (or computation)—the mechanics of addition, subtraction, multiplication, and division. A great deal of successful computation depends on memory (remembering number facts, remembering how to set up problems on paper, remembering in which direction to operate and where to write results of intermediate or partial solutions) until the processes become highly automatic, or well enough understood so that the child can figure out what he cannot remember by rote.
>
> *Applications* (or mathematical reasoning, problem solving)—reading word problems and translating them from ordinary language to a mathematical language and format. Besides depending on adequate bases of concept understanding and computation, application depends on increasingly advanced levels of skill in manipulating symbols and concepts. Teachers have long been aware of children who understand such basic concepts as size, number, and time, who can also do the technical computations accurately, but who cannot find and formulate the mathematical problems embedded in stories of "How many marbles?" "How much change?" "When will the trains pass each other?" Conversely, teachers are also familiar with the children who have a seemingly intuitive grasp of the issues and relationships but who lack

the mechanical skills required for accurate reading of the problems or accurate computation.

The questions in Appendix I will help obtain a focused description of difficulties in mathematics.

Foreign Language. Children with specific language disabilities who have trouble learning to read and spell in their native language almost invariably have difficulty in learning to read and write a foreign language. Depending on the nature of the disability, they may or may not have difficulty in learning to speak the language. Usually, if their difficulties do not involve the auditory–vocal central processing apparatuses, they will adequately learn the language orally, but will fall behind the class when the lessons deal with the written word. However, children weak in auditory discrimination, auditory memory, or expressive language can be expected to have difficulty with learning to speak, as well as read and write, a foreign language.

If the child's class is learning a foreign language, the psychologist should inquire to what extent they deal with the spoken, and to what extent the written, language. Then, the psychologist should obtain as clear a description as possible of any problems the child has in those areas.

Physical Education. The clinician will want to know if the child has any particular athletic strengths or problems. If there are problems, do they limit his performance and make him a team liability? In regard to competition, it may help to know whether the child particularly enjoys it or avoids it. It is also important to know whether he enjoys physical activity and mastery for its own sake. Any difficulties with changing clothes or taking showers should be noted.

Other Subject Areas. Included here are the strictly academic areas such as literature, the social sciences, and science. Also included are the arts and the crafts: music, industrial arts, graphics, home economics, and visual arts. It will be helpful to know whether deficiencies in basic academic skills interfere with success in these areas; whether the child shows particular interest or talent in some subject; and how he manages in general, both academically and socially.

Home-School Relationships

The amount of contact between parents and school is highly variable, ranging from virtually none to almost daily contact. Some schools provide easy communication, not only by their invitations to conferences and parent evenings, but also by the fact that the children must be transported to and from the school by parents, which gives those who wish it a regular opportunity for exchanging a few words with the teacher. Some parents go out of their way to avoid school contact, while others are eager to be in touch, requesting conferences and calling the teacher at home evenings.

The clinician will want to know how much contact there is, who initiates it, and who participates in it—one or both parents, teachers, principal, guidance counselor, or school social worker. Teachers can report on how the parents seem to view the school and the child's problems, and whether the parents are seen as helpful and cooperative, hostile and blaming, anxious and guilt-ridden, demanding or indifferent. Asking both parents and teachers about the home-school relationship frequently reveals discrepancies and misunderstandings that can sometimes be clarified during the assessment. The content of parent-teacher conferences is also important, particularly in regard to how the child's problems have been discussed and whether special help has been asked or offered on either side.

6

Clinical Assessment: Testing

INTELLECTUAL ASSESSMENT

The core of intellectual assessment is almost always an individual intelligence test, either one of the *Wechsler scales* or the *Stanford-Binet* test. Although these tests are frequently misinterpreted and misused because of a tendency to relate only to their various scaled and IQ scores, the fact is that, for most children, they constitute the best single instrument for sampling and analyzing a variety of intellectual operations in a relatively controlled (i.e., standardized and normed) manner. Used sensitively and carefully, these tests provide a wealth of information about cognitive style, strengths and weaknesses in intellectual operations, and the effects of emotional states on thinking and problem solving. In addition, they may signal the need for additional, more intensive testing in specific areas such as learning disability, neurology, and personality.

In some instances the Binet and the Wechsler are not appropriate and cannot be used. The outstanding examples are verbally handicapped children whose disability prevents them from communicating their knowledge and understanding through words. Such children should be given a nonverbal test such as the *Leiter* or the *Columbia Mental Maturity Scales*, both of which tap a broad range of conceptualizing and problem-solving skills. It is an inadequate solution to use only the Performance Scale of the *WISC-R*, since it taps a narrower range of intellectual function, having been devised to complement the Verbal Scale, not to duplicate it.

There is another, far broader category of children for whom the standard individual tests may not be appropriate—these are the children whose cultural background is so different from the dominant culture that the items presented do not adequately tap their intellectual skills and resources. While the newly restandardized WISC-R corrects many of the sampling biases of the original WISC, it cannot compensate for the different cultural experience of many minority-group children. When assessing these children, the psychologist must decide if, distortions and disadvantages notwithstanding, he or she is likely to learn enough from the test anyway to make using it worthwhile. As long as there are no better instruments for gauging broad-range intellectual function, the psychologist will probably opt for using a less-than-satisfactory test and make the necessary adjustments and qualifications in interpreting the responses and scores. The test score should be interpreted as a correlate and predictor of school achievement rather than as a measure of innate or potential intelligence. Properly interpreted, the test can occasionally highlight a disparity between a child's low score and a contrasting high level of intellectual function demonstrated on various cognitive activities, either within the test itself or in other tests or observed activities.

Mercer and Lewis (1977) have developed the *System of Multicultural Pluralistic Assessment (SOMPA)*, which compares the standard intelligence test performances of children aged 5 through 11 with those of children from similar social and cultural backgrounds. In this way, a child achieves an IQ score relative to his own group, rather than to the national norms. Three sets of norms were developed, based on IQ testing of 2100 children, one-third Caucasian, one-third Latin, and one-third Black. The authors suggest that both the original IQ score and the SOMPA corrected score be noted, since the former indicates immediate educational need and the latter "latent scholastic potential." While it is too early to know how widespread or effective such a device may be, it is well worth consideration.

Psychologists vary in their preference for the Binet or the Wechsler, usually according to the test they have become accustomed to administering. In using a particular test, they have accumulated over time, and with the testing of many children, a set of personal norms—that is, familiarity with the responses children tend to make to various test items, and awareness of the oddity or ingenuity of a response or a solution, whether it is formally scored pass or fail. Without claiming that one test is in any general sense superior to the other, many clinical psychologists are aware that because the Binet items are arranged according to age level and the Wechsler items according to type of task, the latter offers a built-in structure of item administration and subtest grouping which more easily lends itself to scrutiny and analysis. For this reason, the Wechsler is recommended in preference to the Binet for the assessment of learning problems.

Before leaving the Binet and looking more closely at the Wechsler scales, it should be noted that the Binet has a number of items that may be usefully added to the testing in order to check out a hunch about a suspected problem. If by chance a Binet has been previously administered, it is worth analyzing to determine in which types of items failures occur early or where success continues beyond the child's average level of achievement.

THE WISC-R

The discussion of the Wechsler scales will focus directly on the *WISC-R*, the scale used for the vast majority of school children, spanning as it does ages 6 through 16. Most of the discussion applies directly to the WAIS and the WPPSI as well, since their Verbal, Performance, and Full Scale IQ's are derived in an identical manner. Their subtests also parallel and often duplicate those of the WISC-R.

Subtest Clustering

A major reason for the general popularity of the Wechsler scales is that they provide separate Verbal and Performance IQ scores, allowing for comparison between the two. Wechsler has expressed his own unhappiness about this source of popularity. His hope was that such a division would lead to a more adequate sampling and rating of global intelligence rather than support the notion that verbal intelligence is true intelligence and performance intelligence a special practical ability (Wechsler, 1950).

There is another reason for dissatisfaction with the division, namely that it is commonly assumed to parallel some basic, underlying dichotomy of intellectual functioning. Neuropsychological research pointing to language and nonlanguage hemispheres with specialized function lends support to such an assumption. However, the division of Wechsler subtests into Verbal and Performance scales does not parallel the theoretical assumptions of the split-brain research, nor does it coincide with empirical factor analysis done on the Wechsler subtests themselves (Cohen, 1957, 1959; Kaufman, 1975; Littell, 1960). In fact, what separates the two scales is the need for speech in presenting and in responding to each verbal item. On all performance subtests, once the prefacing general instruction is given for each subtest, each item can be administered and responded to without speech. The possible partial exception is the Picture Completion subtest, in which the child names the missing part. Yet, even here the child will receive full credit by only pointing to the appropriate place. The underlying cognitive processes required in each task cannot be separated as verbal or nonverbal. On the Verbal Scale, Digit Span is not a task of verbal comprehension or reasoning, and Arithmetic is at best a mixture of verbal and nonverbal cognitive skills. On the Performance Scale, Picture Arrangement seems to involve the use of subvocal speech to put the stories together, the kind of talking to oneself that is occasionally expressed aloud by some children as they work out the sequences. Factor analyses of the WISC (Cohen, 1959; Wallbrown, Blaha, Counts, & Wallbrown, 1974) and of the WISC-R (Kaufman, 1975) bear out the fact that the two scales do not constitute factors in themselves. However, certain subtests do cluster in varying combinations at different ages, which suggests that underlying primary intelligence factors are at play.

Although the verbal-performance separation of the WISC-R is neither theoretically nor empirically valid in any pure sense, it can nonetheless be useful in analyzing learning problems. Seashore (1951) found that in the original WISC standardization sample of 2200 children, about half showed verbal-performance discrepancies of 8 points or more. When the discrepancy approaches 15 points it can be said to be clinically significant. Even so, the individual subtest scores should be scrutinized to see whether one or two tests in each scale have pulled the two scales apart. In that case, those tests may be more significant in their own right than any general verbal-nonverbal issue.

If, as has been demonstrated in the various factor analyses, an underlying cognitive bipolarity is not the differentiating force in a large verbal-performance discrepancy, what might be? There are a number of issues that might be relevant. The clinician can check these out by considering the content of the child's responses and general test behavior, once a sizable discrepancy on the scoring summary has been noted.

One issue is that of language skill—the ease with which the child derives meaning from the language he hears (receptive language), and the ease with which he can manipulate and produce language in order to express his meaning (expressive language). Children who do poorly on the Verbal Scale may have some trouble in the entire language channel of communication, including reception, association, and expression, or in some part of it. The most common language-area difficulty is with expression, in which words, phrases, expressions, and more complex language structures do not readily spring to mind. A child may know the answer, or have a fair idea of what it is, but be unable to express it on demand. Clinicians have occasionally seen an example of this on the original WISC. On the Vocabulary subtest a child would be unable to answer the question, "What is a spade?" A few minutes later, on the Picture Completion subtest, he would look at the playing card and say that a spade was missing.

There may be difficulty with giving good abstract or precise definitions on the Vocabulary subtest: the child may fall back on phrases, examples, or usage in a sentence. There may be problems in labeling the missing parts in Picture Completion; the child may depend on pointing. Some children automatically respond with "I don't know" to questions whose answer does not come immediately to mind. Encouragement to try to formulate an answer (such as "I know it's hard to explain, but I think you know something about this. Try to put it into words.") sometimes produces a good, scorable response. However, one cannot prod a child through every item of the test, and at the end one may be left wondering what other *I don't know*'s might be covering competence and understanding.

Occasionally one can identify problems in language reception or association, but only when a fairly glaring error is made which cannot possibly be explained by lack of knowledge. An example of this occurred in testing a 17-year-old boy on a WAIS Similarities item. In response to the question "In what way are an orange and a banana alike?" he said, "They're both round and they both come off a tree." He was asked to repeat the question; and in doing so, he remembered his response and spontaneously corrected it with some embarrassment. When a general language area problem is suspected, it may be useful to administer the *Illinois Test of Psycholinguistic Abilities (ITPA)* or some other language test which is designed in such a way that specific difficulties in auditory reception, association, and verbal expression may emerge more clearly.

Emotional factors can affect the child's relative success on each scale in a number of ways. Because every Verbal item is administered orally by the examiner, the child must attend steadily, be responsive, and feel relatively positive about the interpersonal relationship which is very similar to the teacher asks–pupil responds relationship. Negative, sullen, aggressively defensive children, particularly adolescents with a history of school failure and hostile interaction with many teachers, may find it nearly impossible to regard the psychologist differently and lend themselves to such question-and-answer confrontations. In contrast, Performance items are literally handed over to the child to work on, with the major interaction taking place between the child and the task, rather than between the child and the examiner. Sullen and angry children thus occasionally have an opportunity to free themselves from interpersonal challenges and lose themselves in concentration on task performance. It is not uncommon for a language problem and interpersonal difficulties to interact and reinforce each other in producing a low Verbal scale IQ. The psychologist must then question the data and determine to what extent lack of understanding and knowledge, a specific language problem, and emotional interference may each be implicated.

A parallel situation exists in considering a discrepancy in which the Performance scale is very much lower than the Verbal. It is parallel in that here also a particular set of cognitive or emotional factors may be in operation, and they are likely in operation together.

On the cognitive side, every Performance subtest deals with some combinations of visual or visual–motor skills. Picture Completion calls for visual closure, which itself depends on adequate visual memory, and a few later items (the missing sock and the cow's hoof) require close visual scanning and discrimination in order to pick up the asymmetry. Picture Arrangement also requires visual scanning and discrimination although in this case the task is more heavily loaded with the contextual meaning of what is seen (e.g., how many lassos on the wall and what that means for the story's chronology). Picture Completion also makes some demands of this sort (in such items as the thermometer and the picture with the missing shadow). In these cases, one does not visually experience the absence of some part (as one does with the comb's teeth and the animal's ear), but rather one turns to considering the use and meaning of what is seen in order to determine what might be absent. Block Design and Object Assembly require the assembly of parts to make a whole; in Block Design the child matches to a sample, and in Object Assembly to a mental concept. Both subtests require alternating or simultaneous attention to part and to whole in order to achieve a visual match. Coding requires visual-motor coordination and spatial orientation for moving eyes back and forth across the code, and up and down between the code and the working area, simultaneously coordinating this with pencil activity. Coding also requires visual memory to avoid looking back every time. While the five subtests vary in their dependence on deriving meaning, they all demand some degree of efficiency in one or more of the automatic level functions involving visual input. Here again the ITPA may be useful in confirming or refuting the possibility that visual processes are a weak area in the child's network of information processing.

The emotional issues that may globally affect the entire Performance Scale are an inhibition about direct and concrete handling of materials and the loss of sustained visual and verbal contact with the examiner (Picture Arrangement is a partial exception). My experience has been that this is a rare occurrence. Anxiety over things in pieces, as in Block Design and Object Assembly (and in a different way, as in Picture Arrangement), may be apparent and may be enough to lower the entire scale, particularly in combination with hysterical anxiety over something missing in Picture Completion. However, this is a matter for individual subtest scrutiny rather than a scale-wide variable. In cases in which anxiety appears to pervade the Performance Scale, the psychologist must make every effort to determine whether the anxiety is in some degree related to visual processing difficulties.

Another rare possibility is that the stopwatch timing on all the Performance Scale subtests drastically affects the child's performance. If the psychologist suspects as much, it is useful to readminister the Performance Scale another time without the stopwatch. Once again, I must point out that even if it is fairly certain that the stopwatch has generated a great deal of anxiety, it is more than likely that its ability to do so is related to the tasks on which the child is being timed.

Rather than looking only at Verbal-Performance Scale correspondence or disparity, it is also important to scan all 11 subtest scores. If the intertest scatter exceeds 7 points, it helps to relist all the subtests and scaled scores in rank order. Thus, it is possible to see how the tests cluster and if there is some discernible common element among the lows or the highs. Attempts to diagnose according to particular Wechsler subtest patterns have been unsuccessful on a statistical basis. This is partly because subtest scores are far less reliable than the IQ scores, and the difference between any two subtest scores must be 3 to 7 points before it is statistically significant (see Anastasi, 1968, Glasser & Zimmerman, 1967, for a detailed discussion and review of research). However, if subtest scores are considered in clusters and analyzed clinically on the basis of the content of the responses, there is little danger of being led astray by random statistical error.

There is one particular pattern of subtest scores that has been noted in the literature as an observed clinical phenomenon associated with learning disabilities (e.g., McGlannan, 1968; Denhoff & Tarnopol, 1971), although as yet there is, to my knowledge, no research evidence to confirm the clinical observation. I refer to a drop in both Coding and Digit Span, relative to all other subtests, which I have come to regard as an indication of automatic level difficulties. These two subtests are the only ones that deal exclusively with nonabstract, nonmeaningful material. They require no complex mediating process or problem-solving behavior which draws on associations to prior knowledge. Automatic-level behavior involves highly organized and integrated response patterns, makes use of the redundancies of experience and rote learning, and is a function of efficient psycholinguistic and psychomotor skills. Sometimes children with average or better scores on subtests that involve reasoning, judgment, interpretation, concept elaboration, and generally complex problem-solving behavior have below average scores on automatic-level tasks. This WISC-R pattern neatly parallels a common description of the classic learning-disabled child: bright, verbal, able to understand what is happening around him and to discuss intelligently, but unable to remember how to spell common words, to recognize a word at the bottom of the page that he sounded out two lines above, or to remember the times tables.

Sometimes Arithmetic is added as one of the depressed scores (Denhoff & Tarnopol, 1971). My experience has been that a low Arithmetic score may or may not accompany a low Digit Span and a low Coding score, but it is worthwhile to check the content and the process of the solving of the Arithmetic items. If the difficulty is in fact only or mainly at the automatic level, there should be evidence that the child has understood the problems presented and known what process to use in solving them, but has had trouble in remembering the numbers read to him or has made computation errors in doing the mental arithmetic. Sometimes these difficulties seriously affect the scores, sometimes not. This depends partly on how flexible or indulgent the psychologist is about time limits and on how efficient the child is in catching and correcting his own errors.

Low scores on these three subtests are often interpreted clinically as indicating depression, anxiety, distractibility, or poor concentration due to various emotional problems. Partly as a result of the ready availability of such an interpretation, psychologists have often failed to consider other, cognitive explanations of this pattern of scores. I do not suggest that failure in these areas cannot be related to anxiety and various emotional issues, but that there are other possible reasons for failure. Psychologists must look to other data and to their own clinical judgment before deciding that they are dealing with anxiety, deficient information processing, both, or something else altogether. If anxiety contributes to the failure, this will be confirmed by other test manifestations of anxiety. If information processing problems exist, further testing will uncover them with greater specificity.

The focus will now shift from clusters or patterns of subtest scores to the individual subtests. The kinds of tasks each subtest presents to the child and what each requires in the way of prior knowledge, problem-solving skills, neuropsychological efficiency, and emotional control will be considered. The handbook by Glasser and Zimmerman (1967), *Clinical Interpretation of the Wechsler Intelligence Scale,* offers an analysis of each subtest in terms of its history, rationale, item composition and difficulty, advantages and limitations, statistical relationships to the total test and to each subtest, and the clinical interpretations commonly associated with it. While based on the WISC and not the WISC-R, there is enough commonality to still make the bulk of the material valid and valuable. This material will not be discussed here, although it shall be referred to from time to time. The questions directing our discussion here are (1) where failures occur, what combination of biological, psychological, and environmental factors should be considered as possible contributors to the failure; (2) how does the test failure relate to school failures; and (3) what compensating strengths in behavior or cognitive skill may be noted which could be exploited in the school setting to enhance learning and academic success.

One general comment should be made before turning to the individual subtests: In learning problem assessments, it is especially important to use the intelligence test as an instrument for finding out how the child thinks; what logic determines his failures; where facile language can cover a lack of understanding; where language inhibition interferes with the communication of genuine understanding; and where in a complex series of mental manipulations he goes astray. The accurate scoring of passed and failed items is as important here as anywhere else, but to concentrate only on scoring is to forfeit a rich mine of information. Glasser and Zimmerman (1967) discuss at some length "extension testing," a term that derives from "extending" efforts beyond the instructions given by Wechsler. They include encouragement to try after an "I don't know"; rewording some questions to make them less personalized; giving suggestions or hints; substituting simpler language for some unfamiliar terms (e.g., "well-organized charity"); substituting easier number combinations in Arithmetic; allowing the child to work on timed items after the allotted time has expired; and actively helping on part of the assembly on Block Design or Object Assembly. To this I would add exploration of any bizarre answers, particularly when one is quite certain that the child knows the correct answer or when the answer reflects some specific attitude or belief. For an example, let us look again at Gila, the child mentioned previously in chapter 3. She is a 6-year-old girl from an Israeli kibbutz where dairy cows are raised. When asked from what animal we get milk, she replied, "Cat." The questioning continued with "*Who* gets milk from a cat?" "Kittens." "Where do *we* get milk?" "Tnuva" (the nation-wide dairy cooperative). "Where does Tnuva get milk?" "From cows." Based on prior parent and teacher interviews, the child's original response was interpreted as relating to her severe emotional problems around mothering. Thus, the question of obtaining milk evoked the image of nursing and the syntax and relationships of the original question were lost. The extension testing was interesting in its spelling out and verifying the psychodynamic hunch, but it was crucial in determining whether or not she had absorbed the factual information and could respond logically and appropriately to a series of questions. In the process, Gila also demonstrated a fairly sophisticated understanding of the dairy production and distribution network.

The Individual Subtests

Information. This test calls for general knowledge, sometimes based on common, personal experience (e.g., How tall is the average American man? How do you make water boil?); sometimes requiring memory for facts usually learned at school (How many pounds in a ton? What is the capital of Greece?); and sometimes requiring temporal or spatial orientation (How many days in the week? What are the seasons of the year? What is the distance from New York to Los Angeles? Where is Chile?). Failures, particularly where there is intratest scatter, should be checked for indications of specific problems in orientation, memory, or insufficient exposure to the common cultural experiences in and out of school. These problems may interfere with arithmetic, the learning of new material, and easy access to formerly learned material in such areas as science and social studies. On the other hand, unexpectedly high scores on Information often indicate a culturally rich home background which has provided wide experience but which may not be backed up by the child's inner capacities for integration, drawing conclusions, seeing relationships, and other more complex cognitive processes. If this is the case, one can continue to capitalize on automatic memory skills and the ability to learn from direct experience, while working more slowly on reasoning and problem-solving tasks.

Comprehension. The earlier Comprehension items test the child's ability to deal realistically and independently with a variety of demands or possible demands of daily life. The later items deal with mores, values, and institutions of the adult world. As such they require that the child deal abstractly with concepts vaguely heard about but not in the realm of personal experience. The specific intelligence factor throughout is verbal comprehension and reasoning. In addition to this, strong emotional reactions are often evoked by questions that consistently involve taking care of oneself and others and coping with one's own impulsivity and that of people and forces outside of oneself. Children whose answers indicate immaturity and unnecessary dependence on others ("Have my mother bandage it." "Tell someone.") may also be overly dependent in school, unable or unwilling to handle work or tasks on their own. The child whose impulsiveness is overwhelming, who cannot inhibit a response about hitting back at a smaller child, raises questions as to whether an inability to inhibit and control his impulses affects adequate self-discipline at school, where uncertainty, provocation, competition, and the demands of the teacher and the group are built-in facts of life. If a child's school difficulty is related to his wish not to grow up, Comprehension items may reflect an attitude of "That's not for me to do (worry about, take care of). Grown-ups know things and do things, not me." If a child with learning difficulties has an unusually high score on Comprehension, it may indicate a good level of emotional stability and control, a capacity for judgment, and a solid, comfortable orientation to his surroundings. All of this will not in itself compensate for academic failures, but it bodes well for the child's being able to tolerate frequent frustrations and adjust relatively easily to the social and behavioral demands of daily classroom life.

Arithmetic. The first three Arithmetic items involve counting and require, as a minimum, adequate perceptual-motor coordination between eye, moving finger, and vocal counting. More skillful children can count silently and group visually with no apparent motor activity, but this performance, too, is based on competence at the lower, sensory-motor level. Story problems in the subsequent items require the ability to comprehend the situation being verbally described, select the appropriate arithmetic operation or operations, and manipulate numbers mentally with adequate speed and precision. Problems in short-term rote memory may interfere with remembering exact numbers. In these cases, the child has obviously caught the sense of the problem (which does not require verbatim recall of the problem as stated), but has lost or confused the exact amounts he is to deal with. Children with difficulty in visualizing will have trouble doing the mental computations involved in the later items (e.g., dividing 72 by 4, finding 3/2 of 28), which they may well understand and could do with pencil and paper. One often sees children "writing" in the air or on the table with their finger, in what appears to be an effort to lend kinesthetic support to efforts at visualizing. Since anxiety, depression, and other emotional states may interfere with memory and visualizing, the psychologist must use additional data from other parts of the assessment in deciding to what extent the child seems to be dealing with a neuropsychological difficulty and to what extent an emotional difficulty.

Children who don't automatically know such combinations as 8 + 6, 12 − 5, or 8 + 3 will generally pass the items where these combinations are involved, within the allotted time, by using their fingers or various other techinques for figuring. However, the failure to respond immediately is a cue to the psychologist to note the process the child used to arrive at his solution. It is often helpful to ask him, "How did you figure that out?" His explanation may indicate considerable aptitude with numbers regardless of his lack of long-term rote memory, or it may point up considerable confusion. Some children will also be revealed as being unable to verbalize the procedure they used. The child who has difficulty understanding the problem as presented is having difficulty with verbal comprehension and reasoning. He is also having difficulty internalizing and drawing on his own experience in such a way as to abstract from it and apply it to hypothetical situations. Exceptionally strong Arithmetic performance suggests unusual ability in the mental manipulation of concepts and symbols. When it occurs in a child with learning problems, it raises questions as to why this skill has not sufficiently helped the child in school tasks. In some cases, a child who shows very good mathematical understanding, reasoning, and problem-solving skills on the test may be doing poorly in school mathematics because he lacks the automatic level neuropsychological skills required for setting up problems on paper and carrying out arithmetical operations. (One such child is Jacob, who will be discussed in chapter 8.)

Similarities. In the original WISC, the first four Similarities items were analogies drawing on common experience and knowledge. While the child had to abide by the framework of the analogy, which required relating his answers to an implicit abstraction ("Lemons are sour, sugar is _____ ." The answer had to be sweet, not white.), all terms of the analogy were so familiar that the responses came almost automatically and the sentence structure definitely guided him to the right association. The WISC-R, (like the remaining twelve items of the WISC subtest) does not provide the momentum or structure that incomplete sentences offer, and some children can proceed only after being given a language stem by the examiner: "they both . . ." or "they both have . . . ."

Besides finding and using the proper linguistic structure, the child needs an adequate information base, beginning with common-experience information and progressing to formal, school-learned information. He must also be able to conceptualize and scan categories. Thus, there is a need for accessible information, to which the child must associate, and a need to properly order the information and manipulate abstract concepts. A fine demonstration of these complex and interwoven demands occurred in the response of a verbally very precocious 7-year-old to the question: "In what way are salt and water alike?" His information base did not include knowledge about basic life requirements (this had not yet been discussed at school or at the family dinner table), but he did know about salt water, to which he associated now, and said that some water has salt in it. However, because his capacity for maintaining the abstract conceptual demands of the task far outstripped his information base, he then went on to say, "But that can't be the right answer, because that's not how they are alike." In this case, the failure demonstrated exceptional competence in verbal reasoning. The reverse situation exists with children who are so captured by their associations that they cannot deal with the more abstract, categorizing demands of the problem and are relatively satisfied with their answers. For example, in item 7, they answer, "The cat chases the mouse." They not only fail to produce the comprehensive abstraction such as "fruit" in answer to number 5 or "animal" for number 7; they also fail to use the technique of mentally visualizing or imagining the objects mentioned, and then searching for physical, concrete likenesses.

Children who cannot abandon or go beyond their own immediate associations, which do not fulfill the conceptual demand of the task, may be having one or more of the following difficulties: (1) lack of information; (2) lack of adequate attribute categories for scanning (e.g., physical attributes, function, origin, composition); (3) difficulties in visualizing; (4) difficulty with the concept of similarity, either in understanding it at all, or in applying it when spontaneous associations have led to some other relationship, such as differences or interactions. Poor performance on Similarities can be probed with extension testing in order to locate the source(s) of difficulty. Extension testing can also be used to assess the extent to which affective states are interfering with efficient cognitive functioning.

Vocabulary. The Vocabulary subtest consists of isolated auditory input. Words are presented out of context, that is, not embedded in a sentence, and without any visual cues. Most children help themselves by providing such cues on their own. Thus, they may visualize the word in order to describe it, or they may reauditorize a phrase or a sentence in which they have heard the word used in order to figure out a meaning within that context. Children with difficulties in either or both areas (revisualizing or reauditorizing) will be handicapped here. The item "spade" was an example noted earlier; it was occasionally missed on Vocabulary and then recognized in Picture Completion. Of course, Vocabulary also demands an adequate knowledge base, and an ability to conceptualize a definition is prized (2 points) over a demonstration of working knowledge (1 point). The Vocabulary subtest provides excellent opportunities for assessing verbal fluency, the quality of abstract thinking, and the child's social and cultural milieu. An example of the last is offered by Glasser and Zimmerman, referring to the WISC: ". . . dull subjects from educated homes may pass uncommon words such as number 21 'shilling' and number 24 'espionage,' but fail much easier ones" (Glasser and Zimmerman, 1967, p. 67).

An example of how Vocabulary may highlight auditory processing difficulties is seen in the protocol of the 17-year-old boy, referred to earlier in this chapter, who slipped on the Similarities item "orange–banana." Here are three of his Vocabulary responses from the WAIS:

> 31. Compassion—having a friend; one of the definitions of love, somebody to fall onto, having a mate to live for, work for.
>
> 32. Tangible—a citrus crop could be tangible if picked and ready to go, it could be tangible, ruined, if left uncooled, and could rot or go bad.
>
> 38 Plagiarize—some type of crime; if you play around writing things about the prime minister you can be accused of a crime, playing with her name or features or something like that.

Compassion appears to have triggered off unconscious associations to *companion* and *passion*, which are here amalgamated into a definition that tries to include both concepts. *Tangible* seems to have triggered off associations to *tangerine* and *perishable*. *Plagiarize* presents a somewhat different issue in that the concrete sound "play" becomes an inescapable input to be made part of this definition, which otherwise reflects correct associations to concepts of "crime" and "writing." What distinguishes this type of error from the more common ones, in which an attempt is made to define words according to similar sounding known words, is that in the present case the process is unconscious and unnoticed. With more competent subjects there tends to be an active, conscious search for connections. Such a performance suggests a tendency to loose, tenuous, vague, and perhaps random associations, which may well influence performance on verbal tasks at school such as class discussions and written examinations and papers.

This boy's performance also illustrates the interplay of neurological and psychological determinants. The content of the response to "compassion" has clear psychodynamic relevance to the boy's longing to belong to someone and something and to his rather passive, dependent attitude. These issues were further delineated in personality measures administered during the assessment. His neurological weakness leaves him open to more global, non-reality-oriented associations, which in turn gives more latitude for subjective, personalized content.

Digit Span. This subtest deals with automatic, nonrepresentative cognitive processes, primarily auditory memory, but also, particularly on Digits Backward, visualizing and visual memory. As mentioned previously, difficulty on Digit Span may signal difficulty at the automatic level. A further refinement is that, no matter what the total or scaled score, when the number of digits a child can repeat forward exceeds the number backward by three or more, it should be considered a possible indicator of difficulty in visualizing or visual memory or both. It is about as difficult to repeat a string of heard digits backwards as it is to sing a song backwards. Auditory sequence exists in time and does not lend itself to reversal as does a spatially organized visual sequence whose shape and cadence does not alter with a change of direction. In general, when faced with having to repeat digits backwards, people use both reauditorizing and visualizing in order to learn the forward sequence, and then read off the visualized sequence backwards.

Some children do relatively well on Digits Backward without ever trying to reverse the sequence; instead they achieve the same end result by repeating the forward sequence over and over (to themselves or under their breath), each time dropping the last digit and uttering aloud the new final digit (e.g., 95368, 9536, 953, 95, 9). This solution leans totally on auditory recall. While the child deserves credit for insight and problem-solving skill, his inability or unwillingness to use visual imagery may be related to reading or spelling deficits, and to difficulties in other academic areas requiring visualization and visual imagery. High scores on Digit Span indicate good rote memory, visual and auditory retention, and the ability to concentrate and persevere on an easily understood but somewhat strenuous intellectual task. When children with learning problems do unusually well on Digit Span, one should look to the comprehension aspects of school tasks for trouble signs, as well as to social and psychological determinants. If the child is lacking in insight or the ability to see relationships, it may be possible to exploit his good automatic memory skills by arranging for him to learn a great deal by rote practice and memory first. This allows insight to come gradually after repeated examples and experience. It will be easier to explain reasons and principles to him once he can relate the explanation to his own built-up and built-in set of experiences.

Digit Span is a supplementary subtest in the Wechsler tests, and in the WISC-R it is not even included in the computation of IQ scores. As a result, it is frequently not administered. Because of the important information it can provide, I strongly recommend that it be administered routinely as part of the WISC-R (or other Wechsler scales) in any learning problem assessment.

Picture Completion. As mentioned earlier, this subtest depends on a visual sense of something missing, or an awareness of illogic. In the former case, the presented picture is matched to a mental image of the object in its natural and complete state. In the latter case, when nothing stands out visually as "missing," the picture is inspected and compared with what one knows about the meaning or function of the presented visual material. Sometimes the visual issue and sometimes the meaning issue dominates. With the cow, a close inspection will reveal that one hoof has a missing line. Knowledge about cloven-hoofed animals may help in the solution, but it isn't essential. Many, if not most, children who solve the item do so because a line is missing rather than because one hoof is uncloven. Children who are not struck visually by the absence of the mouth in the girl's face or of the fingernail on the hand may be indicating trouble in visual processing. They do not merely demonstrate inattention to detail in the picture, but also a failure to relate the picture, no matter how superficially inspected, to the mental image of the natural object. Since the failures on these items are usually in terms of such answers as "the body is missing" or "the arm is missing," an additional hypothesis is that these children also show a tendency toward global rather than differentiated perception. They think in terms of large visual or conceptual wholes rather than differentiated detail. At the other extreme, children who depend totally on some visually outstanding feature or careful inspection, and who don't pay enough attention to meaning, will have trouble on other items. For example, the thermometer's fine lines and numbers prompt some children to persist in searching for missing tiny details rather than considering other, more meaningful aspects. Also, the screw's missing slot is "felt" only by those who consider its functional relationship to a screw driver. One must not overdo the division between visual and meaningful solutions since to some extent they must operate together. However, awareness of what is demanded in each item will help the psychologist sort out which intellectual skills and functions are operating well and which are operating poorly.

The clinical interpretation of hysterical "not looking" as a cause of poor performance does not contradict an interpretation of poor visual processing at a neurological level. The two are very likely to occur together and to continue reinforcing each other. A psychologically based tendency to not look or inspect closely for fear of finding something, or of finding something missing, will lead to a lack of practice and experience in visual inspection and matching. Conversely, neurologically based difficulties in visual processing are likely to lead to an avoidance of that mode. This in turn may lead to seeking out other ways of knowing, which are more dependent on global, subjective impressions and less on a differentiated inspection of externally presented stimuli.

Picture Arrangement. Correct assembly depends on connecting the frames according to a story sequence that develops chronologically and becomes a meaningful, rather than a strictly visual, whole. All items depend on visual comprehension, that is, on deriving meaning from visual input. The visual perception and discrimination requirements are minimal. Solutions depend on experience, general knowledge, and the interpretation of depictions of human emotions and interaction. The further one proceeds in the series, the less obvious and imperative are the particular time sequences, and there is a greater need for verbal reasoning versus visual comprehension. Children who fail early in the series are generally missing or ignoring visual information, either because their emotional needs lead them to a different story or because they cannot adequately process and order the visual input. An example of the first occurs from time to time with "Burglar," in which children produce an extended time sequence that allows them to portray the thief being caught first, and then later going out to steal again. At the other extreme we have Jon, who was described in chapter 3 as having severe difficulties in recognizing and dealing with aggressive impulses. One indication of this was his solution of the "Lasso" item, which he began by showing the storekeeper tied up, and then showed the cowboy as a rescuer rather than a robber. Pictorially, it cannot be done that way, since the number of lassos on the wall in each frame makes it logically and chronologically incoherent. Yet, Jon's emotional need to deny aggressive impulses was a more compelling force in this instance. An example of visual processing problems occurs with "Fire," where the direction of the fire truck makes some children feel that the truck is going away from rather than towards the fire. In later items, children occasionally develop and assemble a story line that does not include all five frames and then may express surprise in the end at suddenly discovering the fifth frame still on the table and not part of the story. They have in fact shut off visual intake at the point where they could not absorb anymore and could still maintain the development of a meaningful story. More aware children, who also cannot make all the frames fit into a logical story sequence, never lose sight of all five frames and will say at or near the end that they can't find a place for one of them.

Children should be asked to tell the story after finishing the arrangement, particularly in a learning assessment. This provides another opportunity for assessing richness and fluency of language, the amount and nature of their rationalization in justifying incorrect and sometimes irrational arrangement, and the use of verbal recital to recheck and correct wrong arrangements. Because this subtest has such a large weighting of verbal comprehension and reasoning, a high performance here in contrast with poor scores on verbal tests demanding vocal expression may indicate a problem in verbal expression. There is another hypothesis raised by a high Picture Arrangement score vis-à-vis low scores on Verbal Scale tests, particularly Information, Similarities, and Vocabulary. It is that the child does well on verbal reasoning tasks based on human experience and interaction, but is handicapped on tests drawing heavily on the more formal and academic knowledge learned from books and from school.

Block Design. This subtest requires visual-spatial perception and analysis, with particular emphasis on part-whole relationships. Visual-motor coordination plays a minor role; clumsiness in handling the blocks is rarely a serious obstacle, but adequate control of the rotation of a block in search of a pattern match is an important aspect, since the child must not swivel faster than he can check the result. Motor control problems are more likely to be an expression of anxiety than of perceptual-motor problems, and children who randomly or impulsively rotate blocks are generally expressing their sense of confusion and helplessness in the face of the task. The crucial cognitive task is to analyze the design, presented as a whole, so as to figure out how it can be assembled from individual blocks. Whether this is done by imagining a grid on the design and then matching block to block, or by a trial-and-error approach in which blocks are combined in various ways until the right match turns up, the processes are essentially visual-spatial perception and analysis, rather than visual-motor coordination.

The child must reproduce various parts of the design, simultaneously keeping in mind the total design to which the part must be integrated, and the overall 2 × 2 or 3 × 3 framework. Some children focus on a certain design aspect and lose sight of other requirements. For example, in Design Number 5, the child may fix on the inverted white triangle in the upper half, search for that white shape among the block surfaces, find it in the white half of a red-white block, and build a design consisting of two red blocks in the lower half, and the red-white block placed above them with its white corner resting on their center point. He has not met the requirement for a 2 × 2 design, nor has he enough red in the right places, but he has satisfied some perceptual match of his own which might be verbalized as "a white shape like this on top of red." A similar solution occurs on Number 6 where the large red center tilted square attracts the child's attention and is matched with a whole red block rotated 45 degrees, around which are clustered the remaining white blocks. At a more advanced level this problem occurs on Number 9 where the red figure is perceived as longer than it is and the 3 × 3 is lost. The older children often recover and correct their mistake, though not always within the allotted time. Younger children occasionally appear to be satisfied with their poor solution of Number 5 or Number 6. The examiner should try to ascertain whether they are indeed satisfied or whether they are saving face despite their feeling that the solution is wrong. Clearly the prognosis is better for a child who sees the mismatch even if he can't analyze the design. He should then be shown how to do it and allowed to try it himself. If he can learn it without too long or strenuous a teaching effort, he should be asked to do it again at some later point in the testing, to see if he has remembered. The IQ score tends to reflect capacity for insight in problem solving, but where school is concerned, one is also very interested in the child's ability to *learn*. That is, is the child able to remember and use what he has been told or shown, even if he did not originally reach a solution by insight and even if his performance is not based on full understanding of the process?

There is a similarity in being so attracted or possessed by a particular visual stimulus as to be unable to focus on wider, more realistic, and integrated demands, and in being drawn by an ideational stimulus, such as occurs in Verbal tasks and Picture Arrangement. In both cases, the clinician wants to know whether other, more appropriate responses can be elicited from the child if he is given more information or support, or if he must persist in his egocentric perception and handling of the task no matter how much one tries to help him reorient or restructure his approach.

A different problem occurs when the child does keep to the general structural requirements but has difficulty in analyzing specific elements and their positions relative to other design elements and to the whole. Angles are the most common problem, and Number 7 often reveals the child's difficulty if it did not show up earlier on Number 3.

Object Assembly. The cognitive demands of Object Assembly are similar to those of Block Design, except for two things. In this subtest one deals with representations of familiar objects rather than abstract geometric designs, which makes the task easier for some children. On the other hand, Object Assembly requires matching to an imagined whole, rather than to a sample, which may make the task harder.

Object Assembly demands considerable attention to visual detail in order to score well. Otherwise, the horse's legs may be reversed, the auto door rotated, and the small lines which dictate the eye assembly in the profile may be missed. The need to build up to an imagined whole is sometimes a problem in the last two items, where the object sought is not named, for those children who do not easily perceive gestalten from fragmented presentations. One 10-year-old boy, who in the end assembled the auto correctly within the allotted time, responded to his first glimpse of the pieces by saying, "It's a gas station." A minute or so later, while assembling the two wheels, he said, "It's two cars." He succeeded in part through paying careful attention to matching up lines and spaces.

This boy has a reading problem—he knows all the sound-symbol relationships and the phonetic rules, but reads slowly, syllable by syllable, unable to visually grasp whole words or short phrases at a single glance. Both his Object Assembly performance and his reading suggest problems in visual closure. Some children demonstrate the reverse problem on Object Assembly. They know immediately upon looking at the collection of pieces that it is a car, but they have difficulty assembling it because they do not analyze lines and spaces carefully, and thus forfeit a source of information and help which in this particular task is quite important.

Coding. Coding, like Digit Span, is a task almost totally dependent on automatic-level cognitive processes. It is a rare child who doesn't understand the task after it is explained and demonstrated, and most children have understood it before the demonstration. The test demands psychomotor efficiency and good spatial orientation. The eye must be accurately directed to the appropriate part of the key in order to locate the proper symbol, the hand must move smoothly along the line of empty boxes, the eye and pencil must meet at the proper box for recording the symbol, and the symbol must be recorded with minimum effort and maximum accuracy. Highly motivated children, children who enjoy moderately compulsive tasks, and children who are eager to please and well oriented and efficient in psychomotor tasks do well on this subtest. Children who resent school-like or routine tasks and who are not particularly motivated to achieve or to beat the stop watch may not do well even if their psychomotor skills are quite adequate. Observing the child during the task will usually provide enough information to explain a poor performance. Those with psychomotor difficulties may be slow in becoming oriented to the location of the numerals they seek along the 1-9 scale. They may have some difficulty finding their place below again, require concentrated effort to make the graphic symbols, or occasionally skip a space. Older children must learn some of the code by heart in order to score well, and those with normal short-term visual retention skill will do so easily.

I have found it useful, at the end of the timed 2 minutes, to cover the key and the filled-in rows with a sheet of paper and ask the child to fill in as many symbols as he can remember on the bottom row. (I tell the child that this part is extra and doesn't count, so that he will be as relaxed as possible in trying to remember and will not feel "tricked" at being expected, but not told, to memorize the symbols.) This provides an easy check on short-term visual memory, in this case memory for paired visual associates. This procedure also occasionally identifies the child who learned all the symobls, but was too timid during the timed test to use his good memory, and kept checking back to the key (thereby probably lowering his score).

A final word about analyzing the child's WISC-R performance. There are two specific cognitive styles in approaching problem-solving tasks and learning in general: one is a global, impressionistic approach and the other a more differentiated and analytic approach. As a rule, both approaches are needed in most tasks, and the flexible thinker automatically switches from one mode to the other as the task demands. Picture Arrangement and Object Assembly both require at first a rather impressionistic scanning in order to get a general notion of what is going on and towards what kind of integration the assembly must lead. However, this must give way to a more analytic approach that attends to detail and sequence. Some children have a very definite preference for or leaning towards one approach or the other. They cannot adjust their cognitive style to the realistic demands of the task. Neuropsychological research, particularly in hemispheric specialization, suggests that such a preference or leaning probably stems from neurological as well as personality factors. The WISC-R, insofar as it presents a sustained experience with a variety of cognitive tasks, offers a rare opportunity for observing the child's approach with an eye to determining if there is a strong leaning in one direction. If so, the clinician will want to consider: (1) how this tendency relates to the child's learning difficulties, cognitively and emotionally; (2) if and how it might be subject to retraining and change; and (3) if it can be exploited in developing remedial programs.

COPYING TESTS

Copying tests, which require a constellation of visual perception, motor, kinesthetic, spatial orientation, and visual-motor skills, are useful in the learning assessment in much the same way that any part of the intelligence test is useful; that is, as an opportunity to observe which skills seem to operate well and which tend to handicap successful performance. Global, impressionistic statements about anxiety, disorganization, possible brain damage, or emotional disturbance will not contribute to the learning assessment. Each figure should be studied with an eye to specific elements such as adequacy of form, size relationships, lack of directional confusion, adequate pencil control, orientation to internalized horizontal and vertical coordinates. Once again, as with all cognitive tasks, notice should be taken of the balance between attention to gestalt and attention to detail.

Copying tests differ from the Wechsler visual-motor tasks in that the child must construct visual forms, not by assembling preformed parts, but by moving pencil on paper, attending to direction, length, and relative size and distance of various segments. The child must make use of whatever visual-motor schema he already knows automatically, such as circles, squares, diagonals, and perhaps diamonds. One way to phrase the difference is to say that in copying the child must create the match from scratch; on various Performance Scale subtests, however, he must manipulate a given set of parts in order to find and recognize the match. Because of this difference, the psychologist can more and more clearly define the specific visual or visual-motor difficulties (the child may have one or more, in various strengths and combinations) if he compares performance on copying tasks, WISC-R Performance tests, and relevant learning disabilities tests.

Success or failure on copying tasks has no one-to-one correspondence with success in basic academic skills, but the clinician can relate various aspects of the child's performance in copying geometric figures to corresponding elements in school skills. Children, for example, who are clumsy and uncoordinated motorically and cannot match their pencil movements to the lines of the drawings, may demonstrate good recognition and analysis of the figures and the gestalten. While such a child is likely to be having problems in writing and perhaps arithmetic, he may be quite successful in reading. On the other hand, a child with a reading problem who analyzes detail and loses sight of the total figure is likely to be similarly handicapped in reading; that is, he tends to get stuck at the analytic level and has difficulty visually grasping and processing larger letter and word groupings.

Of the many copying tests available, we shall consider two of them here: the *Bender Visual Motor Gestalt Test* (1938), an old clinical stand-by, and the *Beery-Buktenica Developmental Test of Visual-Motor Integration* (1967), commonly known as the *VMI*, which was developed with an eye toward the educational assessment and remediation of learning difficulties.

The Bender's usefulness in assessing learning difficulties is limited by its having been designed as a clinical tool for diagnosing brain damage in adults. It has since been used with children as a tool for diagnosing intellectual and emotional status and as a screening instrument for learning problems, but usually in quite an impressionistic manner and with limited usefulness (see Anastasi, 1968). Although Koppitz (1964) has established some developmental norms for children aged 5 to 10, based on specific signs (rotation, perseveration, etc.) the designs are in many respects too difficult for young children. This general difficulty often masks specific problems that would manifest themselves more clearly with age-appropriate designs, and it leaves the clinician to guess about which perceptual-motor functions are creating difficulty and in what way. While the Bender may help in predicting learning problems or indicating neuropsychological dysfunction, it is of little help in analyzing the problems of a child known to experience learning difficulties. Even a "clean" Bender cannot rule out neuropsychological dysfunction, since the copying task does not tap all the relevant neuropsychological functions.

The VMI, on the other hand, is specifically designed for children in preschool and early primary grades, but can be used with children as young as two years and as old as fifteen. It consists of 24 geometric forms, with age norms for each design. In addition, there is a discussion of each design with illustrations of general trends and developmental stages leading to successful reproduction. The sequence of designs is progressive in difficulty and allows the examiner to observe more precisely those elements of design reproduction which are difficult for the child. It also allows the examiner to note the extent to which his or her approach may be overly diffuse or overly discriminating. A section of the manual, addressed to teachers, discusses the varied aspects of visual-motor performance including motor proficiency, tactile-kinesthetic sense, visual perception, and visual-motor integration, and suggests methods for analyzing the child's performance and remediating at the appropriate level. Among Beery's designs are two of the Bender figures: A—a circle and tilted square; and 7—Wertheimer's hexagons. Psychologists familiar with the Bender will be interested in Beery's discussion and analysis of children's reproductions of these designs, and will appreciate his inclusion of age norms.

ASSESSING EXPRESSIVE LANGUAGE SKILLS

It is frequently important to formulate a separate, though informal, assessment of the child's ability to express himself verbally and vocally, since much of his school performance depends on his ability to do so. In this section only spoken language will be dealt with. Although the division is somewhat arbitrary, problems of written expression are discussed in the following section on the assessment of academic skills.

For assessment purposes, expressive language can be divided into four areas:

1. phonology—the child's ability to articulate the sounds of his native language and to discriminate their spoken forms (Can he pronounce *s;* can he hear the difference between *d* and *t* or between the vowel sounds in *pin* and *pen?*)
2. semantics—the child's ability to understand the meaning of words or groups of words, and in expressive language, to understand them actively; that is, to use them appropriately in his own speech
3. syntax—the child's ability to structure sentences according to the linguistic rules of the language, which children normally discover and apply automatically according to a relatively stable developmental sequence.
4. fluency of speech—the child's readiness and willingness to initiate speech, to verbalize spontaneously, and to respond easily

In most cases, the usual assessment procedures will reveal enough information about language usage so that the language assessment is a matter of recording and summarizing information derived indirectly along the way. Articulation problems will be easily noted in the child's speech, and auditory discrimination problems will be indicated through his "mishearing" or misunderstanding what is said to him. If the clinician is uncertain about the presence or extent of auditory discrimination problems, he or she can administer one of several auditory discrimination measures. The *Wepman Auditory Discrimination Test* (1958) is the most common, and the fastest and easiest to administer. It consists of 40 word pairs, some pairs consisting of one word repeated twice and some consisting of two similar-sounding but not identical words (e.g., *cope, coke; rub, rug; led, lad*). For each pair, the child must say if the words he hears are the same or different. The Wepman results depend to some extent on how the clinician pronounces and articulates each word, and it checks a fairly narrow aspect of auditory discrimination. Another test is the *Goldman-Fristoe-Woodcock Test* (1970), which tests auditory discrimination with a specially designed tape recording. It also tests auditory reception against various levels of background noise.

Articulation and auditory discrimination problems may result from atypical psychological or neurological development, but they may also result from environmental factors such as the child's having grown up and learned to speak in a community where the language is different from standard English (or any other regional language standard). If the child is competent at articulating and discriminating the sounds of his own language or dialect, he can be expected to learn that of the dominant culture fairly easily. Depending on his age and the demands of the school system, this may be done with special lessons or simply with the passage of time, during which the child is exposed to the standard language and spontaneously begins to imitate it.

Semantic problems, if they exist, will be apparent throughout the testing, and in particular, on the Vocabulary subtest of the intelligence test.

Syntax difficulties, appearing in faulty sentence structure or incorrect grammar, may also be a result of either idiosyncratic psychological or neurological problems, on the one hand, or lack of adequate exposure to standard language forms, on the other. If the child is known to have grown up in a setting where he has had a chance to hear standard syntax and grammar, the clinician must consider (1) neuropsychological problems in auditory reception, comprehension, or reauditorization; (2) psychodynamic problems relating to infantilism, severe withdrawal, or negativisim; and (3) the possible interactional combinations of any of these.

Inhibition in cursive speech may result from any one or a combination of psychological, social, or biological factors. Children with neuropsychological expressive language difficulties often shy away from free speech. Children from families who do not lean heavily on speech as a form of expressing feelings or ideas, or who speak another language at home, are not likely to be moved to spontaneous or rich language productions. Children who are very anxious or sullen may inhibit speech. On the other hand, cursive speech may be overused to cover a lack of understanding, to fend off the clinicians questions or comments, or as a general response to anxiety.

DIAGNOSTIC ASSESSMENT OF BASIC ACADEMIC SKILLS

The clinician's contribution in assessing basic academic skills is complementary to the teacher's. While the clinician is in a better position to assess underlying cognitive deficits, the teacher is in a better position to know the extent to which deficits actually interfere with daily school performance. Thus, what the clinician learns in this part of the assessment will have its fullest meaning and import when considered in light of the teacher's report.

In outlining an educational assessment by the psychologist, a number of difficulties are apparent. Educational practices and assessments are not the clinician's profession, and outlining an assessment procedure will not make him an educational professional. The following few pages are no substitute for serious training in special education or learning disabilities. Nevertheless, a bridge must be established between the psychologist and the school world of the child. If the psychologist is not sufficiently trained in educational problems and is not fortunate enough to work in close cooperation with a remedial specialist, then he or she must do whatever possible to become familiar enough with various academic deficits so as to understand them in terms of psychodynamic, environmental, and biological determinants.

Before discussing diagnostic measures, a few words about achievement tests and scores would be in order. School achievement is almost always expressed in terms of grade level, so that if a child scores 3.7 on a standardized spelling test, his achievement is at the level of the average child in the seventh month of the third grade. Although most of our assessment efforts go towards diagnostic testing, that is, towards understanding the processes and problems of the child's academic performance, the clinician should have standardized achievement scores at hand whenever possible. This is so that he or she can estimate the child's relative class standing, no matter how handicapped or successful his performance in the clinician's office may appear to be. If the child's achievement score in some area is at grade level and the teacher reports that he is doing poorly in that area, new questions arise: Is the actual level of his class far above national norms? Is his poor school performance not a function of his knowledge and competence, but of psychosocial factors in the classroom? The data from various sources must make sense, and when they don't they must be reconciled. In the reconciling hangs the assessment.

Achievement scores are usually available from school records. They generally come from group-administered standardized achievement tests (e.g., Metropolitan, Stanford), and give grade-level scores in such areas as Word Meaning, Paragraph Meaning, Arithmetic Computation, Arithmetic Reasoning, and Spelling. While the learning problems of some children may render such scores meaningless as a measure of competence, they do sometimes provide a rough gauge as to where he stands in relation to his age group. The achievement or diagnostic test individually administered by the psychologist will provide more information as to what the child actually knows and can do, but the school-administered group test does reflect a daily-life reality which has important meaning.

The clinician is more interested in diagnostic than achievement tests, but some diagnostic instruments provide grade-level scores as well as diagnostic information. They are thus doubly useful in the learning assessment. It will be instructive to compare scores from group-administered school achievement tests with scores from tests individually administered by the clinician.

The Wide Range Achievement Test (1965), or *WRAT*, is an individually administered achievement test consisting of three subtests in reading, spelling, and arithmetic. Each subtest is divided into two levels, one for children aged 5-0 to 11-11, and the other for those aged 12 through adulthood. The three subtests together generally take 20-30 minutes to administer. Many child psychologists and psychiatrists are familiar with this test, having used it for a number of years (it first appeared in 1936). It is a relatively quick, easy-to-administer office test which can give an up-to-date grade-level ranking in the three basic skills. We are interested in it here because it can provide a great deal of diagnostic information if the child is carefully observed during the testing. Each subtest is considered separately as we take up each of the basic academic skills.

Reading. The WRAT reading test consists of about 75 words to be pronounced. For very young children there is a prereading section consisting of recognizing and naming letters. The words to be pronounced are single discrete words, read horizontally across the page but with no textual content. This kind of test checks only technical reading skills: word attack skills; rocognition of basic phonic elements and combinations in the language; and attention to small details within words. There is no context that might aid the intelligent guesser whose technical decoding skills are weak. In listening to and watching the child read, the clinician will note the extent of the child's sight vocabulary (words recognized immediately) and his ability to analyze less familiar words using phonic principles, maintaining proper sequence in pronouncing each sound, and blending the sounds into the correct word. The number of words correctly pronounced will yield an achievement or grade-level score. The nature of the child's errors and the observed reading processes will show the clinician what happens to the child when he tries to read, where he goes astray, and what discriminatory, memory, or sequencing functions are not operating properly. Thus, if the child scores below grade level, there will be diagnostic information as to why. Incidentally, it is always impressive to watch and hear technically skilled children read words far beyond their grade level, which they do not understand and often have never even heard before. They manage to pronounce many of them correctly, a result of automatic-level cognitive processes, operating according to unconsciously learned phonic rules and principles regarding accent and syllabication as well as vowel combinations.

Because the WRAT reading subtest does not include a comprehension check, one cannot be sure from this test alone how well the child understands written material, even if he has technically read words correctly at or beyond his own grade level. Therefore, clinicians using the WRAT reading subtest should supplement it with some reading comprehension test, such as the *Gray Oral Reading Tests* (1967). This test consists of a set of graded paragraphs from beginning first grade level to college level. The child reads paragraphs aloud and is scored according to how many errors he makes and how much time he needs to read each paragraph. Questions on each paragraph allow for a comprehension check. The scoring has been found by some to be quite strict, but even without strict scoring the clinician will get a good idea of how the child manages with written material at various grade levels. The material is quite similar to the paragraph meaning tests which are group administered in school achievement test batteries.

An alternative to the combined WRAT and Gray Oral reading assessment is the more recently developed *Spache Diagnostic Reading Scales* (1972). Designed for children through grade six, with norms through grade eight, it is also appropriate for older children with reading difficulties. The test consists of word recognition lists (like the WRAT), graded reading passages (like the Gray), and supplementary phonics tests which aid in systematic analysis of reading skill deficiencies. The Spache reading passages can also be used to distinguish three reading levels: (1) the level at which the child can read independently with good accuracy and comprehension; (2) the instructional level at which he can read and understand with assistance; and (3) the potential level at which he comprehends material read to him and that usually exceeds his own reading level. The Spache is a more comprehensive reading test and has the advantage of providing the clinician with a single instrument.

Spelling. The WRAT Spelling subtest provides good diagnostic information. Beginning with very simple words like *go* and *in*, the child must use his visual memory, his knowledge of phonic rules, and his ability to maintain proper sequence as he progresses through more and more difficult words. It is helpful, after completing the formal part of the test, to ask the child to look over the words and mark the ones he is quite sure are right. Most children do well on such a task, for even though they may not be able to generate the rule or the mental image that would lead to correct spelling, they are usually aware when their own spelling doesn't look right. With well-motivated, intelligent, not overly anxious children, it is possible to discuss errors, give clues, teach a rule or principle, and test out the efficacy of the teaching by asking the child, for example, to write similar words. This kind of work gives the clinician some idea of how the child responds to individual instruction and what kind of relationship and teaching style are likely to work best in the classroom and in individual remedial teaching.

Arithmetic. The WRAT Arithmetic subtest is the least satisfactory of the three subtests for diagnostic purposes. With the exception of a few very simple items (e.g., how much are 3 and 4 apples?), all items are written computation problems, from simple addition to algebra. The sampling of various arithmetic operations is by necessity spread quite thin since there are a great many specific operations to check on in the space of a short test. The test will yield a grade-level achievement score, but one which can be related only to computation skills. It offers little diagnostic information as to why the child is having difficulty. This is a common problem in assessing arithmetic difficulties, since far less is known theoretically about the brain processes involved in mathematical thinking and operations. Similarly, on a more pragmatic level, we are far less systematic and organized in outlining the specific and integrated neuropsychological functions involved. While we can point to specific tasks and say that the child doesn't know how to do them (e.g., count, subtract with zero's, find the lowest common denominator, extract square roots), we are usually less able to abstract the underlying cognitive problems.

A step in the right direction is offered by the *KeyMath Diagnostic Arithmetic Test* (1971). This test consists of 14 subtests organized into the three main areas of content, operations, and application. Each item is presented on a separate card by the examiner, and except for written computation problems in the four basic processes (addition, subtraction, multiplication, and division), all answers are given verbally. Grade-level scores are available for each subtest as well as for the test as a whole, and the resulting profile will point up areas of special difficulty. This profile, plus the clinician's effort to analyze and categorize the test failures according to the questions below will help to conceptualize the child's difficulties in this area.

1. To what extent do the problems relate to a lack of basic mathematical concepts such as number, size, space and time relationships, serial order, and so on?
2. To what extent are the problems at the automatic level of cognitive organization, such as poor memory for number facts, poor visualizing or reauditorizing abilities, poorly organized written computation, or inaccuracy in reading or writing numbers and symbols?
3. To what extent are the problems related to difficulty in manipulating and integrating concepts so as to apply them to word problems?

Handwriting. To my knowledge, there are no formal tests of handwriting. However, there are some basic criteria for judging the adequacy of writing, and there are several varieties of writing problems related to various psychoneurological dysfunctions.

The two basic criteria for writing are that it be an efficient tool for the writer and legible to the reader. Some children write spontaneously enough and produce each letter without undue effort, but the results are illegible. Some children can produce legible copy only by laboring over the formation of each letter. Children with the most serious problems are those who labor and fail to produce legible results. The various writing problems can be categorized as follows:

Dysgraphia is a condition characterized by an inability to copy. It results from a disorder of visual-motor integration, in which visual and motor skills are intact and function well independently, but not together. Thus the child may accurately perceive, match, discriminate, and even read printed material, and he may be able to draw a reasonably straight line or steady curve from one point to another. However, he cannot copy written material because he cannot transform the visual input into an operative motor plan, or as Johnson and Myklebust put it, "He sees what he wants to write but cannot ideate the motor plan" (1967, p. 199). As the child looks at the figure he must copy, he does not know where to begin, and once begun, which way to move his hand—up or down, right or left—in order to reproduce the figure.

Visual memory disturbance may prevent the child from remembering, that is revisualizing, what a letter looks like, though he will recognize it when he sees it. For example, a 9-year-old boy was asked to spell the word *pal*. He figured out the three letters by their sounds, and wrote *pa*. Then he looked up and said, "I forget what an *l* looks like." The same problem is seen in spelling disorders; the child may have mastered revisualizing the 26 individual letters of the alphabet but cannot revisualize their presence or sequence in a given word.

Motor coordination disturbances create writing problems for the child who knows what he wants to write, can visualize all the letters and words, and theoretically knows how to reproduce the letters, but cannot adequately control his own movements. Lines and curves are unsteady, there are sudden stops or inability to stop in time, and changes of direction are executed with difficulty.

Written expression disturbances sometimes occur in children who have no special difficulty in oral expression, and who have mastered the mechanics of writing well enough to copy and to write from dictation. They have difficulty when they must transfer their own thoughts from inner running speech to paper. On the one hand, the writing does not flow automatically and smoothly enough, and on the other, the flow of thought cannot be properly paced to keep it in synchrony with the writing speed.

Most children with handwriting or combined handwriting and spelling problems show some mixture, and in mild forms, of the above difficulties. They have learned to visualize and to form all the letters, but they may form them in an idiosyncratic way that slows down smooth writing and may be hard to read. They can maintain adequate motor control if they do not have to write too much, or too long, or under conditions that are too frustrating. They find it taxing to write and tend to rush through written work in order to be done with it, thus exacerbating their difficulties.

LEARNING DISABILITIES TESTING

As discussed in chapter 2, a learning disability, by definition, involves discrepancies among various aspects of intellectual functioning. It is not a function of mental retardation. Thus, learning disabilities tests are designed to reveal, and sometimes measure, intraindividual differences in intellectual abilities. With two major exceptions (the ITPA and the Detroit Tests), most learning disabilities tests attempt to measure one particular area of intellectual functioning, although in some instances that area might be defined rather broadly. Thus there are tests of syntax, auditory discrimination, tactile discrimination, perceptual-motor skill, visual-motor integration, and so on. The clinician needs other data, usually but not necessarily from Binet or Wechsler intelligence testing, in order to judge whether a low score in a specific skill area reflects a specific weakness or is part of a larger, perhaps global intellectual weakness.

After it is decided that a child's low score is out of line with his presumed general intellectual ability, the most challenging part of the clinical assessment in this area begins. The low score does not tell what caused it, nor does it tell what relationship it bears to specific academic behaviors. These questions are matters of interpretation, no less so than analogous questions that arise in relation to intelligence or projective testing. While the theoretical assumptions underlying some learning disabilities tests may direct the interpretation in certain ways, in the final analysis it is not the test but the clinician that makes the decision as to whether or not, or to what extent, the child's problems can be attributed to learning disability.

Learning disabilities tests, like all tests, are subject to misinterpretation, misuse, and to seeming to offer more than they can deliver. Many are relatively new, standardized on small populations, and often on samples that do not reflect the population of the country. Bryan and Bryan (1975) describe a number of tests and note advantages and shortcomings. While it is beyond the scope of this book to survey the growing number of learning disabilities tests, three of the most frequently used, the ITPA, the Detroit Tests of Learning Aptitude, and the Frostig Developmental Test of Visual Perception are described in Appendix II. While each presents its own problems in standardization and validity, they can provide very useful information when used clinically for assessing individual children with learning problems.

The learning disabilities tests offer the clinician three specific benefits: they focus attention on intellectual activities relevant to academic learning; they provide an array of age appropriate items for observation and analysis of the child's performance; and within the limits of the standardization population, they offer norms that are helpful in evaluating the performance. While some test makers theorize and many test users believe that specific low scores are directly related to specific underlying mental processes, there are always inferential leaps involved. Thus the tests cannot relieve the clinician of evaluating and interpreting scores, tasks requiring the integration of data from other sources.

For example, there is Ellie, a 4½-year-old cerebral palsied child who could not walk, sat only with support, and got around by crawling. Her nursery school teachers saw her as very verbal and bright. Yet, when she scored at a 3-year-old level on the Visual Association subtest of the ITPA, while other subtest scores were in the 5- to 8-year-old range, there was concern about her conceptual abilities with visual stimuli. The ITPA was standardized on a middle class, predominantly white (96%) population; and it is not appropriate for lower class children, who are unfamiliar with many of the items presented. Ellie is from a highly educated professional family, but her experience with visual materials turned out to have been severely limited by her lack of mobility, so that on this subtest she was in essence a culturally deprived child. Her family and community environment was culturally rich and stimulating but her perspective from the floor was extremely curtailed. She could not rummage in drawers or walk around the neighborhood. When she rode in the car, her car seat did not put her high enough to see out the windows. So she did not recognize pictures of a flag, an ambulance, a safety pin, or a book of matches. (In retrospect the parents recalled that her neurologist had also noted that she didn't recognize a number of pictures he showed her, but as an isolated finding in an otherwise very intelligent, verbal child, nothing was made of it.) Since Ellie's language and conceptual development seemed more than adequate, the standard interpretation (Kirk & Kirk, 1971) for Visual Association difficulties did not seem a likely explanation for her low score. Nevertheless, the ITPA did point up a significant discrepancy. While, according to Carroll (1972), there is insufficient data for saying that the test is in general a valid diagnostic and remedial tool, Ellie's case illustrates how the test can provide a flexible and sensitive clinician with useful data.

Another example involving the ITPA illustrates its usefulness in a manner closer to that for which it was designed. Margaret had a congenital hearing loss which was not diagnosed until she was 5 years old. When she was 8 she had a language evaluation that included an ITPA. The major concern was to see how the hearing impairment might have affected her vocabulary development and general comprehension. Her overall age-equivalent score on the test was very close to her chronological age, and nine out of ten subtest scores were within one standard deviation of her mean test performance. The tenth, in Visual Closure, was 2⅓ standard deviations below the mean. It was the first indication that there might be anything in the visual, rather than the auditory sphere, to be concerned about. When a full psychological and educational evaluation was done shortly afterwards, a number of visual, motor, and visual-motor difficulties became apparent. WISC-R testing confirmed the ITPA indications that language development, including comprehension and vocabulary, were normal in spite of the hearing impairment.

Margaret's case also illustrates what the ITPA cannot do (nor, to my knowledge, can any other learning disabilities test)—that is, to indicate for individual children whether they do or will have difficulty in specific academic skills. The research does not yet make it clear whether the ITPA can even distinguish between groups of average and disabled readers (Carroll, 1972). Margaret's reading skills, particularly in decoding and individual word recognition, were very good; she spelled beyond grade level; and her handwriting, although large and somewhat uneven, was totally legible and produced with speed and ease. The best evidence for what a child can actually do in basic academic skills is a teacher's good observations plus academic skill testing. The learning disabilities tests can help discover, in the case of a child who is known not to be achieving, why he is not learning.

Eddie was such a child: at 13 he was reading at second to fourth grade levels. He had severe emotional problems and a very chaotic family life, and had been attending school for the past 5 years in classes for the emotionally disturbed. IQ testing indicated average nonverbal abilities and low verbal skills (WISC Verbal IQ 75, Performance 100). His learning problems were understood to be basically psychogenic. However, the teacher was so discouraged that she requested further testing with the hope that something new might be found which would clarify the problem and perhaps suggest a different way of teaching him. The psychologist noted in administering reading and math tests that Eddie misspoke once or twice, saying, for example, "big handle, top hand," when he meant the big hand of the clock. Furthermore, Eddie could not remember the numbers he was given for mental computation. He knew almost none of the vowel sounds nor the sound of an isolated *ch*, though his middle name was Charles. He managed to read at fourth grade level when reading paragraphs, making extensive and clever use of context clues. However, word lists were far more difficult, since there were no context clues; and with no reliable knowledge of the vowel sounds, he was almost totally dependent on visual memory and guessing from the consonants alone. These observations lent more meaning to the WISC verbal-performance discrepancy of previous testing, and together they suggested the possibility of auditory, automatic level difficulties, particularly in auditory memory.

The Detroit Tests include one subtest on memory for sentences, called the Auditory Attention Span for Related Syllables, which is similar to the Binet items, except that the Detroit sentences start at 3-year-old levels. Eddie was given this test, and scored at the level of a 5-year-old. It was noted that although Eddie could not remember the exact wording of sentences, nor the sequence of various phrases, he did understand the sentences at more advanced levels. He could state the gist of the sentences, and he also knew that he was not repeating the sentences verbatim. He was attentive, motivated, cooperative, and dismayed at not being able to remember—in short, the examiner had no reason to believe that emotional problems were interfering in this task, nor in those undertaken earlier. This subtest illustrates that test names cannot be taken at face value as accurately describing what they measure. The name "Auditory Attention for Related Syllables" suggests that a child who does poorly has problems in auditory attention. Eddie, according to any reasonable definition of the term, was attending. He listened, absorbed the content, and struggled to repeat it back. His difficulty was with memory, not with attention.

The advantage of the Detroit subtest here is that it provided an extensive array of prepared material, 43 sentences, ranging in length from 6 to 26 syllables. Moreover, it provided norms, which even though very old (1935), pointed out a severe discrepancy and offered a better estimate of Eddie's relative ability on this task than a clinician's best guess. The test did not diagnose or label; rather, it gave the clinician more data on which to base a judgment of whether or not Eddie had a learning disability in addition to emotional problems.

PERSONALITY TESTING

Every learning assessment requires some level of personality assessment. This may be achieved with or without personality testing, depending on the presenting problems of the child and the experience and style of the clinician. There is no particular personality test battery recommended for assessing learning difficulties. Whatever the psychologist finds most useful in helping him or her understand the child's characterological makeup will, by extension, shed light on the psychological aspects of the learning problems as well.

A few places in the routine clinical battery occasionally evoke conscious associations to school and learning, and thus may more directly illuminate the learning issues. One of these is TAT Card Number 1, the violin card, which may draw an expression of attitudes about success and achievement, about working towards a goal, about feeling pressured by parent's in the face of one's own sense of inadequacy or lack of interest, and about disappointing others.

TAT Card Number 2, the farm scene in which the young woman has an armload of books, often leads people, particularly adolescents, to voice attitudes towards learning, including aspirations, the expectations of others, and the perception of learning as being in conflict with other life roles and activities.

The *Tasks of Emotional Developmental Test* (Cohen & Weil, 1971) is a TAT-type test designed for children and adolescents, with pictures touching on various critical developmental issues. There are four sets of pictures, one each for latency boys and girls and adolescent boys and girls. The pictures in general evoke more material relating directly to interpersonal issues of youngsters than does the TAT, and there are one or two cards in each set which deal directly with school issues.

The "Three Wishes" question occasionally brings forth such wishes as "I'd wish I were the smartest in the class" or "I'd wish I never had to go to school again." With some children it is possible to pursue these thoughts and have the child amplify and elaborate them.

Another source of associations that sometimes relate to school are those gathered in connection with figure drawings. Questions about the drawn figure—what makes him happy, sad, worried, or angry—enable some children to express feelings about school at a safe remove. If the child has drawn both a male and a female figure, and associations are collected for each, the comparison of feelings and attitudes about school attributed to each sex may be illuminating.

In personality assessment, my own practice has been to administer almost routinely the "Three Wishes" question, the *Cole Animal Test* ("If you could be any animal in the world, which would you most want to be?" "Which would you most not want to be?" "Why?"), and usually a "Draw-A-Person." These are sometimes given all at once, and sometimes spread through the intelligence and academic testing. They are short, usually interject a relaxing change, and often provide an adequate perspective on the child's psychological status for our purposes. When the resulting information is not sufficiently enlightening, I then add a TAT or TAT-type test, the *Rorschach*, and perhaps additional drawings. In those cases where the child's problems are clearly very complex or serious and I want as thorough a personality assessment as possible, I may decide quite early to administer a full projective battery.

Although direct references to school or learning may be sparse or nonexistent in the projective materials, there is invariably data pertaining to dependency and independency, attitudes toward authority, the handling of aggression, task orientation, and the need for achievement. These should shed light on the learning difficulty, and not only in pointing to what contributes to it. In some instances personality testing will point up strengths that help the child to perform as well as he does, in spite of various other obstacles.

REFERRAL FOR MEDICAL OR PARAMEDICAL EVALUATION

In some cases, test results, observations, or parent or teacher reports will indicate a need for further examination or consultation, and the clinician will want to refer the child to another specialty area. Most referrals fall into three areas: vision, language (or speech and hearing), and neurology. To be considered here are the indications for such referrals, the findings and recommendations to be expected from the specialist, and ways of relating the results to the child's educational program.

There are some general principles that apply to all referrals. It is important to discuss the referral possibilities with the child's pediatrician or family doctor. He or she may have some information in the child's record about the problem being considered, such as complaints from earlier years, prior examinations, reports from examining specialists, and his or her own observations and examinations. Even if this material does not negate the need for an examination or consultation at the present time, it is likely to add to the current picture and make the referral more precise and informative.

The psychologist and the pediatrician should decide together who will handle the referral process and who will talk with the parents about it. They may be able to help each other in suggesting and contacting the appropriate specialists. Whoever handles the actual referral should see to it that they each receive copies of the subsequent reports. Since in most cases the child will be followed for a longer period by the physician than by the psychologist, it is especially important that when the psychologist handles the referral activity, he or she sees to it that the physician is kept informed and supplied with copies of reports. If the child has no regular physician or pediatrician, perhaps the family can be referred to a local family care program in which they are continuously followed by one doctor.

It is strongly recommended that the referral be made in writing, with the referral reasons clearly spelled out. The specialist should know about the learning difficulties which prompted the assessment, and about the specific indications which are prompting the referral. This will enable the specialist to focus his or her own examination and to report back in such a way as to better meet the needs of the assessment.

It is also recommended that the referral letter include any specific questions that the clinician wants answered. These usually have to do with the significance of the noted behavior or symptoms and any finding or recommendations affecting schoolwork that would be important for the teacher to know.

Whenever possible, it is wise to refer to specialists familiar with learning disabilities, since so many of the phenomena encountered are but minimally abnormal, show no blatant pathology, and assume significance only in the wider context of a spectrum of neuropsychological dysfunction and learning difficulties.

Vision

Lawson's (1968) comprehensive review of the literature on ophthalmological factors in reading problems concludes with a statement of consensus that while ocular factors do not cause reading retardation, they can aggravate a learning disorder and impede remediation. A number of ocular factors, including ocular motility, accommodations, and binocular fusion, can, when not operating properly, cause discomfort, eyestrain, headaches, and fatigue. These not only make reading more taxing for a child with visual processing disorders but also discourage attempts to read. Since only extensive reading practice will help the child overcome his reading difficulties, anything that discourages spending time at reading constitutes a serious impediment.

The clinician should be alert for signs or reports of squinting, eyestrain, fatigue after short periods of reading, eye rubbing, headaches, and any other complaints of eye discomfort. He or she should also watch for difficulties or errors related to vision; for example, losing the place while reading, not noticing words at the extremities of lines of print, difficulty in keeping track while counting WISC-R trees, Bender dots, and the like. Children with any of these signs should be referred for a thorough eye examination. The standard school eye examination using the Snellen chart is not sufficient. Even children already wearing glasses cannot be assumed to be adequately corrected or to have had all the relevant visual processes checked. Lawson's review mentions a 1962 study of poor readers in which, of the eight children already wearing glasses, only two were considered adequately corrected.

While glasses can correct some visual problems (refractive error or farsightedness, for example), other problems such as jerky ocular movements or poor binocular fusion must be treated by eye-training exercises or "orthoptics." There is today no agreement as to whether orthoptic training makes a significant difference in learning to read, although there is frequently tangible improvement in learning to use the two eyes together more efficiently and more comfortably.

One of the findings from Lawson's own research is that among children with learning disabilities, those with positive ocular findings are inferior in locomotor coordination when compared to children with learning disabilities but no eye disorder (1968, p. 172). This suggests that learning disability children with poor coordination are, as a group, at high risk for eye problems. Therefore, special attention should be paid to establishing their visual status.

Among the questions that the psychologist may want the eye specialist to answer are the following: Could visual problems be interfering with reading? If the child is to wear glasses at all, under what conditions is he to wear them at school? Does he need to sit anywhere in particular in the classroom? Are there particular recommendations for types of material to be used in reading or writing?

Language

There are two types of language problems likely to prompt a referral; the first and more common has to do with the mechanics of speech and hearing, and includes problems of auditory acuity, auditory discrimination, articulation, and fluency of speech. When the psychologist notes during the assessment any suggestions of poor hearing, difficulty in discriminating or articulating sounds, or poorly regulated speech flow, he or she may wish to consult with a speech and hearing specialist.

Depending on the age of the child, the seriousness of the problem, and the extent to which it interferes with academic learning, it may be advisable to assess the difficulties with more precision and to consider the need for special treatment. Questions to raise include the following: Are auditory difficulties interfering with learning? If so, is there any corrective treatment recommended? Are there speech problems that can be treated now? Is there a recommended treatment program? Does the teacher need to do anything or avoid anything in particular?

The second type of language problem is the more general and comprehensive one having to do with the meaning of language, that is, aphasia. If present, the clinician will have noted such problems throughout testing, and a test such as the ITPA will have helped to delineate them. In cases where the deficit seems extreme and raises questions about extensive neurological involvement, and where it seems to be seriously interfering with the ability to handle academic learning, it is wise to look to a language pathologist who may be found among speech and hearing specialists, neurology specialists, or in the area of language and learning disabilities.

Neurology

Some clinicians (in this instance the term includes psychologists, psychiatrists, and pediatricians) feel that every child with learning problems should be given a routine neurological work-up, including an EEG. Others feel that every child whose learning problems seem in any way related to central processing dysfunction should have such a work-up. Still others feel that only when there are suggestions of lesions or convulsive disorders is such an examination warranted. At the present time there appears to be no general rule or consensus and decisions tend to be based on more extraneous factors, such as the availability of facilities, cost, the interest of local neurologists in studying children with learning problems, and the presumed negative or positive psychological effect that a neurologist's involvement is likely to have on parents and teachers.

Where learning problems are concerned, the neurological examination and EEG may be used to determine if drugs are to be tried, and to establish baseline responses before drug trials. Drug research with children is still in its very early stages, and the great majority of studies done to date lack good experimental controls.

However, there does tend to be agreement about some basic issues, which are summarized by Connors (1971):

> In general, older drugs with known absence of toxicity, such as the stimulants, are drugs of first choice. Routine prescription of medication without careful physical examination and laboratory studies in children is never justifiable. Multiple points of observations, such as from a clinician, parent, teacher and the child himself are recommended for proper evaluation of therapeutic effect; the use of standardized objective measures of cognitive function is also recommended. (p. 296)

Denhoff and Tarnopol (1971) list three groups of children who appear to benefit from medication: (1) those with convulsive or subconvulsive tendencies; (2) those with hyperkinetic behavior syndrome, which includes hyperactivity, short attention span, variability in behavior, impulsiveness, irritability, and explosiveness; and (3) those with behavior disorders that reflect anxiety, aggression, or neurotic behavior. Connors (1971) discusses the use of drugs with children who have none of these symptoms, with the hope that the drug may affect central processing competence and thus enhance learning. This is a newer and more radical use of drugs and results are as yet inconclusive.

If it is decided to try a drug regimen, it must be well established how and by whom it is to be regulated and monitored. In this instance, the concern is not with specific questions but rather with an ongoing cooperative communciation arrangement.

In general, I recommend referral for neurological examination for one of two reasons: (1) when it is believed that drug treatment might alleviate a condition, such as seizures or severe hyperactivity, possibilities that a pediatric neurologist can most competently evaluate; or (2) when there is some reason to suspect an underlying neurological abnormality, which should be documented if it exists, ruled out if it does not, and kept in mind as a possible factor if it cannot be ruled either in or out. Among the reasons to suspect such abnormalities are notable sensory and motor deficits, including odd gait and carriage; extreme discrepancies in intellectual abilities (such as observed in a 5-year-old boy whose range of intellectual abilities on the McCarthy scales spread over 5½ standard deviations); suspected seizure disorder; and the presence of extremely unusual or bizarre responses which do not clearly relate to psychodynamic problems. An example of this last was the WISC-R Block Design performance of a 12-year-old boy on Design Number 6 (the tilted square). He used four all-red sides, each representing a corner, and placed them at the four corners of an imaginary diamond, none of them touching any other. This boy had a Full Scale IQ in the mid-80s, with a discrepancy between verbal and performance scales of 15 to 20 points (he had been tested four times). Yet, neither the dull normal IQ nor the consistently weaker visual-spatial abilities could account for such a deviant, primitive solution without further examination.

The elements of assessment, that is, the data collected from interviews, reports, tests, and behavior observations constitute the building blocks from which the clinician must construct a model of the child as learner. The task is a demanding and creative one, for the building blocks do not bear notations about how they fit together. The shape, and the relative value and importance of each element in the final construct depend on the individual clinician's talent, experience, theoretical leanings and, not least, fidelity to the data. The resulting characterization must be a creative, but not a fictional rendition, highlighting the dynamic interaction of the child's aptitudes, style, attractiveness, character, and preoccupations, along with environmental supports and constraints. The validity of the assessment cannot be statistically or even scientifically verified, although we can say with certainty that no assessment is ever complete or perfect. If the assessment picture derived resonates well with those who know the child and if predictions based on the assessment come to pass or remedial plans built into it work out well, the clinician can enjoy some measure of satisfaction.

7

Case Illustrations

There are few generalizations that one can make about learning problems or about the people who have them, and there would be little value in trying to define categories of learning problems. While we can categorize the determinants of learning problems, the individual learning problem, like the individual who has it, will always have unique characteristics, depending on the determinants involved and the interaction among them. For this reason, the case illustrations chosen for this chapter are not offered as a representative sample of learning problems, but rather as illustrations of the interaction of biological, psychological, and environmental determinants in a number of individuals. For the most part, the cases are presented in groups, each group having some common characteristic of age, sex, or general referral complaint. The final illustration, about Susan, is an exception; she is presented singly, and as I try to indicate, she probably does represent a great many other children.

THREE BOYS—DANNY, CHIP, AND GEORGE

I have chosen these three particular boys for discussion because each demonstrates the interplay of biological, intrapsychic, and environmental determinants in their learning problems, both in the creation of the problems and in the ways that each boy has developed for coping with them. These three boys also illustrate, in the similarities and differences between them, some of the critical issues involved in the resolution of difficulties that each child must ultimately come to, whether that resolution is successful or not.

Before presenting each boy individually, some general facts about all three will provide some structure for the material that follows. Chip and George are very similar "demographically." Each was 14 and in the eighth grade at the time of referral for evaluation. Both boys were perceived as learning disabled by their parents and at school; both had been diagnosed in the fourth grade; and both had received special learning disability tutoring in the public schools since that time, while spending the major portion of the school day in regular classes. Chip and George both had IQ scores between 100 and 110. Both of their mothers had become trained as learning disabilities teachers after learning of their sons' problems. Both fathers were businessmen. Both families were self-referred for assessment, each having decided to go outside of the school system for a reevaluation of their sons. Both families saw the boys as definitely learning disabled, were concerned when their respective school systems raised questions about emotional problems, and sought the evaluation when they did because the boys were approaching high school entry and it was time to make a plan for the next four years.

On the other hand, Danny was 8 and in the third grade when referred by his psychiatrist for evaluation. He had been in treatment for 3 years, and the referral was prompted by an aunt's suggestion to Danny's mother that he might have a learning disability. The mother discussed it with Danny's therapist and the referral was made. In contrast to Chip and George, Danny's problems had been seen as largely emotional by his parents as well as his therapist. He was described as unhappy, whining, infantile, and disorganized. While the mother was very eager to pursue the question of a possible learning disability, she was also very anxious that Danny's psychotherapy continue. She found his demanding, disorganized behavior draining and was not put off by the idea of his having emotional problems. Danny's parents pursued professional and academic careers and Danny's WISC-R Verbal IQ was 133 (Performance 105, Full Scale 122).

It is apparent that Danny's general situation is quite different from Chip's and George's although all three come from solid middle-class families living in communities with good school systems. As will be seen from the following case histories, age is a major factor in determining the issues with which the boys deal. Furthermore, while Chip and George deal with the same stage-determined questions, they handle them quite differently. We begin with Danny.

Danny

Danny, 8, was the youngest of three children. He got along well enough with his sister, 2 years older, but quite badly with his 11-year-old brother, who tended to lord it over the younger boy and generally tried to demonstrate his own superior knowledge and power. Danny retaliated by being a pest and a tattletale, thereby earning considerable disfavor from the whole family. He seemed to refuse to be independent. He insisted, for example, that his mother make him a sandwich when he could make it for himself, or that someone else read the Monopoly dice and tell him how much he had rolled. His third grade teacher was not concerned about his academic work or progress. His reading was not very fluent, he was slow and disorganized in arithmetic, and his handwriting was labored and rough. However, the teacher saw him as a very bright and verbal youngster, itchy and immature, and she believed he would eventually outgrow his difficulties. She did not find him difficult in class, but he was frequently sent out of the room by the music teacher who complained of his talking and singing out of turn.

Danny got along well enough with the children in his class, but he had no particular friends in the group. In his neighborhood he felt somewhat intimidated by the other children. He spent a lot of time hanging around the house, watching television as much as he could get away with. He did not initiate after-school play arrangements with other children, but would respond gladly if he were invited to play.

Danny was small for his age, and during three testing sessions he was never still. He squirmed on his chair, jiggled a leg, poked at the knees of his jeans with a pencil. Even when he seemed calm and content, working at some task he enjoyed, he would hum or make noises with his tongue. His frequent restlessness, his apparent need to be in motion even when contentedly absorbed in a cognitive task, and his small stature contributed to a general picture of developmental (constitutional) immaturity. In addition, his behavior in dealing with people was often immature. It was not uncommon for him to drop down on all fours and crawl around making growling animal noises in reaction to a denied request or some other disappointment.

Testing indicated a mild learning disability. There were processing difficulties in visual areas, contrasted with exceptional verbal and language skills. The 28 point discrepancy between his Verbal Scale IQ of 133 and Performance Scale IQ of 105 resulted from a range of 13 through 18 on Verbal subtests (excluding Digit Span which was 9), and all Performance subtest scores of 10 and 11. Nevertheless, he enjoyed the Performance subtests and would say, "I love doing this kind of thing." In several instances he achieved correct solutions of difficult items when given more than the allotted time. Thus, Danny's relatively weaker skills in this area did not cause frustration, nor did he have any sense of doing less well than anyone else.

The less skillful visual processing was also apparent in his reading, which was sprinkled with omissions and the misreading of small words and suffixes. In spite of errors, he managed to read through and comprehend fifth grade material. In contrast to his pleasure with the Performance subtests where his skill was just average, he was distressed with his reading ability. When the psychologist told him that he was reading fifth grade material, he said, "So what—some kids in my class read sixth grade books." It was apparent that, in reading, not only did he experience the dysfluencies in his technique, but he also felt a general sense of not measuring up to his self-selected reference group. Furthermore, it seems likely that he experienced the discrepancy between his superior comprehension and vocabulary levels and his approximately average but rough technical skills.

Danny's comment about reading was in keeping with his general perception of the world and his ability to manage in it. He saw himself as too young, too unskilled, and too unsocialized to get along at the level he believed was expected of him and had come to expect of himself. Being small and the youngest in the family set him up for such a perception, and the situation was further heightened by his mother's eagerness for him to grow up and become independent as quickly as possible. In addition, the whole family tended to see any dependency on his part as being intentional, designed to provoke and to gain special attention and favors. Here the mild learning disability played a role, for some things that one would expect of a very bright verbal youngster were in fact more difficult for Danny—such as reading quickly and accurately the number of spots on the Monopoly dice. The irritated response of parents and siblings to his failure to do what was truly difficult for him intensified his feeling of not being able to make it in the outside world of school and neighborhood. This feeling, in turn, contributed to his use of regressive behavior as a major defense mechanism and worked against his trying to organize himself in a more grown-up way to overcome his mild learning difficulties.

In school, Danny was relatively comfortable and relaxed so long as his teachers accepted his constitutional immaturities as nonhostile, nonprovocative, and capable of being outgrown. If his noises and fidgets could not be readily absorbed into ongoing classroom life, a cycle of blame, guilt, and retaliation was likely to ensue, similar to what sometimes transpired at home. Danny's very high verbal intelligence helped to compensate for his behavioral immaturity and for some of the ill effects of his lower nonverbal skills. The fact that the latter were at average levels relative to the general population also made the realistic difficulties with academic work slight (for example, in comparison to another child whose discrepant abilities would yield scores of 82 and 110). The biological items of developmental immaturity and verbal-nonverbal imbalance were intertwined with an immature, regressive behavior style, which thereby threatened a self-perpetuating cycle of immature behavior, blame, recrimination, and reactive regression, anxiety, and guilt.

In Danny's case then, it appeared that biological and psychological determinants contributing to learning problems were such that they could be mitigated by sensitive and appropriate handling at school.[1]

Chip

"Chip" was a nickname and the name by which he was known everywhere. Chip's real name was the same as his father's, and he was the oldest of three sons. His father was very closely identified with him, partly because he had a severe reading problem himself. The father related that when he himself was in third grade, his teacher told his mother that he was a moron and would never learn to read. His mother worked with him every evening for the next three years and taught him to read. The father remained a poor speller, but he wrote freely and had his spelling corrected by his wife or secretary. He had two nephews with learning disabilities, and Chip's next youngest brother had shown some signs of the same problem though to a lesser degree, perhaps partly due to earlier recognition and remediation. The youngest was developmentally very immature, having begun to lose his first teeth only at the age of eight.

[1]. Several months after this material was written, Danny's mother wrote to the psychologist to share the news of his progress:

> I think a small success story is always positive to put in one's files. I want to tell you how Danny is doing in 4th grade. In short—"dynamite."
>
> To elaborate, his teacher has really pushed him, and to his surprise he has ended up proving to himself how well he can do. He is an "expert" in math—he uses a calculator at home to check himself and for "fun" also does long division problems, the harder the better. His joy comes from doing his tables at school in 2 minutes 49 seconds—having worked at his speed, which was five minutes a month ago. He writes magnificent poetry, a sensitive journal and READS!—easily, without mistakes. He is now consumed with Cortez's tortures of the poor folks and Montezuma's revenge.
>
> He has a much better self-image—functioning well in just about everything—the only problem (if one can even call it that) is legible handwriting. He has announced that he needs to practice—also that he needs to quietly say numbers aloud before writing them down because he "backwards" them. If he remembers to check himself his work is perfect.

Chip had friends in the neighborhood and at school, where he was quiet but not isolated. In the two years before referral, he had had quite an active social life, and had seemed more successful at school as well. This year he seemed to be working as hard, but was getting poorer grades, stayed at home most of the time, and saw only one friend with any regularity.

His father worked with him a good deal on homework, and also on hobbies, hoping to get Chip interested in something he could enjoy and excel at. Chip did well in these activities, but the father was uncertain about how much the boy really liked them and how much he just went along. Chip never expressed great enthusiasm about them or initiated requests or projects, but he always agreed to his father's suggestions. Chip's mother had worked with him on reading, but in recent months he had resisted her help.

Chip had repeated first grade, had been given some remedial reading help in second and third grades, and in fourth grade after an outside evaluation, had been recognized as having a serious learning disability. After this, Chip was given more extensive special services in the schools. He was weak in a variety of automatic-level skills. In reading, his comprehension was above grade level, but his reading was slow because of poor word recognition. He could sound out any word in his spoken vocabulary, but the need to sound out so many words made reading painfully slow. If he tried to read at a normal speed, which he often did, he was prone to misreading small words, prefixes and suffixes, and look-alike words. If the material was complex, a few errors of that sort were sufficient to distort the meaning entirely. Reading at a low speed allowed for greater accuracy, but often left Chip at the end of a section not remembering what he had read at the beginning. Some of his school reading had been transcribed for him onto tape; by this method, Chip could get through material much faster and with good comprehension. Technically, Chip's reading measured at about sixth-grade level, meaning that at this level he could read with good comprehension and without excessive technical errors. Spelling was at fourth- to fifth-grade level on a formal test, but he could write *doe* for *do* and not notice that anything was wrong. Chip's arithmetic skills ranged from fourth grade to mid-high-school levels, with his best performance in conceptual understanding and his poorest in computation. Cursive writing was painfully slow and difficult, and Chip had recently asked that he not be made to practice and use cursive script. He had become "automated" enough with printing to be comfortable, though slow, with it; and it was legible.

WISC-R testing confirmed the general picture of good verbal and nonverbal conceptual and reasoning abilities and poor automatic-level skills. Chip had scaled scores of 6 on Digit Span, Arithmetic, and Coding, 12 on all other Verbal subtests, and 9 through 12 on the other Performance subtests.

The psychological picture was of a boy deeply concerned about making his way in the world. He was involved with becoming independent, trying to wean himself from his mother's protective help, and wondering how well and happily he could do on his own. The major recurrent theme was of failing to achieve what he aspired to and having to settle for something less, with the added feature that in aiming high he would not only fail but be injured in the process. He felt in a general way that he would get along, but without distinction or great happiness. In the projective materials and in parent and teacher accounts, Chip appeared to be moderately depressed. He studied, he tried, he produced with great effort, and he made slow progress.

For Chip school had value as a social setting and as a place where he could continue to strive for academic success. He wanted to be able to go to college, and high school achievement was, among other things, the means of getting into college. The learning disability severely hampered Chip's achievement, but the striving continued, despite occasional periods of despair. A family history which helped him to see his problem as something other than personal inadequacy; good intelligence; supportive parents and teachers; and an achievement-oriented father, who was constructively identified with his son's difficulties and aspirations helped Chip to cope as he did with his serious learning disability.

George

George, 14, had two sisters, one 3 years his senior and another in her 20s, married and living in another city. His parents had had a stormy, conflict-laden marriage for several years, and George had witnessed many violent arguments. In some of these arguments, George saw his mother struck by his father. (The mother described the father as a mild-mannered person with a vile temper.) When George was in the third grade, his parents were divorced. The children lived with their mother, but saw their father, who lived nearby, quite frequently. The relationship between the parents remained a difficult and verbally combative one. When the oldest daughter had married and moved away and the younger two children were adolescents, a conflict developed around the second girl, who decided to go live with her now remarried father. She stopped visiting her mother at all, whereupon the mother declared that George was not to visit his father anymore. George did not complain about the ruling. When asked some months later how he felt about not being allowed to visit his father, he indicated that he was relieved that he was forbidden to go. Although he was fond of his father, he complained, "They yell and argue a lot over there." George himself had always been quiet and shy, and at times openly fearful. He hesitated about going anywhere new or crowded, and he seemed fearful of strangers and unfamiliar places. He had spent most of his time at or near home until a couple years prior to the evaluation; then he began spending several afternoons a week at a nearby kennel.

George had received extra reading help at school since the early elementary grades. By the time he was in eighth grade, his reading was at grade level in technical skills and above grade level in comprehension. His spelling was poor, with errors related to poor visual memory and poor phonic analysis in words of more than two syllables. His handwriting was cramped and jerky, and any written work took him a very long time. In arithmetic, George's conceptual understanding and basic computational skills were good, but he made careless errors and made little effort in active problem solving. What he could do easily and automatically he did rather well. The solidity of his knowledge of early computation skills and the absence of any familiarity with fractions and decimals suggested that he might have worked more actively up through perhaps fourth or fifth grade, and that in more recent years he had been making less of an effort to master new concepts and materials. In general, spelling, handwriting, and arithmetic were three to five years below grade level.

George's eighth-grade teachers consistently noted that he was quiet, well-behaved, and "a loner" in classes. He could not do regular class work in most subjects; and those teachers who were willing to modify or provide special assignments for him complained that he did not pick them up, complete them, or even work on them in class unless the teacher were right next to him. Metal shop was the only class where his work was satisfactory, and even in that class he was the one student who worked alone rather than at a bench with others. He had no friends in the neighborhood. George's major interests were in outdoor survival skills, and he occasionally camped out alone near his house. He had also become interested in a dog-breeding farm located in a nearby community. In the last couple of years, he had taken to spending several afternoons a week there doing any general work that might be found for him, including cleaning the kennels and exercising the dogs. He was apparently well liked by the owner and workers there, although he was no more open or communicative there than he was at home or at school. It was evident, though, that he felt happy and comfortable at the farm, perhaps more than anywhere else. In the last year he was being given some special handling lessons in exchange for his work, but until then he had been happy to work for nothing, just for the sake of being around the animals.

Testing sessions with George revealed the shy, uncommunicative, pleasant-faced boy, and also some of his more covert hostility and rage. Direct expressions of feeling were noted in his initial refusal to leave his mother's car and enter the psychologist's office, in a fleeting scowl quickly covered with a shy smile, and in a routine he developed of ringing the doorbell each time he entered and left the office. Otherwise, George was the quiet, compliant boy described by his teachers. A mild learning disability was noted in relatively weak visual memory and visual-motor skills, but the overriding impression was of severely curtailed energy and investment in academic tasks. Simple arithmetic calculations were done carelessly, and numerals were overwritten with no concern as to whether or not they could be read.

Projective testing produced surprisingly rich protocols. The Rorschach was almost totally devoid of affective expression (F% = 94), but it was a product of long and thoughtful effort with 34 responses. Like the TAT, it began with very very long initial reaction times, but in each case George began to respond more easily after dealing with the first few cards. The sense of affective distance was maintained throughout. George did his best to never handle any of the cards, and he told long elaborated TAT stories while sitting hunched over his knees, often staring at the floor, occasionally with his head buried inside the front of his windbreaker jacket which he had not taken off. An outstanding characteristic of the TAT stories was the implication that expression of feeling is tantamount to loss of control. Even George's stories of happiness led to celebration, drunkenness, drunk driving, and consequent manslaughter or suicide. The major theme, however, was not happiness but retaliatory rage against some aggressive act. In some instances the hero was guilty of the original wrongdoing, in some instances he was the avenger of some wrongdoing against another. Almost invariably the resolution was a life in solitary isolation, living away from other people in a forest, on an island, in a lonely lighthouse, or a fortified castle. It was only by way of withdrawal from the affective, and seemingly disastrous demands of people that George believed he could handle himself, be at peace, and feel effective in providing for his own basic needs. It appears that George's identification with his father and what he perceived as his father's destructive violence, contributed to a reactive pattern of trying to hold on to feelings for the sake of self-preservation. By controlling and even dissociating himself from his feelings, George has also turned off a major source of energy supply for active learning.

The psychological picture that emerged from testing sessions with George helped bring about an understanding of the nature of his relationship to school and learning. The pleasant "loner" whom the teachers described had learned a nonobtrusive style with which he could keep his feelings in check and avoid more than minimal contact with other people. When directly confronted, George would do what was asked of him, but there is no indication that he actively wanted anything from learning or from relationships at school. It is against this background that the relatively mild learning disability existed preventing George from doing with relative ease what he otherwise might have done if spelling patterns, handwriting, and arithmetic computation came to him more automatically. The additional frustration and failure which the disability engendered undoubtedly added to the load of feelings, which George believed he had to keep in check, and to the general lack of comfort that he apparently experienced at school. This is in contrast to his more relaxed demeanor at the dog farm where he knew that he could do whatever was expected of him.

School did not engage George. He wanted nothing from it but to be left alone. He had no hope of finding or achieving anything there, neither friends, increased self-esteem through accomplishment, nor the means to attain the other things that follow from school success. George was not devoid of wishes for friendship, success, and happiness, and like everyone had fantasies of being loved, appreciated, and admired. However, he could fashion little or no connection between school and what he wanted for himself. Given this situation, it would take an exceptional school environment to help George overcome his learning difficulties. He would not only need patience and understanding but also active help in developing relationships with peers and teachers and in turning his energies outward and onto school-related issues and activities.

All three boys, Danny, Chip, and George, have a learning disability, characterized by difficulty in some kinds of information processing and evidenced in test score discrepancies and academic task performance. Chip and George clearly have learning problems in that they have difficulty in doing the school work expected of them. It is not certain that one could say the same of Danny; his mother would probably say that he does and his teacher that he does not.

The comparison of the three boys' learning disabilities and learning problems highlights a number of issues regarding the interaction of learning and learning difficulty with age, intelligence, and emotional problems.

Learning Problems and Age. The boys illustrate the difference that age makes in the meaning that school, with its attendant successes and failures, has for children. Danny's struggles revolve around industriousness, applying and controlling himself, and conforming to the expectations of parents and teachers and to the standards of his classmates. If he is successful, he stands to gain acceptance in his family-school-neighborhood world, and the self-esteem and sense of personal well-being that these afford. As Erikson (1950/1965) points out, "School seems to be a culture all by itself, with its own goals and limits, its achievements and disappointments" (p. 259).

Chip and George, on the other hand, are entering a period in which identity and eventual independence are critical concerns. It is not enough to work hard and do assigned, expected tasks in order to feel right with one's self and with the world. Their thoughts and concerns are to a large degree about the adult roles they are to play in the wider world. School success or failure has implications for their future ability to get along independently and to make their own happiness through new relationships and experiences.

Learning Disability and Intelligence. Danny and Chip, whose Wechsler score patterns are so clear-cut, demonstrate the effect of overall intelligence on the extent to which a learning disability can impair learning success. Danny's discrepant scores are low Performance subtest scores of 10 and 11 and a high score of 18. Chip, on the other hand, has lows of 6 and highs of 12. Danny's superior verbal skills and average visual-spatial abilities helped compensate for a perceptual-motor deficit so that he could perform at grade level in math and above grade level in reading comprehension. Chip, having solid intelligence but very deficient automatic skills, was totally unable to keep up without intensive extra help.

Learning Disability and Emotional Problems. Chip's learning disability, along with his normal intelligence, meant that he had to struggle hard to keep up with his class. George's learning disability was less severe, but his emotional problems, originally unrelated to his school situation, were severe enough to interfere with learning and to aggravate the difficulties that a mild-to-moderate learning disability would create. Chip was not free of emotional difficulties, but they were basically secondary to the learning disability. George was likely to have had learning difficulties even if he had not had a learning disability, while Chip was likely to have had little or no difficulty with school had he not been learning disabled.

MR. MEYER AND MR. ROSSI—ADULTS WITH LEARNING DISABILITIES

Compared with children, it is relatively unusual for an adult to seek evaluation of a learning problem. Usually, by adulthood, an individual has come to terms with or made some kind of adjustment to whatever learning difficulties he experienced during his school years. For many people, the completion of required schooling constitutes a liberation from the steady confrontation with failure and the negative aspects of one's self-image. Population figures on the retarded demonstrate that many identified retardates of school age disappear into the general population as adults, managing their family and working lives competently and independently. Something similar apparently happens with a number of learning disabled pupils, who manage their subsequent careers, occasionally at high professional levels, with comfortable and workable circumlocutions of their specific difficulties. Those who are intellectually talented and characterologically strong enough may work in positions of authority, where their problems with automatic skills are almost invisible. Poor handwriting is almost an asset when one has only to scrawl a signature; poor spelling is irrelevant if one dictates to a secretary or tape recorder; and inability to learn a foreign language is unnoticed if one works only in his native language. Even inefficient reading skills can be tolerated in many business positions, where language style and vocabulary tend to become routinized and familiar and there is no demand for accurate perusal of large quantities of narrative prose.

From the limited number of adults who see a psychologist for assessment of a learning problem, we can learn in retrospect about a group of undiagnosed learning disabled students who got through school in various ways and, in many instances, established successful family and working lives. In my experience, adults come for assessment when some specific and often idiosyncratic circumstance precipitates a move to seek a remedy for a long-standing problem. Given the number of adults with suspected learning problems who do not seek help, one must assume that those who do come for help constitute a very small percentage of those who have had learning disabilities throughout their lives. We are going to discuss two men who sought help for a learning problem, Mr. Meyer and Mr. Rossi, both of whom had learning disabilities. They are not presented as being representative of adults with learning problems or even of adults with learning disabilities, but rather as people who are articulate about their past and current learning problems, and whose experiences can help us in understanding children as well as adults with learning difficulties.

There are advantages and disadvantages in retrospective pictures such as those Mr. Meyer and Mr. Rossi provide. The disadvantages include the inability to check out and round out the necessarily subjective picture of how things were twenty to thirty years ago. The great advantage of course is in seeing what people have been able to achieve, in spite of their handicaps, and how they deal with remaining problems. They illustrate the great importance of psychological and environmental circumstances in determining how learning deficits are experienced and dealt with. They offer us a perspective on the children we encounter, allowing us to speculate, with somewhat clearer parameters, on how they might manage in their adult years.

Mr. Meyer

Mr. Meyer was 32 years old when he became newly concerned about his spelling problem. He was the owner of a small and successful business, married and the father of an infant son. He did almost no writing at all. At work he wrote nothing more than the names of customers in the appointment book; at home his wife handled all correspondence. He had been resigned to and relatively untroubled by his inability to spell correctly, until some months prior to his son's birth. During his wife's pregnancy, he began noticing how the young children of their friends were apt to ask, "Daddy, how do you spell _____?" He began to be concerned that his son would one day do the same, and the thought that he would be unable to spell words for his children touched off a flood of anxiety and concern about his own self-worth and about his ability to be a good male role model for his boy. He went first to a psychiatrist, who, after hearing the despairing remarks about spelling and handwriting several times, asked Mr. Meyer to write something and bring it in the next time. After the psychiatrist saw the exceptionally poor results, he suggested that the poor skills be assessed in their own right.

Mr. Meyer had been raised in England, in an Orthodox Jewish family. From the age of five he had attended a bilingual day school, where he was taught in both English and Hebrew. He was a poor student from the very beginning and always at the bottom of the class. He did not learn to read English with confidence until he was fourteen, and a year later he quit school. He wandered around the Continent and eventually to the United States, working at various odd jobs for a time. Towards the end of his travels, he got considerable training and experience as an apprentice in a highly valued skill. In his late 20s, Mr. Meyer opened his own shop in the same community in which he lived. He employed about five assistants and operated a successful business.

Mr. Meyer spoke easily, with good articulation and a well-developed vocabulary (he had a scaled score of 12 on the WAIS Vocabulary subtest). After he spoke of his spelling difficulties, he was asked if he had any trouble with reading. He said no, but added that he did not read much because he tended to get a headache when he read. He said his reading was pretty much limited to the sports page and a few other items in the newspaper. Nevertheless he agreed to read aloud, and in the course of the first two sentences it became clear that Mr. Meyer did indeed have a reading problem. His reading was similar to that of the boys discussed earlier in this chapter, Danny and Chip. It was imprecise, omitting or misreading small words, omitting or adding final *s*'s, misreading inflections of tense and prefixes and suffixes in general. Mr. Meyer, however, unaware or denying his reading difficulty, failed to ever go back and correct himself as the boys often did. Instead, he would continue, and if the words he came to later in the sentence did not agree in tense or number with what he had previously misread, he would alter the later words to fit what he had said earlier. For example, if a sentence read "The boys in the house say they want to come out," Mr. Meyer might start out with an initial misreading and say "A boy . . ." When he comes to "say they want . . ." he might perceive the words accurately, but realizing that they are grammatically incorrect in combination with what he has just read, he adjusts his reading to what sounds right rather than checking any of the words more carefully, and continues on. One can now speculate about why Mr. Meyer gets a headache when he reads, being so frequently confronted with the disagreement between what his eyes tell him and what his ear (for inner as well as spoken language) tells him. Impressionistic, inaccurate reading such as this may often convey basic information, but if the errors are frequent, the amount of made-up reading must increase to compensate for them. Before long, the inner narrative has little to do with the written page.

It is useful to speculate on Mr. Meyer's style of handling his reading disability, which seems to fit in many ways the psychiatrist's general description of him as a pleasant, eager to please, hysteric person. His nonawareness of any problem and his somatizing of the difficulty fit that picture, as does his tendency to ignore indications of error and to gloss over disonance in reading that sounds all right but fails to match the visual message. Although the kinds of errors Mr. Meyer makes are highly characteristic of reading disability, and would seem to be more biologically than psychologically determined, his way of handling them appears to be determined in considerable measure by characterological factors.

Mr. Meyer did better in reading discrete words, scoring a grade level of 8.7 on the Wide Range Achievement Test. With no context clues he was forced to rely on word analysis more than his good ear, and his well-developed vocabulary helped him to correctly guess at some words which he only partially analyzed, such as *unanimous* and *contemptuous.* He still made errors, usually of the type where an incomplete or inaccurate analysis touches off associations to a word with similar visual elements; thus, he read *biographic* instead of *bibliography, imagine* instead of *image, deceive* instead of *decisive,* and *integrating* instead of *ingratiating.*

Mr. Meyer's spelling was at about second-grade level, and indicated (1) difficulty in tracking consonant sounds (*interuite* for *institute*); (2) poor visual memory (*belive* for *believe, hevan* for *heaven*); and (3) no awareness of basic spelling conventions such as *q* always followed by *u,* and an *ee* sound at the end of a word signified by a *y* (*eqepment* for *equipment, mejroti* for *majority,* and *qontoeti* for *quantity*). Lack of reading experience quite likely has a significant effect on visual memory for words and awareness of spelling conventions, but failure to spell phonetically suggests more basic and more serious difficulty.

Mr. Rossi

Mr. Rossi, a fireman who turned to the Yellow Pages rather than to a psychiatrist in seeking help with his spelling and writing problem, found a community-sponsored, psychological service organization that referred him for assessment. He was 42 years old at the time, married and the father of three. He had just completed a two-year college-degree program financed by the federal government (part of a GI Bill to which his Navy service of some twenty years earlier entitled him). He had a better than B average in the program, but had experienced difficulty in writing compositions. Not only was his spelling poor, but he found that because of his poor spelling he tended to alter what he planned to say so as to express it in more easily spelled words—and in so doing, he produced less effective written work. (That is a common problem and a common solution, with both children and adults, when there are spelling difficulties in native or foreign languages.) Mr. Rossi was interested in improving his spelling because he wanted to continue his college education and prepare himself for a new career after he retired from fire fighting thirteen years hence.

Mr. Rossi was the twelfth of thirteen children and the son of immigrant parents. He grew up in a moderately poor section of the city, and he was one of only two children in the entire family who completed high school. He might easily not have graduated, for his father insisted he quit school after the eleventh grade and get a job, so as to contribute to the family income. Mr. Rossi did so, but managed to attend night school as well, so he graduated from high school on schedule. Mr. Rossi had no recollection of any difficulty in school; on the contrary, he recalls enjoying school, doing well, being well behaved, and being liked by his teachers.

Several months after graduation Mr. Rossi went into the Navy for four years, where he worked in damage control (which was mostly fire fighting). When he came out of the service he worked in a series of unskilled jobs, and then at age 35, at someone else's suggestion, he applied for his present job. He now realized it was a natural place for him given his training in the Navy and regretted not having thought of it earlier. He had recently taken and passed the captain's exam and was on the list for promotion to that position.

In the meantime, when the government was encouraging veterans to go back to school by paying their tuition plus a salary, Mr. Rossi began school again and maintained his job as well. He said, "At first I went because of the money, but now I like it." The two-year Associate of Arts degree whetted his appetite for more schooling, but his problem with written work made him skeptical about being admitted to more advanced training or professional work.

Mr. Rossi spoke in slightly dysfluent language, with occasional grammatical errors, slurring, and dropped word endings. It was the speech style characteristic of the neighborhood in which he'd gone to school, worked, and lived all of his life. Although testing could not rule out some possible language area deficit, his speech and language background accounted well enough for his current language ability and usage.

Like Mr. Meyer, Mr. Rossi also said that he had no reading problems, and he added that he did not read much because he had a pretty active life. He said he used to enjoy detective novels but stopped reading them after his sister-in-law said it was a waste of time and that he ought to be reading "culture books" instead. He tried that, got bored after a few pages and quit, but did not return to the detective books. When asked to read at the evaluation, he demonstrated the same kinds of difficulties that Mr. Meyer had, but Mr. Rossi tended to catch and correct his errors. He also commented, when trying to decode long and unfamiliar words, that he had difficulty in breaking up words and getting them out right. He said that his wife would sometimes tell him he was not reading a word properly.

Mr. Rossi had a less sophisticated vocabulary than Mr. Meyer; he had a scaled score of 9 on the WAIS Vocabulary subtest. On the WRAT his reading score was 6.8. He read many multisyllabic words almost correctly, omitting a single letter or two, but his unfamiliarity with the words made it impossible for him to recognize the word and correct his pronunciation of it. He did better with prose passages, reading at about an eighth-grade level. In silent reading his comprehension level was considerably higher, approaching college levels.

Mr. Rossi's spelling was at fourth-to-fifth grade levels. Words misspelled were usually spelled phonetically, although words of more than three syllables, which he did not use regularly, were occasionally spelled with missing or reversed letters and syllables.

Mr. Rossi was asked to write two short pieces, one a report of a fire such as those he logs in at work, and the other a summary of a two-column news magazine article which he had just read silently. Both are reproduced below:

> 10:10 Reported by tower on line phone #58 to Rossi of car fire at eastern parking lot responded with E-1 and E-7 and 6 men. On arrival saw smoke and fire coming out of hood of car. We hit it with a 20 lb dry chemical extinguisher then follow it up with the Boston line of E-1. When the fire was out the battery was disconnected. Called the garage and state police to come and

removed the car. The car was a 1974 Blue Ford Reg. M-123456—owner is Mr. X from 123 West St. Boston. E-1 and E-7 returned at 10:30

With the talk about energy promblem through out the world, America is talken about solar power. Solar power comes from the sun. it is a knowed fact that the sun give 25 time more power then all the surce we have in our plantet. Congress is talk about giving more money to master the solar system. We do have a small amount on solar system being use in the west coast they use it for heating swiming pools. Boeing Co is working on some plants now. They use mirrows which are very expensive They have tryed less expensive mirrows but donot get the same results. The big concern is the cost   They say that the cost for solar power is in the 8,000 bracket were nuclear power plant are only about 1,000 in kilowatt. We have one rep. from Wastington who dose not believe that solar system will work now or by year 2,000   So I believe that cost is the great problem now but when money is no longer a great facture solar will come into it own.

The comparison between the two paragraphs is striking in that the first, of about 100 words, has two errors (*follow* instead of *followed*, *removed* instead of *remove*), while the second, of about 175 words has over 25 errors. The errors are of three major types, and almost equally divided among them. There are misspelled words, omitted or incorrect grammatical word endings, and faulty word usage and sentence structure. There would surely have been more spelling errors in the second paragraph if Mr. Rossi had not had the news article in front of him, so that he could copy such words as *kilowatt*, *nuclear*, and perhaps *system*. That the first paragraph has only two errors seems due to the fact that Mr. Rossi writes that sort of report regularly, has learned by conscious effort the correct spelling of such words as *extinguisher* and *battery*, and has become used to the prose style appropriate for the job. It is conceivable that anxiety was a contributing factor in the greater number of errors in the second paragraph. Yet, there seems to be no question that the new information, the need to summarize and develop sentences for relaying the information, and the need to write it as he thought it, all combined to constitute a far greater load on the information processing apparatus than would be the case with material in which vocabulary, content, and style were familiar and practiced. To put it another way, the material in the first exercise made use of some preexisting structures which allowed for more automatic processing.

Comparing Mr. Meyer and Mr. Rossi on the extent to which they used, and used effectively, basic academic skills, it is apparent that Mr. Rossi's skills were more functional and integrated in his daily life. He used them at his job and their rough quality did not deter him from completing high school, or from going to college more than twenty years later. He even turned to reading for pleasure and relaxation in picking up detective novels. At the same time he was more consciously aware of his difficulties and, while self-conscious about them, could talk about them in a direct and well-differentiated fashion.

Both men had average intelligence, and Mr. Meyer might seem to have an edge with his better vocabulary and richer language environment in childhood and in his current neighborhood. It seems somewhat paradoxical that the higher expectations of Mr. Meyer's family contributed to his feeling of failure and need to escape, while the lack of expectation for academic achievement in Mr. Rossi's family made any success of his a notable achievement. It was clearly not just a matter of family, but of cultural environment and expectations. Mr. Rossi grew up in a neighborhood where completing high school was not automatically expected, and Mr. Meyer in a community where not completing high school was most unusual and regarded as a significant failure. Mr. Meyer developed a characterological style including denial and avoidance, while Mr. Rossi was more able to face certain shortcomings directly. How much these characterological features are related to the ways in which their learning disabilities were accepted in family and school settings, and how much to other aspects of development, it is of course impossible to say. One can say, however, that for each one the quality of his self-image as a learner has had a significant effect on his perserverance with academic tasks, and that the self-image was in some measure determined by the family, cultural, and school reference groups in which each grew up.

FOUR GIRLS

Due to a random statistical quirk, it happened that during one 13 month period in the mid-70s, I saw four girls aged 14–8 to 15–9 for learning problem evaluations. All had been referred because of a general difficulty in keeping up with their schoolwork. In each case there was a specific reference to a reading problem—in reading retention, reading comprehension, or reading speed. They were the only teenaged girls referred to me during that period, so the similarities between them were especially striking. All attended different schools and had been referred from different sources, and thus their appearance did not reflect a special concern of one or two schools or clinical practitioners.

They are presented here as a group, rather than individually, because only as a group do they direct attention to a particular kind of reading and learning problem that otherwise tends to go unnoticed. All four were attending academically demanding private schools at the time of referral. While in each case it was inability to meet the intense academic demands that had precipitated the referral, it became apparent that a particular and longstanding pattern of interests and abilities, consistent in all four, underlay the problem. Greater academic demand had brought to light what was previously a subclinical problem, although as we shall see, less "sub" in some cases than in others. The problem would be of little or no general interest if it only affected girls suddenly having trouble in difficult private schools. However the girls had also had mild difficulties in their earlier school years, and the pattern of strengths and weaknesses they present can be found in other youngsters and in adults as well.

At the time of referral, two of the girls were in the ninth grade and two in the eighth. All four had come to their current schools in the previous one to four years, three from public schools in their own upper-middle class communities, and the fourth, Julie, from a succession of four schools, including public and private community free schools. The two eighth graders had each repeated a grade when transferring to their current schools (one in the fifth and one in the eighth grade). Their families and schools had recognized that the girls were ill-prepared to compete with age-mates in their new schools.

The girls resembled each other in other ways, aside from their similarity in age, kind of schooling, and presenting problem. All were well liked by classmates and teachers, and had presented no social or behavior problems. Three of them were specifically noted as being exceptionally conscientious, hard-working, and responsible students; comments such as "she's really a plugger" were heard from parents and teachers. Julie, who had had the poorest earlier education, knew that she could not pass the year nor return to the school and had stopped seriously trying to do her work. Each girl was not only well liked but also had the reputation of being sensitive to the feelings of others, of being a person that other children or adolescents could confide in or turn to for understanding. For example, when Ruth's parents were asked about her general role and position in her family of six siblings, they answered, "She's the one that can get along with any of them." Julie's teachers commented about the help and support that she had provided to a girl in her class who was having a particularly difficult time. Three of the girls also had in common a notable talent in some physical skill. Two were excellent athletes and the third a competent ballet dancer. They also had skills in ceramics, painting, and crocheting. The fourth, Diana, was by no means clumsy or awkward, but had not gotten actively involved in extracurricular interests other than piano lessons. An indication of her smaller scale or smaller-muscle visual-motor organization is apparent in her Coding scaled score of 17. And finally, each was pretty and spirited. Had they ever been together, an observer would have been struck by the attractiveness of the group.

Another set of similarities was revealed in the testing results. All four girls scored somewhat higher on the Performance than on the Verbal scale of the Wechsler, with differences ranging from 7 to 14 points. That is not particularly surprising, considering their reading comprehension problems and their motor and visual-motor skills. More striking is the pattern of their Verbal scale scores. With a single exception—Ruth's low score on Similarities—they all scored lower on Information and Vocabulary, and higher on Comprehension, Similarities, and Digit Span (see Table 7.1).

Again with the exception of Ruth, they scored lower on Arithmetic. Actually, Julie and Diana each solved two additional problems correctly but needed more than the allotted time.

The pattern of scores suggests a discrepancy between verbal reasoning, judgment, and problem solving, on the one hand, and information absorption and retention on the other. There is no evidence of difficulty in concept formation or in understanding ab-

Table 7.1 WISC-R Verbal Scaled Scores for the Four Girls

	Betsy	Julie	Diana	Ruth
Information	11	7	8	6
Vocabulary	11	9	9	8
Arithmetic	10	9	9	14
Comprehension	14	12	11	11
Similarities	14	12	10	7
Digit Span	14	12	10	11
(Full Scale IQ)	121	108	102	100

stractions; rather the difficulty is in processing information at the pace at which it is presented, recognizing some aspect of it, and associating it with relevant prior knowledge. The difficulty that the girls experienced on Information and Vocabulary subtests was not related to the verbal presentation in the test session, which allows them to take their time and consider the information available to them. Rather, the difficulty is related to their failure to have picked up and stored or assimilated, in the course of their routine life experiences, such information and associations as the sun setting in the west, February having the additional day during Leap Year, and Edison inventing the light bulb. They have also failed to note, store, or assimilate such words as *material, latitude, migrate, espionage,* and *duel.*

Awareness that it is not verbal presentation per se, but the pace and the references in it to assumed prior knowledge, makes it easier to understand why the girls could do well with Digit Span. In dealing with short term, nonrepresentational material, they are not handicapped for there is no need to hunt for connections and draw upon relevant associational material. This indicates that the problem is not one of the *auditory mode,* but of *language,* and of representational material. The girls have trouble with the written word as well as the spoken word (which is in fact why they were referred in the first place).

Diana most clearly showed the problem in association to words. We present here two illustrations, one from the testing and one described by her mother in the initial parent interview. During the WISC-R Information subtest, Diana was asked from which country the American colonists gained independence in 1776. Her answer went as follows:

> Washington—Oh, that's a state. Country, country, what's a country? Like X (here she named her own community)? No, that's a town. I saw that play *1776.* (Question: " Do you remember what it was about?") About the states getting together—independence.

That was as far as she could go. Two questions later she was asked which two countries border the United States, and she answered quite easily "Canada and Mexico." When asked later how she knew that, she explained that she was going to be traveling across the country during the summer, and had been looking at a big map to see where they would be going. So, given a context, she could use her visual memory to see what bordered the United States. The term *country* in isolation had failed to touch off relevant associations.

Diana's mother related the following incident. Diana came out of her room one afternoon, where she had been doing her homework, and asked her mother, "What's a political party? I have to write a report on political parties in Vietnam, and I don't know what that is." Her mother answered, "Yes you do, you worked for the Democratic party in the city last year when they were trying to elect Senator Jones. That's one political party, the Republicans are another." Her mother's making the association for her was enough to tell her what she needed to know. The concept was not lacking, or hard to understand. The problem was that the phrase did not trigger the association, the verbal label was not solidly enough connected to the concept it labeled. A related lapse is seen in Diana's offering excellent definitions for both *migraine* and *migrate*, but not knowing which was which.

Several of Ruth's teachers commented on her difficulty in understanding verbal directions and instructions. The gym teacher noted that she would catch on to what she needed to do by watching or trying it herself, but got little or nothing from the verbal explanations. The history teacher reported that Ruth often called out for her to stop in the middle of homework explanation, unable to keep up with the pace of the teacher's remarks or, perhaps, not understanding the language. Ruth's only failed item in the WISC-R Arithmetic subtest was due not to any mathematical difficulty, but rather to inability to understand the question as it was worded. The questions reads: "Tony bought a second-hand bicycle for $28.00. He paid 2/3 of what the bicycle cost new. How much did it cost new?" Ruth looked very puzzled and troubled. When the question was reworded so that she understood the situation being presented, she did the mental calculations swiftly and accurately.

In arithmetic, language was a factor for all of the girls. On the WISC-R Arithmetic, Diana had trouble organizing all the elements of the problems as she heard them, but could recover and solve them accurately if she took more time. She was getting a straight A in algebra at school, and was similar in that regard to Ruth, who could work through long and complex algebraic equations so long as she did not have to derive the algebraic formulation from a word problem. Ruth scored above grade level on the Wide Range Arithmetic test, where there are no word problems. At school she met daily with her math teacher for help on translating word problems into mathematical statements.

The expressive, as well as the receptive language of the girls also showed some weaknesses, both in speaking and in writing. Julie used a number of neologisms during the testing sessions, such as *disencourage, confliction, commendment.* Her meaning was generally clear and reasonable, but her failure to find the right word or to recognize that her productions were not real words was striking. Diana had a slight tendency to repeat sentence fragments, as though she did not remember having said them already, and to use idiomatic expressions that were almost but not quite right, such as *in my point of view.* All of the girls' teachers commented on the general immaturity of their writing, referring to their vocabulary and very simple sentence structure. It is important to distinguish here between self-expression and high level language usage, for all of the girls could express themselves verbally, both in writing and speaking, with clarity, directness, and some liveliness. They lacked the sophisticated vocabulary and sentence construction which give verbal expression intellectual richness, but they were not lacking in sensitivity and awareness, in the ability to grasp concepts within their ken, nor in basic communication skills.

All of the girls read well, technically. On the Wide Range Reading test they all scored at tenth-grade level, indicating competence in decoding the written word to its sound equivalent. They made errors predominantly in the kinds of words that one is unlikely to pronounce correctly if not familiar with them, in the sense of recognizing them as having been heard before. Thus, for example, Julie read *oligarchy* and *sepulcher* pronouncing the *ch* as it sounds in *chair, prevalence* with a long *a*, and *pugilist* with a short *u*.

Their reading comprehension varied with the kind of material they had to read. On short reading passages they all read quickly enough and could answer questions well enough to score at grade level. They tended to do better on questions requiring inference about mood and feeling, and to have difficulty in remembering facts or ordering them easily.

They all had trouble getting through and understanding school reading assignments, particularly in social studies. They complained of being slowed down by repeatedly having to look up words in the dictionary, and then not remembering those same words if they came across them later. Betsy said she could understand her history book if she read the material three or four times, but not if she only read it once or twice. Ruth got through much of her work by doing it with her mother. They took turns reading sections aloud to each other and discussing their meaning. It was not uncommon for her to enter the house and say to her mother, "Boy, have we got a lot of homework to do today." Betsy and Diana had individual tutoring outside of school, and Ruth also moved from her mother to a tutor. Only Julie did not have supplementary tutoring, which may in part explain why she could not make it through the year.

The girls could not take in and comprehend the complex school material they read, at the rate at which they could technically read it (in the sense of decoding the words). While everyone has to slow down their reading speed when dealing with dense, complex, new material, these girls were not adequately helped by simply slowing down. Lack of adequate information and vocabulary and difficulty in processing verbal material, written or spoken, interfered with their understanding and integrating the material as they read it.

Once again, it is useful to scrutinize the three major categories of determinants—biological, psychological, and social—to specifically consider an array of possible reasons for their deficit areas. I have implied in the foregoing material that the problem is in some measure neuropsychological. There is additional evidence for this in at least two of the cases, Ruth and Diana, whose parents report language difficulties in the girls from early childhood. Diana was very late in talking, and her nursery school teacher reported that she used nonsense speech at times. Her mother said that Diana's speech came out backward and nonsensical, and that when Diana was six, her three-year-old sister spoke in more complete and coherent sentences than she did. Ruth had very unclear speech for many years; at the time of evaluation she still had a mild speech impediment (with *s* sounds occasionally slushy), and her parents said her speech was much clearer now than it had been until quite recently.

It seems likely that the personality organization and interests of the girls also contributed to their difficulties in becoming familiar with historical and scientific information. They were all so much more focused on interpersonal matters than on the wider and more objective world of scientific and historical concerns. It is possible that their not noticing, absorbing, and remembering what they heard and read in these areas had to do with their being more interested in the reality of their personal and immediate circle of involvement. (Of course, it is also possible that difficulty in retaining less frequently presented information encouraged the turning of their interests closer to home and self.)

Environmental determinants certainly played a role, more in some cases than in others. The degree of interest and experience each girl had in wider-ranging intellectual areas certainly depended in part on their exposure to those issues at home and at school. The girls' families varied in the intellectual atmosphere and direct encouragement they provided their daughters. Ruth's family probably provided the richest intellectual atmosphere and Betsy's the leanest, but all of them were above average, as far as the parents' educational and occupational achievements were concerned. Two were lawyers, one was an architect and one an educational director. The public schools they attended also varied in how much structure and stimulation they provided, but again none was below average. Betsy, who had the highest IQ score in the group, also had the least intellectually stimulating home and school environment—by no means was it impoverished, but laissez-faire; no one went out of their way to provide enriching intellectual experiences. It is conceivable, in her case, since she had no specific language anomalies, a generally high IQ, and weak areas no lower than average, that a more structured elementary school program and a more enriching home atmosphere might have made a significant difference in her ability to handle more demanding work. That would not rule out a neuropsychological element, but we might be more likely to cast it as a matter of differential "talents" rather than as weakness or deficit.

Julie was raised in a very stimulating academic community. However, her chaotic school career (five schools in nine years), with seven of the first eight years spent at schools which philosophically did not believe in the structured teaching of basic skills, may have been the critical factor in her downfall in ninth grade.

Acknowledging the contribution of personality and environmental determinants does not gainsay the presence of some language-related neuropsychological condition, which in my view merits recognition as a learning disability. It is not a perceptual or perceptual-motor problem as Wepman et al.(1975) have defined learning disability (see chapter 2, p. 26). It is more related to association, integration, and memory, those middle intermediary processes between perception and motor response. Whether it should receive the label of learning disability, language disability, or something else is a matter that time and usage will determine. It is important that however it is labeled, teachers and clinicians be aware of it. We will consider remediation of this kind of problem, along with others, in the following chapter.

SUSAN

Susan was in the fourth grade when her teacher, Mr. King, came to consult the school psychologist about her. He explained that Susan was an excellent student in most areas, and quite talented in language areas. She had recently written, with a classmate, a 30-minute puppet show, which was so clever and entertaining that it had been performed for several groups in the school. All in all Susan seemed a very well adjusted, happy, friendly youngster. The only problem was math.

Susan had always had some difficulty with math, but her teacher felt she understood the concepts involved and was not as bad at it as she seemed to believe. Whenever she was given a math assignment she made a face and asked, "Do I have to do it?" The teacher would say that she did, and then urge and encourage her, reassuring her that she could indeed do it. In her school journal she wrote one day, "I feel guilty because we had a choice of doing a math quiz or something else, and I didn't choose the math." Another day she wrote, "I'm glad I can do my math at home where I can cry." The situation came to a head when Susan's parents called the teacher one evening, saying that Susan had come home with a math test on which she had only 8 out of 40 problems right. Susan was crying, saying she couldn't do math, wanting her parents to help her but getting upset when they tried. Susan's parents were concerned about her unhappiness and also about her very poor paper; they wondered if they ought to consider special math tutoring for her.

The teacher explained that the math paper was part of a unit they would be working on all year, called the 4-40, in which the children had four minutes to do forty simple arithmetic fact problems—basic addition, subtraction, and multiplication combinations. No one was expected to complete all 40 within 4 minutes at first; they were to do it periodically throughout the year, graphing the results each time, so that as they improved they would see a rising graph line. By the end of the year, each child could be expected to be more fluent in math facts and to have learned something about graphs as well. While the parents now understood that the math paper in question was not an indication of failing work, they were still concerned about Susan's general distress over math, as was the teacher.

A meeting was scheduled for the parents, teacher, and school psychologist. The parents were again apprised of the teacher's evaluation of Susan's math abilities—not the best in the class, but solid and adequate. The parents raised the question of whether her overreaction could be due to a need for attention. She was the older of two girls, her sister was a year younger. If the school staff felt Susan needed more attention at home they could give it to her in other ways, rather than in sitting with her over her math. The parents also mentioned that her third grade sister was a whiz in math, which raised the possibility of Susan's distress and sense of incompetence stemming from the comparison between the two girls. The psychologist had wondered if her excellent language skills had contributed to a feeling of needing to excel in everything in order to be valued.

Midway through the meeting, while talking of the third grader's good math skills, it was also mentioned that the younger girl was excellent at jigsaw puzzles, which Susan had never liked and had stopped doing altogether. The family occasionally did a large puzzle together, and Susan would join them in the family room with a book to read, rather than at the table with the puzzle. It was this bit of information that started the psychologist thinking along neuropsychological lines—not that Susan was learning disabled in the usual sense of the word, but that she might be weaker in the automatic processing of numerical and spatial information, as distinguished from verbal information which she handled so well.

A plan was then devised, based on the assumption that Susan's major difficulty in math was neurogenic rather than psychogenic, and that her hysterical overreaction should be ignored or circumvented for the present. The plan was experimental; it cost next to nothing in time and energy, and if it didn't work within a few weeks it could be abandoned and a more intensive evaluation considered.

The plan consisted of four parts. The first was to ask the parents to stop all math help at home, since it did not help anyway, and only reinforced the notion on all sides that Susan could not do math. If she complained at home about not being able to do math assignments, she was to be referred back to her teacher for help. The parents were relieved and agreed.

The second part of the plan concerned the 4-40 quizzes. The psychologist had suggested that the pressure of the clock was perhaps creating in Susan a sense of panic. If she were relieved of that pressure, perhaps she could do better, using whatever ability she had and not being distracted by the anxiety around timing. However, if she were not timed, what would happen to the graphing project? Mr. King had a solution to that. He said that Susan could take as long as she wanted to do the problems, but could note how long it took her and graph that each time. He added that there were a number of children in the class for whom that would also be a better plan.

The third part of the plan was that the teacher would explain to Susan that her problem seemed to be not one of understanding math, but of not having the numbers come into her head as quickly as they should. She needed more time to think things out, and so she was to take that time, even with the 4-40. The more practice she got doing it slowly and in her own way, the more easily she would eventually work into doing it faster.

The fourth part of the plan was a selected piece of behavior modification. The teacher was to stop being so solicitous when Susan complained about every math assignment. Rather, he was to tell her yes, she did have to do it, and save his warmth and affection for after it was done—thus rewarding the doing rather than the resistance.

All of this took place in October, after which the psychologist heard no more. When the teacher was asked from time to time how Susan was doing, the answer was "fine," but then Mr. King would go on to speak of some more pressing problem. The feedback finally came during the last week of school in June. Susan's mother saw the psychologist at a school assembly and said, "I want to thank you for that meeting we had last fall; we haven't heard a word or a whimper about math since then." The teacher said to the psychologist, "I never used to believe in behavior modification, I thought it was all levers and M&M's. You should see her graph and how that time line goes down down down." Most gratifying of all, Susan, who never knew she was a "case," said to the teacher on her last day in class, "Thank you for teaching me to know that I can do math."

Susan's story contains many lessons. The first is that not every learning problem requires a full assessment procedure. When the problem seems limited to one or a few areas, when the reports of parents and teachers sound as though they can be taken at face value, and when enough clues come through to suggest a plan of action, there is little to be lost in trying it—perhaps only a wasted week or two—and much to be gained. The teacher remains the major problem solver and change agent, the child is dealt with in the most natural setting, and the psychologist has more time to help other teachers and children.

The second lesson concerns the importance of detailed information about relevant classroom activities, lessons, and so on. Relevant here means relevant to the problem—one can never have detailed information about all aspects of the child and his classroom life. However, when the teacher and psychologist together can focus in on specific details concerning the problem at hand, the psychologist is helped to make tentative hypotheses, and the teacher is more apt to generate specific remedial measures.

The third lesson involves the effects of a close, cooperative working relationship between psychologist and teacher, with each having his or her own job to do but also sufficiently attuned to the professional concerns of the other. In this instance the teacher was as concerned about Susan's anxiety as he was about her math, and the psychologist was concerned about what would happen to the graphing lesson if there were no time limit. The teacher's acceptance of anxiety as a possible reason for changing the assignment also made him free to dream up the revised version. Most important, the plan eventually devised could never have been thought up by either the psychologist or teacher working alone.

The fourth lesson has to do with remediation. Although that is the subject of the next chapter, one of the most important aspects of remediation is illustrated here; that is, the identification, as specifically as possible, of what the class is doing that the child cannot do, and the determination of what adjustment to make in order to bring them back into harmony. It is no great trick, though it is an expensive one, to call for a special tutor to work with the child individually so that he can catch up—and in some cases that is no doubt necessary. But not in all cases, and not in Susan's. She did not need to learn new material, facts, or procedures; she needed to learn that she knew what she had to know, and that her difficulties were with style and timing, which she could learn to live with and make adjustments for.

The fifth lesson involves the relationship of specific learning difficulties and psychodynamics. An early hypothesis about Susan's problem was that she was playing for attention from the teacher, using math as a vehicle. At this point, we add another part of Susan's story. Her teacher, instead of simply not encouraging complaints about math and reinforcing the doing with a smile, had explained to Susan that this was his plan. She was explicitly told that she would get her smile when the work was done. Although this had not been the psychologist's intent, this was the teacher's understanding of the plan and thus it was conveyed to Susan. And her subsequent behavior was instructive—she transferred her dramatic behavior from the beginning to the end of the math paper, making sure she got her smile each time or teasing for a bigger and better smile. Thus her dramatic, provocative style and prepubescent interest in her teacher did not change; they were only relocated and no longer used as a way of dealing with the anxiety generated by a mild speed and memory inefficiency. As to the learning problem itself, it had been masked, not created, by the dramatics, and only by recognizing this could one attempt to deal with it.

Finally, one can only wonder how many cases of math hysteria have similar origins, where lack of talent in speedy calculation or visual-spatial conceptualization is experienced as an inability to do math.

8

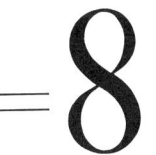

Remediation

Remediation, the process of helping children to overcome learning difficulties, is a concern that pervades the assessment process. The evaluating clinician will repeatedly be asking questions (of himself or herself and others) about the extent to which a problem area interferes with school success, why a problem has persisted in spite of efforts at remediation, how the child has responded to the school's program for him, how he reacts to the clinician's extemporaneous efforts to teach him during the course of the assessment, and what can be suggested to parents and teachers about working with the child in the future. While few clinicians actively engage in remedial work themselves, they need to be sufficiently familiar with the major issues and processes of remediation so that they can participate in planning a remedial program. The term remedial is used here in a broad sense, to include any special educational placement or procedure which is employed to enhance learning success. In this chapter, we consider some of the basic issues in remediation, sample some problems and approaches in the remediation of basic skills, and finally, suggest some pragmatic guidelines for the clinician in remedial planning with children, parents, and teachers.

SOME BASIC ISSUES IN REMEDIATION

Problems and Goals

What and how to remediate is essentially determined by the answers, tacit or explicit, to the following two questions: (1) What is the problem? and (2) What are the goals of remediation? These are simple questions, but they cover a complex array of facts, findings, values, and aspirations that do not yield simple answers. What the problem is, or more precisely, how it is construed or defined will depend not only on test findings, but on the experience and theoretical orientation of the clinician interpreting them. The goals of remediation, while partly dependent on the testing results, will also depend on a number of subjective and qualitative factors, such as the motivations, aspirations, and values of all those involved—child and parents, and also teacher and clinician. In addition, both problems and goals will be affected by such variables as the child's age, his general intellectual ability, emotional sturdiness, and the resources which family and school can provide.

An example will illustrate. In chapter 6 (pp. 177–178) we considered Eddie, whose test protocols revealed a number of difficulties in language areas, including auditory memory. At almost 13, Eddie was four to six years behind in reading skills, and exceptionally deficient in his knowledge of vowel sounds. He had fairly low frustration tolerance in the classroom, and a disturbed family setting that could not offer him educational, financial, or emotional support for his studies. Eddie had perhaps another year or two in the special school he was then attending; after that, although his schooling might continue, he was unlikely to get intensive reading help. Thus, it seemed that in the year or two left for remediation, Eddie was likely to have neither the time nor the patience to handle a remedial program centered around the learning of individual sounds. Rather, with his normal conceptual ability and visual processing skills, it seemed a better bet to work on the recognition of visual patterns in words—endings such as *ly* and *tion*, prefixes and suffixes, and word families—and to devote a good deal of time to building up a sight vocabulary and reading from texts. While it would be impossible to completely avoid the learning of sounds, that sort of drill could be kept to a mininum, with alternative ways and mnemonic devices used wherever feasible.

It was not Eddie's difficulty in auditory processing that dictated the kind of remedial work, but rather the life circumstances that accompanied that difficulty: his age, the continued schooling anticipated for him, and the emotional lability with which both Eddie and his family continually struggled. A younger child with similar auditory processing difficulties might be amenable to a program for learning sound-symbol relationships with a lot of repetitive drill couched in games and play activities, but Eddie did not have the ego strength to tolerate such a program; he would feel humiliated by simple, "babyish" tasks. He was still willing to try, so long as his teachers believed in him and were willing to help, and so long as a task was sufficiently dignified as well as manageable.

In general, it has been my experience that as long as older non-readers and poor readers are attending school, they can generally find enough support from the structure of school itself to put up with continued reading lessons, even though they are deeply discouraged and sometimes overwhelmed by their sense of failure and continuing frustration. Once a person has left school and settled into some other daily-life framework, it is extremely difficult to maintain a steady remedial program. If routine activities allow for the avoidance or covering up of deficit skills, it is easy to give up any further attempts at improvement.

It is almost impossible to overemphasize the importance of age in assessing problems and determining realistic remedial goals. The child's age in great part determines how much time will be available to work at the academic deficits within a structured school program. Along with school history, age helps determine the rate at which the child will respond to intervention. Age is also the most immediate indicator of the social and psychological forces that are likely to enhance or detract from a remedial program. Fear of peer group criticism, years of failure experience, and a face-saving opportunity to avoid further learning (such as a job which does not require reading or writing) may combine to force an adolescent or adult out of any remedial regimen. On the other hand, there are some individuals (such as the adults discussed in chapter 7) who can only seek remedial help after they are settled and established, strengthened by the self-esteem they have gained from success in other areas.

It should be stressed that the major effect of age on readiness or ability to learn is motivational and not biological. The question is often asked, "Is it too late to learn to read (or write or spell)?" The answer to that, in my opinion, is a qualified "No." Except for the older student's need to extinguish previously acquired incorrect habits or assumptions, there is no evidence that academic skill learning is biologically easier for children than for adults. Spelling rules, phonic regularities in reading, conventions for handling fractions and decimals, and so on—all are conceptual tasks that should be at least as easy for adults as for children. Adults learning foreign languages show no particular problems in learning to perceive and discriminate graphic symbols and to associate them with their sound equivalents. Perceptual learning among adults presents a problem only for learning new sound elements in a foreign language. Learning to pronounce sounds which do not occur in the native language is more difficult for adults than for children. With the exception of foreign accent and perhaps the need to unlearn poor handwriting habits, adults do not appear to be at any physical disadvantage in learning basic academic skills.

Remediation in Light of Behavior Modification Principles

The principles of behavior modification have special relevance for remediation. While many teachers make use of these principles without formal knowledge of label or theory, there is value in delineating the ways in which successful remediation is grounded in learning theory and behavior modification.

At the heart of most behavior modification approaches is the notion of reinforcement, that is, the reinforcement of desired responses. In considering the array of responses associated with learning problems, it is useful to distinguish between right and wrong answer responses on the one hand, acceptable and unacceptable behavior responses on the other. Most of the literature on behavior modification applied to children with school problems deals with behavior responses. The focus is on conduct inappropriate to school and learning and on the reinforcement programs used to reward desired behavior and extinguish disruptive behavior (for literature reviews, see Kazdin & Bootzin, 1972 and O'Leary & Drabman, 1971). There are reports of associated improvements in academic functioning, apparently as a by-product of the improved behavior and the additional time spent studying, but as Bryan and Bryan (1975) point out, ". . . if the child does not have the necessary skills within his repertoire, no amount of reinforcement will elicit more complex skills" (p. 362).

Then how does remediation with the skill-deficient child relate to behavior modification? That is the question we will consider next, noting how principles and techniques of behavior modification are applicable to teaching in general and to remediation in particular.

One of the unrivaled advantages in the human learning process is the potency of success as a reinforcer. The gratification from feeling competent often appears to equal or surpass that which derives from food, tokens, or praise. When Skinner shaped the behavior of his pigeons so that they would press a bar to get food, subsequent bar pressing was attributed to their interest in getting more food, rather than to the pleasure of achieving mastery over the apparatus. By contrast, children who manage to read a line or to do a particular arithmetic procedure are generally more moved by the fact of having succeeded than by the information or answer acquired. "I did it!" is one of the happiest phrases a struggling student utters, and it is among the most gratifying a teacher hears.

Since success is such a powerful reinforcer, good teachers attempt to build it into their lessons as much as possible. Of course, this does not mean giving children assignments comprising only tasks they have mastered. Not only would they fail to learn new material, they would quickly become bored and discouraged, knowing they are only repeating easy work and not making progress. A common complaint of children attending special class, or sittting in regular classes unable to do the work that the others do, is illustrated by one child who said, "The teacher keeps giving me adding and subtracting to do. I want to learn times and division. I'm not getting anywhere." The double demand of providing work that simultaneously allows success and advances learning is a constant in all curriculum planning. The work must not be too easy, and at the same time it must not be so difficult that mastery is unattainable or too long postponed. While this is true of all teaching, it is particularly important when dealing with children who believe, realistically or not, that they are less competent than their classmates.

Among all children there are differences in learning rates and previous experience that affect the speed and degree of mastery. In regular classroom teaching, presentations of material to the whole group are based on the assumption that most of the children will accommodate themselves to the teacher's style and pace, even if some find it too simple and repetitive, and others find it difficult and confusing for a time. Children without serious emotional difficulties can tolerate confusion or boredom for a while; and children without serious learning problems will eventually understand the material with little or no special assistance. Those who cannot make the accommodation need remedial assistance, and it is these children who concern us here.

Remedial help means providing a successful learning experience for a child who cannot achieve it under regular classroom conditions. Some children requiring remedial aid can master the regular classroom material easily enough if they are helped to keep their anxiety under control and to persist until they have finished. In these instances, the special remedial input is largely one of emotional support. Other children cannot master regular curriculum material in its ordinary format, even under the most benign and supportive individual tutelage. In either case, one of the first tasks of the remedial teacher will be to figure out what happens when the child tries to learn, and fails; to determine what part of the learning situation he can handle and what factors (emotional or cognitive) or combination of factors make the task unmanageable. At what level of emotional stress or cognitive complexity can the child do his work satisfactorily? That will be the place to begin, presenting tasks that offer the reinforcement of success, and gradually introducing new demands for mastery.

Breaking down a task to the point where it allows success is at the heart of most remedial work. Robbie, for example, was failing in the third grade, doing poorly on tests and often regressing to infantile behavior such as crawling on the floor or dissolving into tears. On individual testing he scored at grade level, but only when given exceptional amounts of support and encouragement. One evening he was working with his father on division problems, and claimed he could not remember how to do them. His father suggested that Robbie dictate to his father the numbers he had calculated, and his father wrote them in the right places. After doing several problems that way, Robbie was ready to do them alone. It was not clear whether the father's writing gave emotional support or demonstrated where the numbers were to be written, or perhaps both. It is clear, though, that relieving Robbie of some part of the task made it possible for him to work successfully, first with assistance and then without it.

Another example of breaking down a task can be seen in what Vera spontaneously did for herself. She was a 30-year-old dyslexic with average to low-average general ability, who read at approximately second grade level. This meant that she could read very little—neither newspapers nor highway signs nor job applications. She could cook, however, using a cook book or the package directions. She did not read the cookbook instructions or the package directions; she read only the lists of ingredients. She was able to do so because they are generally written in larger type and in list form, not imbedded in frightening paragraphs of finer print. Furthermore, Vera knew enough about cooking to anticipate most of the ingredients, and had developed a reliable sight vocabulary for frequently appearing words such as *eggs*, *milk*, *cup*, and *flour*. A remedial program for Vera might well have started with cookbook recipes, having her read the ingredients list and then try advancing to the prose directions. It would be pointed out to her that although the print is smaller and more dense, many of the words included in the prose are taken directly from the list which she can read.

A more complicated example of breaking down a task concerns a preacademic skill that most of us take for granted and that rarely has to be taught—the skill of hearing rhymes. Most children are so innately and intuitively able to hear rhymes, that "teaching" what a rhyme is usually consists of illustrating with several sets of rhyming verses or words and providing the label "rhyme" for them.

Hearing rhymes is important for reading. A child is more likely to be able to read and to spell a new word such as *hose* if he already knows how to read and spell the word *nose*. Hearing and seeing similarities in parts of words is an integral part of reading, aiding as it does the recognition of significant segments of otherwise unknown new words.

Some children do not spontaneously recognize rhyming sounds, but they can be helped to do so if the task is broken down. For example, one might first give several samples of words that rhyme, telling the child that they do, but not asking him to explain what that means or to produce any himself. He is then given examples of words that do not rhyme and that are also different from each other in additional ways, such as in the number of syllables and component letters. For instance, *sing* and *wing* rhyme, and *up* and *yesterday* do not. The next step would be to say a pair of words to the child, either a rhyme or very dissimilar sounding words, and ask him to say if they rhyme or not. Most children will be able to answer correctly, although it may be for the wrong reason. Another variation is to give them one word, such as *now*, and ask which of the next two words rhymes with it—*how* or *Tuscaloosa*. This may be hard because it requires holding three words in mind for comparison. (Three words can also be presented via pictures—for example, pictures of a sock, a rock, and an elephant—with the child identifying the two that rhyme). Once the child is proficient at distinguishing rhymes from very dissimilar words, less dissimilar pairs may be introduced, words of equivalent length or with a number of letters in common, such as *jump* and *will*, or *later* and *trail*. Eventually he should get to words that have considerable auditory similarity, such as *strike* and *street*, and recognize them as nonrhyming.

Rhymes, like number concepts and many other abstract concepts, are difficult to teach because they cannot simply be told as facts for later recall. They require a kind of concept formation to which the teacher can contribute only by offering examples and demonstrations. The perception, the awareness, the click of understanding what in the words constitutes "rhyming" can come only from within. One can direct the child's attention to the ends rather than the beginnings of words. Yet, by the time he can distinguish between beginning and ending word sounds and between final syllables and final letter sounds, he can usually hear rhymes too. The drill described above provides a continous series of exposures with focused attention to rhymes, and a question-and-answer or puzzle format which offers challenge and success.

A final example of breaking down a task is found in arithmetic computation. A child who cannot add long columns of numbers might need help, praise, and practice in writing the numbers in straight columns down the page (without which correct addition is very difficult), before any stress is laid upon correct calculation of the problems he has copied. He can, of course, be working on addition during the same period, using problems in a workbook or problems that the teacher has written down.

Practice is another major component of remediation. It may be useful to think of practice as a two-stage operation, with intensive drill when a skill is first learned and periodic review, rather like a booster shot, to refresh the memory and keep the skill in working order. There often seems to be a positive relationship between the time it takes to understand a new skill and the amount of practice required to make it an efficient and useful skill. Thus, many of the children who cannot learn new material at the rate demanded by the regular curriculum are also in need of more than usual amounts of practice on that material once it is learned. This is in order that it be well learned, that is, integrated and readily available. Many children must literally "go through the motions" repeatedly in order to learn to make certain letters of the alphabet, to memorize the multiplication tables, or to master the mechanics of multiple-digit multiplication and division. Similarly, others must have repeated practice in learning vowel sounds, using new vocabulary words, or hearing bits of information in various contexts before they are truly assimilated.

It is not an oversimplification to say that remedial teaching consists of two things: (1) breaking tasks down into their component parts and (2) providing adequate practice. Doing these two things is not so simple; complex tasks can be broken down in a variety of ways and to a variety of degrees of fineness; and the teacher must take the task apart according to the child's particular cognitive and emotional strengths. Practice has to be consistent but varied, so that the child is not bored to distraction nor made to feel that he is not progressing, and also so that he can learn various contexts in which to apply new technical skill. In short, remediation in the acquisition of basic skills depends on the teacher's providing a series of successful learning experiences, which in turn depends on her developing an appropriate sequence of component tasks and a reasonable schedule of drill and review. Whether this set of procedures is thought of as operant conditioning, behavior modification, or remedial education, the steps are surely familiar to teachers, and to clinicians who remember their own schooling. My experience is that the concept of "shaping behavior" is a useful one for teachers, providing a sense that their planning a sequence of activities directed towards a defined goal can in fact lend shape and direction to a child's efforts to develop academic skills.

Two Important Dualities in Remediation

Two issues in remediation fall quite easily into dichotomous positions: (1) teaching to strengths versus weaknesses, and (2) emphasizing automatic versus representational information processing.

Teaching to Strengths versus Weaknesses. It is by now fairly common practice for educational test reports to point out a child's intellectual strengths and weaknesses, both in terms of acquired knowledge and also in terms of specific abilities in processing information. One of the most frequently noted differentiations, for example, is that between visual and auditory processing skills. Once such distinctions are made, questions arise about how best to make use of that information in remedial teaching, and the central question is often whether to teach to strengths or work at strengthening weaknesses.

For example, a child who reads haltingly and consequently has trouble completing his assignments may be able to understand faster and better if the text material is presented to him on tape. If he can handle information better when it is heard, should he then be given his assignments on tape, or should he be pressed to work at improving his reading by confronting the printed page for information? Similarly, should a child with poor and labored handwriting be trained to dictate onto tape, or use a typewriter, or should he persevere with handwriting? Clearly, the answer to such questions depends on how problems and goals are assessed. When accomplishment of the current task is paramount (in order to pass a course, to experience success, etc.), or when the assessment suggests that the problem is too great or the time too short for remediation of weak areas, one tends to opt for exploiting the strengths and bypassing the weaknesses. In the two examples cited, it is apparent that using strengths will in no way contribute to improvement of weak skills. Listening to tapes will add to knowledge but in no way contribute to improved reading, and turning to typing or dictating will not advance handwriting skill. On the contrary, lack of practice is likely to result in further diminished competence.

Ideally, one would like to help children on both fronts. In reading, that would involve keeping up with current assignments by using tape and setting aside additional time for reading practice. Unfortunately, there are not always adequate hours or resources for such double programming. There are some instances, however, when teaching to strength does inherently help remediate weak areas. One of the most dramatic examples of this phenomenon has occurred with severely handicapped children, some of whom are described as autistic, who have extreme difficulty in making any sense of spoken language but who demonstrate competent and even exceptional visual processing skills. In one case, a child could not understand, repeat, or recognize the word *cocoa*, until his teacher wrote *ko-ko* on a piece of paper while pronouncing the word and simultaneously pointing to a cup of cocoa. Showing him a visual representation of the sounds helped him to perceive the repeated syllable in the spoken word and to recognize it when he heard it again some time later. In this instance, the child's strong skills in visual analysis are being used to help him develop in auditory analysis.

Thus it is apparent that there is no simple and no single answer to the question of teaching to strength or weakness. The raising of the question, however, helps stimulate an analysis of the costs and benefits attached to various remedial plans.

Emphasizing Automatic versus Representational Information Processing. This issue is rarely raised in any formal way when remedial planning is discussed, but it is a practical matter that influences the planning and teaching of all lessons. It is a question of the extent to which learning is to be fostered by drill and rote memory on the one hand, and by conceptualization, reasoning, and verbal mediation on the other. An example can be seen in the teaching of multiplication tables. If the teacher emphasizes automatic responding, the children will be instructed to memorize the tables, drilling on them repeatedly until they have nearly reflex responses to the various number combinations. If the teaching emphasizes representational processing, the children will be shown ways to figure out the combinations which they do not know ("If you know what 2 × 8 is, you can figure out what 4 × 8 is.") and they will not be pressed to learn them quickly by rote. In emphasizing automatic processing, the stress is on getting the right answer quickly. In emphasizing representational thinking, the focus is on understanding *how* a particular answer is arrived at and *why* it is the right answer.

Most intellectual tasks require both automatic and representational level organization. Rote knowledge without understanding is useless when it needs to be extrapolated to a new context, and understanding without an efficient system for performance may be so unwieldy as to be useless. In arithmetic, for example, a child who can recite the eight tables by rote (from 8 × 0 through 8 × 12) but does not firmly grasp how they are derived, will be helpless if asked to figure out 8 × 13. Conversely, a child who understands how multiplication facts are derived but has not learned them by heart, will be hopelessly stalled if he has to figure out each combination from scratch when doing long division. In reading, a child with an extensive sight vocabulary but poor word analysis skills will read quickly when he deals with familiar words but have no way to figure out a new word. His opposite is the child who can sound out every word he sees if given enough time, but cannot automatically recognize many words and so reads at a pace so slow as to impede comprehension.

Rote, automatic learning and conceptualized, representational learning tend to be mutually reinforcing. Rote knowledge helps in the learning of underlying principles and concepts, and conceptual understanding often speeds up rote memorization. In normal learning, the two types of processing proceed in some roughly parallel fashion, and whichever the teacher happens to be emphasizing at any given point will be incorporated into the child's particular learning matrix. In short, the teacher is likely to encourage both types of learning, and the child with general learning competence can manage to assimilate both.

Such is not necessarily the case with children requiring remedial instruction. Those whose problems are mainly of the learning disability type are, by definition, generally poor at automatic processing and rote memory. Some children who handle rote learning quite well are slower at grasping new concepts or explanations and at seeing underlying relationships. The remedial teacher is better able to analyze difficulties and plan remedial lessons if one of the variables he or she takes into account is that of automatic versus representational organization. It is not so simple as deciding that "Bob learns best by rote and Bill learns best by understanding." Children and cognitive processes are not so nearly categorizable, and in the end, what counts is the teacher's ability to understand (whether formally or intuitively) both the child and the cognitive demands that the task imposes. Then she will arrange lessons with drill and with conceptual explanations as they are appropriate.

An example which occurs in teaching simple spelling patterns provides an illustration of the blending of automatic and representational cognitive organization. One of the basic spelling patterns in English is the sequence of consonant-vowel-consonant (*c-v-c*). The pattern holds true for many of the words in the basic reading vocabulary of early primary grade children, words such as *can*, *red*, *big*, and *hut*. It does not hold true for some other common vocabulary words such as *less* and *will*, although from the sound of these words they would seem to be of the same type. Most children learn how to spell *will* and *less* without any special teaching, because they see them so often that remembering how they look (i.e., revisualizing them) presents no problem. If you were to ask them how they know how to spell those words, they would probably say they "just know." The common error of children who do not "just know" how to spell *will* is the failure to add the extra *l;* they have overgeneralized from the typical *c-v-c* pattern, having failed to notice (perceive) or to store (remember) the difference in this particular word.

Probably the most frequently used method to remediate this kind of error is to drill the child on the word he has misspelled (in this case, *will*). This amounts to giving him more frequent, repeated exposures to the word, and also making him aware that he must pay attention to the spelling of this word. If the tactic works, when he has to spell it again he will have a better memory for what the word looks like, which may come to him automatically, or perhaps be preceded by some thought such as "Oh, I know that word, I was practicing it, now how does it go?" The tactic relies almost exclusively on automatic level organization, verbal mediation being employed only for focusing attention.

Another way to learn to spell a difficult word, such as *will*, is to discover its inclusion in a group of words which have a similar spelling pattern; in this case, one-syllable c-v-c words in which the final consonant is doubled. It turns out that four consonants are often doubled in this position: *f*, *s*, *l*, and *z;* thus we have *cuff, miss, tell,* and *buzz,* as well as *will*. One teacher made up a mnemonic device for a few second graders who had trouble remembering which words had double letters at the end. She taught them the sentence *Sam likes fried zuchini,* in which each initial letter is one of the frequent doublers. She taught them how to use the mnemonic, and gave them practice in applying it by dictating lists of one-syllable words for them to spell, some with a single and some with a double consonant at the end. The children had to invoke rote memory to recall the sentence, but once they had that, they could generate the correct spellings of many words, including *will*, using representational, verbally mediated reasoning and not relying heavily on visual memory.

To stay with the present example just a bit longer, it is the teacher's job to decide, given what he or she knows about the child and what he or she has in mind for future lessons, how to handle the learning of *will*. It is the teacher's ability to know which child to urge to look carefully, and which child to tell about Sam's liking fried zuchini, which makes the teacher something more than a follower of teaching prescriptions. He or she might also choose to deal only with *will* now, and at some future date use it to illustrate a group of words. The point I wish to stress is that awareness of both automatic and representational levels of organization will assist the clinician and teacher in characterizing the manner in which children learn and the methods for helping them learn more easily.

A SAMPLING OF LEARNING PROBLEMS AND REMEDIATION APPROACHES

A sampling of fairly common academic problems is presented here in order to demonstrate an approach, or perhaps it would be more accurate to say an attitude, towards remediation. Once the assessment process has as comprehensively as possible identified sources of learning difficulty and noted specific deficiencies warranting remedial attention, the active process of bringing about change gets underway. There are, of course, the particular methods and techniques of remediation, the devices and materials that specially trained teachers are familiar with, which cannot all be taught or summarized in a chapter such as this one. But the attitude of innovative problem solving in remedial work is an aspect of the special teaching situation that clinicians can more directly and immediately appreciate, and to which they can make important contributions.

I will begin with a variety of reading problems and will follow with examples of arithmetic and handwriting difficulties. The arithmetic and handwriting concerns are fairly self-explanatory. The reading problems require a short introduction.

There are many kinds of reading problems. Most can be categorized as either technical skill problems or comprehension problems, and some children have both. By technical skill problems I refer to those that interfere with accurate and fluent decoding of the words on the page—what is sometimes known as "word calling." Comprehension problems are those in which the meaning of the material is not grasped, even though each word is properly sounded. Here are some sample sentences in the various categories with which most competent adult readers would have difficulty:

1. Technically difficult to read but easily comprehended if the code is known. hereW illw ouy be omorrowt? (The first letter of each word has been transferred to the end of the word.)
2. Technically easy to read but difficult to comprehend. "There is, I think, good evidence that the transformational component applies to an initial phrase marker with more than one cyclic category in a definite and

regular manner, namely, cyclically (hence the term)" (Chomsky, 1975, p. 85).

3. Difficult to both read and comprehend. *Isopyrocalciferol* is a thermal decomposition product of calciferol; a stereoisomer of pyrocalciferol and ergosterol. (Stedman, 1972)

Below are three case examples of technical reading problems, followed by a discussion of the common reasons for reading comprehension problems.

Dennis

Dennis had high average intelligence and came from an emotionally supportive, upper-middle class professional family. In second grade, he had not yet learned the sounds of many consonants. If he were shown an *f* one day and told the sound it made, he could remember that sound through the school day, but by the next day he could not answer when shown the letter and asked to tell its sound. After closer examination, it turned out that Dennis could not recite the alphabet from *A* to *Z*, a shocking lack in an intelligent child from a culturally rich background. There was little likelihood that Dennis would learn to read more than a few words until he could name and identify all the letters, and so there the remedial work began. It is easier to learn to sing the alphabet according to a tune (the most common one seems to be "Twinkle Twinkle Little Star"), than to merely recite it; the melody appears to add some momentum and associative connection. If Dennis could learn to recite to himself all the letters of the alphabet in order, he would have within himself a set of information which could be used for the next step, that of learning to match the letter name or sound with the graphic symbol.

Dennis's parents were told of his inability to recite the alphabet and asked if they knew the alphabet song, which might make learning easier. That Friday the family, including three older siblings, drove the two-hour trek to their weekend cottage, singing the alphabet song all the way. Sunday they drove home singing again. It was a painless drill and review and when Dennis arrived at school on Monday he knew the alphabet. He had to sing it to get through it, and if interrupted he had to begin again at the beginning, but within himself he had knowledge of the names of the 26 letters in order. (He also had the intense pleasure of having achieved a childhood milestone which ranks in importance with being able to tie shoes and ride a two-wheeler.)

Once Dennis could recite the alphabet, his teacher printed it on a long strip and taped it to his desk. Now he could match any letter symbol with its name by reciting the alphabet as he counted off the symbols on the strip. So, if he needed to know what letter the *f* represented, he could locate it on the strip and then, beginning at *a*, follow with his finger and recite the letters from memory as he went along. When his finger landed on the *f* he would be saying *f*.

Dennis learned to recognize and identify the letters of the alphabet, but reading continued to be a very difficult skill for him to learn, a fact probably predictable from the special methods required for learning individual letters. He did learn to read, but he learned very slowly, with special techniques required at almost every step along the way.

Ken

Ken's WISC-R scores were in the low 80s, and he was plagued with severe eczema which distracted him with itching and which itched more when things did not go well.

Ken was enthusiastic about learning to read. He had a good sight vocabulary, but had gotten stalled around the more analytic decoding skills because of a particular difficulty with learning vowel sounds—a relatively common cause of difficulty in beginning readers. He had a good memory for the general gestalten of words, and could decode initial and final consonant sounds, but he could not distinguish *pit* from *pet* nor *big* from *bag*. The short vowel sounds are among the most difficult symbol-sound correspondences that children must learn, and many children learn to read without first learning these in isolation. They get enough information from the rest of the letters in the word and from the context to permit intelligent guessing. Eventually, having learned enough words containing the short vowel sounds, they intuitively generalize the sounds into new words with similar linguistic patterns. Thus, for example, if a child has the word *big* in his sight vocabulary, meaning that he recognizes it on sight without having to sound it out, he will be able to sound out a new word, such as *fit*, by transferring the sound of the *i* in *big* into the spot between the *f* and *t* sounds. Children who do not develop enough sight vocabulary or who do not spontaneously make the abstract generalization and transfer of short vowel sounds (which appeared to be Ken's problem), must be taught in a more concrete fashion some way of knowing or remembering those sounds.

A remedial program was devised for Ken around this particular stumbling block. While he was encouraged to go on reading from sight vocabulary and context clues, he was also given some exercises in which he would have to discriminate short vowels with no context clues. For example, he might be given the three words *pot*, *pet*, and *pit* and three corresponding pictures, and have to match word with picture. Given such a lesson, he would also have to be given some way of figuring out the solution, of finding which of the middle letters represented the sound he heard in the word *pot* for instance. The teacher made up a key to the five most common short vowel sounds: the *a* in *cat*, the *e* in *hen*, the *i* in *pig*, the *o* in *pot*, and the *u* in *sun*. On a large card she printed each of the five single letters, and next to each one the key word using that letter, and a picture of it.

For the key she chose nouns that Ken knew fairly well and that could easily be depicted with simple, unambiguous drawings or pictures. Deciding to include Ken in the project from the beginning, she had him find or draw the key pictures. Focusing his attention on five particular vowel sounds was an important first step in the project, introducing him to the idea that they could help him figure out some words, much as he had already learned that beginning and ending consonants could help do. Whether he actually learned to transpose the sound from his key to another word, or whether he learned the sounds at a more intuitive, automatic level by simply being exposed to them with greater frequency and focus, he did learn those sounds over a period of weeks and used them to decode new words.

Dennis and Ken both illustrate an important principle in remedial work, that of equipping the child with enough information or technical assistance (charts, keys, etc.) so that he can independently find or figure out the answers he needs. Instead of having to ask a teacher or another child, he has within him the means to derive solutions. The advantages of such independence are both concrete and psychological. The child does not have to wait until someone is free to help him. He learns that he is capable of figuring things out and working independently. He also tends to learn the new material more quickly, because he actively confronts the material and the processes involved in handling it rather than passively receiving a piece of information. As we have noted before, "going through the motions" often reinforces and speeds learning.

Eileen

Eileen was beginning tenth grade when her parents requested a reading evaluation. They had become aware of her reading problem only when she was in the eighth grade. She had always done well in school, and the problem was discovered during her eighth grade only because she commented one day to her mother that she had a bad habit of sometimes writing numbers down backwards. Her parents had known that she hardly ever read voluntarily and that she had poor handwriting and spelling, but they were unaware that she did almost no reading at school. Testing in eighth grade disclosed that she was able to read almost any word, but at an incredibly slow rate—25 to 40 words a minute, with pauses of half a minute or so on an occasional long word. She had been getting by in school on her high-average overall intelligence and with help from her friends. She gleaned enough information from class lectures and discussions to comprehend most of the material; she could also write in grammatically smooth sentences, though with largely phonetic spelling, and so was able to turn in assignments regularly. She lived in a small community with an average school system, and had managed well enough so that she rarely if ever experienced school failure. She had, in fact, incorporated her academic difficulties into a strong-willed, independent style which asked that she be accepted as she was. For example, she wrote in her notebook beginning on the last page and working towards the front, insisting that because of being left-handed this was easier for her.

By the tenth grade, her teachers and family had all made accommodations to the reading problem. Her teachers did not call on her to read aloud in class, and left it to her to get the material in whatever way she could. Her reading ability allowed her to read short exam questions and even to do homework assignments. The latter she did by reading the questions at the end of the chapter, and then skimming the bold-face headings to find the paragraph which contained the answer she needed. Her father read the chapters of her biology book into a tape recorder, so that she could listen to them in order to study for an exam. Most teachers accepted her written work for its content and did not grade her down on spelling. She was active in sports and had a job behind the counter at the local pharmacy. Her voluntary reading was confined to the daily Ann Landers column and to the captions on pictures in magazines.

It was because Eileen had aspirations to go to college and study for a career in marine biology that her mother asked for a reading evaluation. Teachers, parents, and Eileen herself believed she could get through high school in the same fashion that she had gotten to tenth grade. The question was whether she could be helped to read well enough to do college reading and to read for pleasure.

The assessment presented a straightforward picture of problems in visual memory, unclouded by other deficit areas or by psychosocial difficulties. A strength which allowed her to be more successful than most youngsters with similar difficulties was her ability to express herself clearly in speech and in writing, although she wrote slowly and with idiosyncratic letter formations. The visual memory deficit was apparent in the lack of whole word recognition, poor spelling, and inability to do mental computation. The need was clear enough: to arrange for as much reading practice as possible, with the hope that the speed would increase with repeated exposures to the written word.

A school conference was set up for Eileen, her parents, her teachers, and the high school remedial teacher. The English teacher offered to give Eileen credit for the course if she spent the class hours doing special reading with the remedial teacher rather than coming to regular English class. Eileen, who had managed for so many years as a "regular" student was unhappy about being seen entering the remedial classroom, but she eventually agreed. Beyond this, however, she was not willing to sacrifice her out-of-school time for reading practice; that would have meant giving up sports or her pharmacy job, and she was not ready to do that.

At follow-up four months later Eileen seemed a little more realistic in acknowledging her difficulties. She had done her remedial stint without complaining, but had tried to answer comprehension questions without doing the reading. Most encouraging, she had read her first book—a current paperback best seller then making the rounds of her high school group. The group had been discussing it, and one girl had offered to read it to Eileen. Eileen retorted that she could read it herself, and the friend teased her, saying she bet Eileen couldn't. Eileen took the book and stayed up till 3 A.M. reading. She did not read every word, to be sure, and skipped long descriptive sections; but she spent 6 to 8 hours with it and went from the first page to the last. At the follow-up there was no indication of increased reading speed; that would take considerably longer to achieve, if in fact it could be achieved at all. The major change was in the greater willingness to attack reading, rather than to circumvent it. It would still take some time to help her shift from an attitude of "how to get by without really reading" to one of getting in as much practice as possible. She still was tending to fight the imposed need to practice, and it is perhaps characteristic of her that she read the book on a dare, as it were. Her mother was simultaneously trying to add reading practice by cutting out occasional interesting newspaper items, to supplement the daily Ann Landers column. With the clue provided by her reading of the novel, the psychologist and remedial teacher decided to try having her read romantic fiction during the remedial period, rather than the usual reading exercises.

There are countless children (and adults) like Eileen, who theoretically can read anything handed to them, but who require an inordinate amount of exposure to written material before developing spontaneous recognition of even a rudimentary sight vocabulary. Rather than getting that high frequency exposure, they get far less than normal readers, because they avoid reading whenever possible. The problem thus becomes self-perpetuating and grows progressively worse from lack of practice. As with most problems, the earlier it is detected the easier it is to alleviate, in this case mainly because it is easier to provide sustained reading practice at appropriate levels of difficulty when the children are in the lower grades.

Reading Comprehension Difficulties

Nearly everyone has had the experience of reading several sentences, or even several pages, and suddenly realizing that he has comprehended none of the material because he was not paying attention to the content, although his eyes had in fact taken in every word and some inner voice had strung them together in sequence. Most people have also had the experience of reading with attention and concentration, and still failing to understand because although they can decipher the words, the meaning of the whole sentence or paragraph escapes them. It is the latter situation we refer to here in discussing difficulties in reading comprehension.

Sources of difficulty are either semantic or structural; that is, the material is not understood either because the words or concepts are not familiar, or because the style in which the material has been organized for presentation is overly demanding.

Semantic problems stem from lack of experience with what is being written about. It may be unfamiliarity with specific words; this is a common and basic source of reading difficulty, and one of the reasons why vocabulary building exercises continue to be included in reading and English curricula through high school. It may be unfamiliarity with concepts which cannot be understood simply from reading their labels and understanding the component words. Thus, for example, the concept of "survival of the fittest" is not likely to be understood as thoroughly by one unfamiliar with Darwinian theory as it will be by one who knows it in that context, although both may understand the meaning of the words *survival* and *fittest* equally well. It may be unfamiliarity with the general topic, such that what is written cannot be related to the reader's experience and therefore is difficult to integrate. Thus, instructions on how to build a model airplane will be more difficult to understand for someone who has never built, or even seen one, even though he may understand all the terms used.

Problems of structure have to do with the pace at which information is presented, and the complexity of organization. Long, complex sentences usually demand that the reader get through to the end, before he can achieve closure on a complete thought. Sentences that contain several ideas and a number of subordinate clauses do not give the reader much opportunity to mentally catch his breath or digest ideas until the period at the end is reached. Consider this example, in which the reader must move quickly through the direct quotation in order to maintain the connection between the opening of the sentence and the conclusion of the idea which follows the quote:

> Ace says that he can remember certain details of his own birth—"The Doctor picked me up and slapped me once, and lo and behold, there I was, one minute old, with a strangulated hernia and no Blue Cross"—but he manages only a highly selective recall of the rest of his childhood and adolescence.[1]

Sentences such as this require greater speed than do short, simple statements, and they also require greater accuracy in reading, because one or two errors in small words, or an unnoticed comma, can render the whole statement meaningless. Here is an example of a complex sentence, with quite simple content and vocabulary, which is far more difficult for one who reads somewhat slowly or haltingly than would be the transcription of that sentence into the four sentences that follow it.

> A small boy wearing a light shirt was on his way to school when suddenly, noticing dark clouds in the sky, he began to run, hoping to escape the coming rain.
>
> A small boy was on his way to school. He was wearing a light shirt. Suddenly he began to run. He had noticed dark clouds in the sky and hoped to escape the coming rain.

[1]Mark Singer, "Profile of Goodman Ace," *The New Yorker,* 4 April 1977, p. 45.

Another aspect of structure that makes comprehension more difficult is chronology in presenting material. Stories which intersperse dialogue with descriptive or explanatory passages, or which insert flashback or parenthetical material, require greater concentration and conceptual sophistication than do chronological narratives.

When a reader has a comprehension problem it is usually due to some combination of semantic and structural overload. In addition, children who do not read fluently, in the technical sense, may have comprehension difficulties because so much of their energy goes into decoding that their cognitive energies are not free to focus on the content. Listening to their reading and their answers to comprehension questions usually provides a good deal of information as to whether technical reading ability is adequate or not, and whether there are semantic or structural demands which they cannot meet.

Technical reading difficulties are the only ones that can be directly attacked through reading practice. Comprehension problems are generally approached by discussion and analysis: breaking down the reading passages, looking for main ideas and items of information, finding the difficult vocabulary words and unfamiliar concepts and explaining them both in isolation and in the content of the reading passage. When the problem is that the subject is totally unfamiliar, a more introductory level presentation is in order, provided either by discussion or a different book. As a rule, structure becomes more complex as reading material becomes more demanding in content. For the most part, when readers are technically competent, and also familiar with the vocabulary and concepts of the subject they are reading about, they are also able to manage the structural demands.

Jacob

Jacob had difficulties in all academic areas. With high average intelligence and a warm supportive family, he was plagued by multiple learning disabilities in visual and auditory processing and in language and motor production. At 13, he read at first grade level, had very poor auditory discrimination for similar vowel sounds and some consonant pairs, spoke with alternating stammer and press of speech, and wrote haltingly. Three years of twice weekly tutoring brought him to a general competence level in reading of third-to-fifth grade. His spelling and handwriting were very poor but also improved slowly. His arithmetic skills are what interest us here because they demonstrate how very discrepant skills may be within a given area. The discrepancy is perhaps best illustrated by the fact that he could calculate 48 × 25 in his head, but could not compute it on paper.

Jacob had an excellent sense of number and of quantitative relationships. He explained how he had done the mental calculation as follows: 48 × 100 is 4800; 48 × 50 would be half of that or 2400; and 48 × 25 would be half of that or 1200. On paper however, he could not do the calculations because he lacked a number of skills that to most children come far more easily than does the above mental calculation.

The first difficulty Jacob would encounter would be the reading of $\begin{smallmatrix} 48 \\ \times 25 \end{smallmatrix}$ in such a way as to recognize that it asked the same question as did the verbally presented inquiry "How much is 48 times 25?" Rather he saw it as a set of numerals that he was supposed to manipulate in some predetermined, patterned set of movements which he could never remember. The failure to perceive the problem in a pattern of numerals is not confined to learning disabled children. A frequent error on the Wide Range Achievement Test is with the problem $\begin{smallmatrix} 75 \\ +8 \end{smallmatrix}$. Many first and second grade children can calculate the problem in their heads (and on their fingers), but written out it presents an unfamiliar stimulus. They may not yet have learned the formal process of carrying in addition, and if they have, they may not be accustomed to adding a one-digit number to a two-digit number. Most interesting is their failure to realize that they can solve the problem, that 75 plus 8 is not an unfamiliar exercise for them. Arranged on paper, the numbers appear to require manipulation, not comprehension.

We return to Jacob and his variety of difficulties. His poor handwriting and spacing made it difficult for him to copy the problem in a fashion that would allow him to solve it. When he tried solving it, the additional numbers he wrote were very hard to keep in manageable columns. He could not remember the sequence of procedures which, since they are not meaningful to an elementary school child, can be mastered only by rote. Consider that rote sequence: (1) You must remember to multiply the top row of numbers by each number in the bottom row (many children want to multiply two numbers in the same *column*, probably because that is the critical relationship of numbers in addition and subtraction computation); (2) You must remember the sequence to follow in multiplying the top row and the sequence of bottom row numbers

A Sampling of Learning Problems and Remediation Approaches   245

to be used; (3) You must remember where to write down each line of new numbers, and to move each successive line one place to the left; and (4) You must remember that the rows you have written are to be added (not subtracted) to achieve the final answer.

Jacob could remember none of this from his school lessons, and he also had the more common problem of not knowing the multiplication facts by heart. Once it was clear that his conceptual understanding was more than adequate to the task, and that the problems he had were exclusively with automatic processing (memory for facts and sequence, and motor-spatial organization), it was a relatively simple matter to begin practice exercises in the weak areas. The matter was simple in the sense that no sophisticated method of analysis or teaching was necessary; but it was not simple for Jacob to learn. The problems were tackled individually. Jacob's tutor talked with him about the difficulty and the importance of keeping the numbers in straight lines, and she continued to praise and remind him on that score until that part of the routine went automatically. The multiplication tables were dissected and catalogued, as together they discussed which combinations he knew very well, which he was hesitant about, and which he could figure out quickly enough even if he could not recall them immediately. They made flash cards for him to practice at home, a few at a time (alone or with family assistance, as he wished), and to be reviewed at every lesson with the tutor. The lessons included time spent on practicing the process of multiplying one to three-digit numbers and manufacturing mnemonic devices wherever possible until the procedure was fully automatic. It took months for the process to be fully automatic, but it was haltingly successful before then. When Jacob was certain enough about the steps, his homework regularly included a few multiplication problems to do, using the number combinations which he knew well or was then working on. Jacob's tutoring lessons were an hour long, twice a week, and were devoted mainly to reading. The time spent on arithmetic averaged perhaps 10 minutes a lesson, and he spent about 30 to 40 minutes a week on it at home. The arrangement was hardly ideal, but it was all that could be managed. Even such a minimal amount of time, however, paid off. Within a few months Jacob had mastered the process and most of the tables, and he continued to learn them all, as solidly and automatically as possible, and to review the process periodically as he moved on to learn division.

The remedial work described above illustrates what is meant, and what is not meant, by the idea that tasks have to be broken into component parts and taught bit by bit. The task of multiplication is broken into specific aspects for Jacob, according to where he encounters difficulty, and each is addressed separately. Addressing them separately does not necessarily mean working on them one at a time. It was not necessary to have him practice only the writing of legible numbers in straight columns until that was fully automatic. On the contrary, he would have become bored and discouraged if only allowed to set up problems. On the other hand, it would not be wise to give him homework problems before he had sufficiently mastered the process, and it would be overloading him to have him trying to memorize all the multiplication facts within a month or two. Good remedial teaching only starts with basic principles such as breaking tasks down into component parts and providing sufficient practice and success. It is maintained through ongoing programming, both carefully planned and spontaneous, according to what works and makes sense in each case.

Van

Except for his signature, Van could only print. He attended a school for disturbed and disaffected adolescents, and was referred by his teachers for an assessment of basic academic skills. He had been labeled dyslexic in childhood and, although he now could read, he had difficulty with spelling and handwriting—problems commonly encountered by former dyslexics.

Van was angry and embarrassed at having his poor skills scrutinized. This was particularly so in regard to his handwriting. He muttered that he did not know how to write, hoping that would end the matter. He was then handed a sheet of paper with 52 squares ruled off, and asked to fill in the letters of the alphabet in cursive writing, once in small letters and again in capitals. Any letter he did not know how to make he could just skip. It turned out that he knew how to form all but six of the small letters, and about half of the capitals. He was then asked to write a few short words, dictated to him and using only the letters he knew how to form. In this way it was possible to see what he knew about joining letters.

Based on this amount of information, it was recommended to his teacher that he start a regular handwriting program in which Van could be shown how to make the letters he did not know and given opportunities to practice them systematically. Once he realized that his lack of knowledge and ability was finite and could be overcome, he cooperated willingly with his teacher's program, even agreeing to work in a handwriting workbook designed for 8 to 10 year olds. When his teacher had approached him with the workbook and had started to explain that he could use it or not as he wished, so long as he practiced writing somewhere, Van interrupted him to say, "I know, it's for little kids, I don't care, give it to me."

Within two weeks he had learned the remaining small letters and was writing full sentences in a careful, even hand. He had not yet mastered the art of connecting those letters which end at the top of the letter rather than down on the line—*b, o, w,* and *v*—so that was the next objective. After that, he moved on to learn the capital letters.

Van is but one of many adolescents, mostly boys, who failed to learn cursive writing when it was taught in elementary school (usually in second and third grades) and gave up on ever learning it. Some children are not ready to move from printing to script at the moment that the shift is introduced at school. This is not necessarily because script is harder, but because they have not mastered printing well enough to be comfortable with it. Shifting too soon often results in a hodgepodge of letter forms, with mixed capital and small letters, cursive and print. Others attended schools in which cursive writing was not formally taught at all, or it was introduced for only a brief period and never reviewed or reinforced. Most children can devise a form of cursive even if never formally taught, and can read other people's cursive writing. However, those with learning disability problems may have difficulty with both the reading and writing of cursive script if left to their own devices. Those who reach high school with continuing and severe problems in a number of basic skills, such as Chip, who was discussed in chapter 7, are probably best left alone with their printing, if their energies are still required to master lagging reading and arithmetic abilities. Others, like Van, have overcome many of their earlier difficulties and are capable, with minimal but systematic attention, of finally learning cursive writing. Once they have learned all the letter forms, they need only to exercise it periodically in order to maintain cursive writing as a functional skill, much like the use of a foreign language.

There are two main reasons why those who can should be encouraged to learn to write more than their signatures in cursive script. The most practical reason is that a number of learning disabled readers who ultimately learn to read and write printed material and have not learned to write in cursive script are also unable to read it. While one can get along fairly well never writing in cursive, he will be at a disadvantage in many situations if he cannot read the cursive writing of others. Learning to write cursive script will not guarantee the ability to make out everyone's penmanship, but it will increase the odds.

The second reason to teach cursive, when possible, is the general sense of increased competence and self-esteem which it affords to those who have felt deficient and odd in their inability. While some adolescents boast about not being able to write, our experience has been that when they discover that they can be taught, most welcome the opportunity and are more than willing to give up their badge of exceptionality.

THE TEACHER-STUDENT RELATIONSHIP IN REMEDIATION

Whatever the problem and whatever the setting for a remedial program, the relationship between the child and his teacher(s) is probably the single most critical factor. Several aspects of the relationship are of special interest to the clinician, for they parallel his or her own assessment work with the child and touch upon matters he or she may want to discuss with parents and teachers. Because of the one-to-one or small-group arrangement, remedial teachers are in a particularly good position to sponsor or provide the following: reality-based support, independence, structure, and innovation.

Reality-Based Support

One of the similarities between special teacher (or tutor) and therapist is that the tutor, like the therapist is both more aware of problems that may be covered over in front of others, and also more accepting of the imperfections and supportive of attempts to overcome them. Paralleling the psychotherapist's stance, the tutor's attitude conveys, "Nothing you do not know or cannot do will shock me. Any learning problem you might have can be looked at here. Anything you do know and can do may help us in working on the problem areas. I can help you learn."

A realistic evaluation of the child's difficulties underlies much of the supportive teaching and encouragement that make up remedial work. Some children need help in acknowledging what they are unable to do; others need encouragement to keep from being overwhelmed by their perception of being incompetent. All of them need support that acknowledges (rather than overlooks or makes light of) real difficulties that hamper achievement and pleasure.

An incident with Jacob, whose arithmetic difficulties were discussed a few pages back, illustrates the need for support which is cognizant of ongoing difficulties and attuned to the child's feelings. Jacob was in the seventh grade and, after a year or so of reading tutoring, had made significant progress—from first to early third grade competence. One day, after an especially productive reading lesson, his tutor commented on the good progress he was making with a remark such as "That was very good reading today, you've been doing very well lately." When Jacob failed to respond, she said, "You don't seem pleased. Don't you know that you are doing well and making progress?" He then answered, "Yes, but what good does it do? I still can't do any of the work in my class." The tutor acknowledged his discouragement and disappointment, and reassured him that he would continue to make more progress, reminding him of what he had not been able to do before but could do now—such things as reading billboards and movie marquees and figuring out street signs. Her willingness to acknowledge the difficult reality and her care in not promising easy or total success in catching up, while still pointing out the positive aspects from a different perspective, kept the relationship honest and supportive, thereby further strengthening it.

Independence

By its very nature, the remediation process tends to promote dependency in children. The special teacher is seen as one who knows a great deal and who is especially willing to give individual aid and attention. It may be necessary to foster some dependency at first, while the child develops a sense of trust in the relationship, but helping him to become increasingly independent in his work is an ever-present objective. The teacher can use his or her special relationship to achieve this goal rather than to maintain dependency. The teacher can help children to work alone, to develop confidence in their own judgments about the quality of their work, and to assume responsibility for doing, checking, and turning in their assignments.

Some children have great difficulty in sitting alone to do schoolwork, needing someone alongside to reassure that the work is correct, to keep them from day dreaming, or to keep them company for some more global, anxiety-reducing purpose. These children must gradually be weaned away from dependence on a live body next to them. Some children will work if given directions about where, when, how, and how much to do, but they will not take the initiative or assume responsibility for starting to work. They do not persist when work is difficult, seek out assistance when they can do no more, or look over their work for errors. Some children remain overly dependent on teacher judgment as to whether a paper is neat enough; they do not think to exercise their own judgment, and have no confidence in it.

Lack of independence can easily go unnoticed in one-to-one or small group remediation where teacher availability tends to forestall anxiety and avoidance. There is no substitute for individual instruction when it is needed, but it can also become a counter-productive crutch. One second grade boy who was getting after-school help from his classroom teacher stopped trying to do any class work at all, because he knew he would get individual help later. He also came to believe that he could not learn with the class. Similarly, a sixth grader who had overcome most of his reading lag in the course of three years of tutoring had come to assume that what he did not pick up in class sessions would be repeated to him individually later on by his teachers or fellow students. As a result, he allowed himself to tune out from time to time during class. When his teachers noticed the pattern and called it to his attention, he was able, with occasional reminding, to pay more consistent attention and to wean himself from depending on repeated, individualized lessons. The sixth grader's situation illustrates the importance of teachers who are sensitive to fine discriminations and can make judgments as to when being helped by one's classmates is useful and when it is not.

Structure

As a rule, difficulty in handling academic work is accompanied by a general sense of confusion and incomprehensibility. The more a child knows of the material, the greater his sense of its structure; and the greater his sense of structure, the easier it is to learn new material. Thus, a child who can count by rote to 30 is in a better position, than one who cannot, to realize that the sequence of 0 through 9 as final digit is repeated through each decade of numbers. And conversely, awareness of this pattern will make it easier to continue counting beyond 30.

In addition, a sense of structure can help provide reassurance to the child that he is capable of learning what has thus far eluded comprehension. Van was mentioned earlier in this chapter; once he was aware of what he did and did not know about cursive writing, he was better able to try learning it. Structuring the problematic material makes the task appear more finite and manageable.

Children tend to create a sense of structure by measuring learning in terms of workbooks or readers completed, and the unsuccessful student measures his failure in the same terms. The remedial teacher can offer structure more closely related to content and concepts, and can demonstrate goals and progress in terms almost as concrete as workbooks. A child who knows he is working on the five common short-vowel sounds, three of which he has already learned fairly well, is aware not only of the progress he has made and the goal in sight. He is also more aware of short vowels in his reading and more likely to integrate his newly learned skill. Charting progress with check marks is another expression of the same principle.

Innovation

Innovation in this context does not require the use of modern methods and equipment in the teaching field, although there is certainly no need to rule them out. It is more a state of mind of the teacher, a watchfulness for unexpected difficulties, an altertness to usable events and materials, and a readiness to incorporate serendipitous occurrences into the lessons. A card game or commercial educational toy may suggest a better way of presenting material. A recent or proposed family trip may offer a background of experience or curiosity which promotes learning in a related academic area.

Innovation and spontaneity must be subject to control, so that the remedial situation maintains the requisite degree of familiarity and predictability, and so that lessons continue to be lessons even if they are uncommonly enjoyable and effortless. One of the most common pitfalls of remedial teaching, particularly with emotionally disturbed children whose anxiety pushes them to avoidance tactics, is the abandonment of teaching in order to allow the child to relax or get something off his chest. Although there are of course times in any educational setting when lessons must be abandoned under exceptional circumstances, remedial sessions are especially vulnerable to such occurrences. Teachers must be particularly vigilant to preserve the educational objectives.

The greatest demand for innovation arises from the special sticking points the child encounters in learning. The child may not remember on which side of the paper to begin writing, or which way to make a proper *s* rather than a reversed one. He may not hear the difference between *sad* and *sat* or *lift* and *left*, or he may not maintain sequence in spelling out a word. The teacher has to find a way to explain or demonstrate how to do these things and a host of ways for providing continued practice. The more prompt the teacher is in recognizing and dealing with a problem, the less the child is exposed to feeling failure and inadequacy. One tutor working with a second grader who confused *b* and *d* made rings for her to wear on each hand, the right hand ring carrying a *b* and pictures of a ball and a box, the left ring showing a *d* and pictures of a doll and a dog.

As in most interesting jobs, the teacher's success depends largely on his or her own experience, wisdom, and imagination, but the teacher is not working alone. He or she can sometimes get assistance from the child in devising ways to remember and practice difficult material. Saying "I'm trying to think of a way to help you remember this" can elicit imaginative suggestions from children, and simultaneously encourage their taking initiative in helping themselves. One clinician, seeing a third grader who occasionally reversed 3s and 5s, mused aloud, "How can we help you remember how to begin a 3 so it comes out right?" The child looked at the paper for a moment and then said, "I know, it starts like a 2 does." The clinician, elaborating on the child's idea, then suggested that a way to remember how to do the 5 was that it starts the way 4 does.

SOME CLINICAL ISSUES IN REMEDIAL PLANNING

Some aspects of remedial planning which warrant particular attention by the clinician are: reporting assessment findings to parents and relating them to remedial recommendations; giving some feedback to children; considering various arrangements for remedial help; and planning the role parents are to play in a remedial program.

Reporting to Parents

Remediation comes in for serious discussion when the clinician reports to parents about the assessment findings. Parents differ in their specific concerns about their children's academic competence, but most have certain hopes and fears which will need to be addressed. Three particular tasks of the summary conference are worthy of specific mention: (1) presenting an honest, realistic appraisal of the child's academic abilities in terms of intellectual achievement and emotional factors; (2) considering together ways for dealing with any learning deficits or problems; and (3) answering any remaining questions raised by the parents when they initially requested an evaluation.

Presenting a realistic appraisal of the child's academic abilities requires not only that the clinician report findings in an organized form and straightforward language, but also that he deal with parent reactions. Their response may have less to do with the actual abilities and success of the child than with their own assumptions, aspirations, and concerns about the child. The parents of a retarded youngster may be delighted to hear that their child can be expected to learn to read, while the parents of a child with high average ability may be disappointed to learn that he is not highly gifted. A common problem in recent years has been with parents who need to believe that their children's problems stem from learning disability and not emotional disturbance. With schools often providing special educational services according to diagnostic label, the pressure on clinicians is even greater to certify learning disability. The clinician has a responsibility to present his or her appraisal honestly, and to do so in a way that will help parents accept unpleasant realities and plan the most helpful remedial program. Often this is made easier by pointing out strengths and positive aspects, some of which parents may be overlooking. Obviously, these must be genuine strengths and not merely sops to the parents.

Katherine, for example, was 24 when brought for evaluation by her parents. She was severely retarded as a result of encephalitis at the age of 7 months, but she was able to read and write a bit. She watched certain educational TV programs religiously, with a notebook in hand for writing down new words, and wrote letters daily to a friend she had met at a boarding school for the handicapped. The parents wanted to know what kinds of educational and vocational training would be appropriate for her.

Testing with the WISC-R resulted in age-equivalent scores of 6 to 7 years on all subtests, indicating that no matter what training she might receive, she could not be expected to do other than the most routine work, particularly if unsupervised. At the same time, some aspects of her emotional level were most similar to young adolescents. It was important for the parents to know that her reasoning and judgment abilities were at the level of a young latency child, but it was also a shock, particularly to the mother, who had hoped Katherine might be able to do some semi-independent work. Her reading skills, at second-grade level, indicated that she might well benefit from further instruction. With her rather good automatic language processing skills, interest, and persistence, it was certainly worth a try.

The mother had mentioned Katherine's occasional stubbornness about certain things she would or would not do. During the summary conference, this was pointed out as a characteristic that accompanied her perseverance with some tasks and as more useful to her than would be apathy or more total compliance. When the stubbornness was perceived as the same strong will at play, it might be easier to tolerate the irritations it created. This discussion also highlighted the pleasure Katherine took in tasks and activities at her intellectual and emotional level, thus signaling the potential for happy and productive years ahead, though they would be spent under supervision.

Even if parents reject the assessment findings and remedial recommendations, the clinician must, without nagging, do the best to make his or her own view clear. While parents may not be able to accept it at the time, it may become more meaningful at a later date if events begin to bear out what the clinician has said. Leonard, for example, was in the ninth grade at a special school for slow learning and disturbed adolescents. He had done quite well and wanted to return to a regular high school, and his parents requested an evaluation to help them decide if he were ready for that or perhaps needed another kind of school altogether. The parents made it clear at the initial interview that they believed Leonard to have learning disabilities which had resulted in some emotional problems. The school records, Leonard's therapist, and previous diagnostic testing all indicated that Leonard had a long-standing, and to some degree free-standing characterological problem manifested by fear of his peer group, withdrawal to endless TV watching, and an inability to discipline himself in connection with school work and home responsibilities. The current testing indicated average and above-average basic skills, and no sign that learning disabilities were now hampering Leonard. In the psychologist's opinion, Leonard might not be able to manage the regular high school program, but had a good chance to profit from a special school that stressed confrontation with one's own behavior and responsibilities in a highly supportive setting. The third possibility was to continue in a protective special school, which could handle problematic behavior that a regular school could not, but which was not designed to push for more adaptive behavior. Although the chances were great that the parents would resist the psychologist's recommendations for the more actively therapeutic school, it was important that the recommendation, and the reasoning behind it, be articulated. Even if Leonard attended another school, it was possible that during the next three years there would be occasion to recall and make use of the clinician's reasoning and recommendation.

Reporting to Children and Adult Patients

Most children and all adults who have had a learning assessment require some feedback from the clinician, even if it is only a few sentences at the end of the last testing session. With young children it often takes the form of reassurance—either that things are going well, or that in addition to those things that go well there is a particular area which needs some attention in order for it to go more smoothly. If there is to be added help, small children may be told who will be helping them, and some older children are responsive to being told the rationale behind the help being planned for them. Awareness of the area of difficulty, be it academic or psychosocial, presented by a nonjudgmental clinician, can assist a child in understanding what is making life difficult for him, though he may not understand it with the greater depth or objectivity available to the professional. Furthermore, the pinpointing of difficulty accompanied by the knowledge that there will be someone to help in overcoming that difficulty usually provides reassurance and hope. With learning disability problems requiring extensive practice, the clinician can aid by explaining something of the nature of the difficulty and noting that steady practice is the main ingredient in making progress. Almost all children, and adults too, need outside support in maintaining a regular schedule of drill and review. Some understanding of how the practice helps may provide "inner support" as well. I have often used the analogy of practicing a musical instrument or learning to swim, pointing out that some children catch on or "get it" more quickly and with little practice, while others have to work longer before they reach the stage where it goes easily.

With some children, the psychologist can also begin the process of encouraging the child's active involvement in helping himself. The psychologist can suggest things the child can do alone or on his own initiative which will speed up the remedial process. These are mostly additional practice times, beyond the minimum set in the remedial program.

Varieties of Remedial Programming

There is no clear line between a regular classroom program, which attends to individual needs, and a remedial program. However, for purposes of discussion here we will consider the latter to be any planned intervention in a child's education that offers individual or small group instruction, and in which the content or pace of instruction is altered to meet individual learning ability.

Remedial programs vary in how much time is allotted to them and who does the actual instruction. The most salient variable for characterizing and categorizing them is probably the extent to which they supplement versus replace regular educational programming for the child. The mildest and generally simplest program is one which supplements the regular school day with additional lessons afterwards, one or more times a week. In-school remedial sessions, which take the place of regular class instruction, may involve anything from one period a week to full time special instruction. The most extreme form of remedial help removes the child from regular school altogether and places him in a school designed entirely for special needs children. On occasion, children who do not attend school at all may receive some kind of home instruction.

Part of the clinician's task is to consider what type of remedial program, if any, is most appropriate for the child. This will depend in large measure on what and how well the child can manage academically within his regular class, but also on what remedial facilities are available. The quality and flexibility of local private and public schools, the financial resources available to parents through public funding or private means, and the availability of qualified teachers are among the first set of conditions affecting remedial program decisions.

When appropriate-sounding programs are financially and geographically accessible, they must be considered in some detail as to how well they can provide for the child's particular constellation of special difficulties and normal developmental requirements. No school will ever exactly meet a given child's needs, even if these could be perfectly assessed and quantified, but some will come closer than others, and the clinician can be instrumental in helping to determine the best fit available.

The critical areas are usually academic and social, and certain questions commonly arise as to how well various needs in these two areas will be accommodated. In the questions that follow there are no specific right amounts or conditions of instruction. What is "adequate" and "appropriate" must be ascertained for each child.

A. Academic
1. Can the program provide adequate instruction in deficit skill areas?
2. Is the program geared to the appropriate level of ability in other school subjects? For example, will a child who is interested and able in science or social studies or art be challenged and

encouraged to develop further? Will a child who can not do grade-appropriate work of any kind receive appropriate instruction in content areas and nonacademic subjects?
   3. Does the program offer a reasonable division between intensive work on skill deficits and general education?
B. Social
   1. Is the school population appropriate for the child, in terms of his current social competence, both interpersonal and independent?
   2. Is the program likely to contribute to social development, as distinguished from tolerating and maintaining current levels of adjustment?
   3. To what extent will remedial instruction be at the expense of working as an integral member of a classroom group?
   4. Conversely, to what extent might efforts at mainstreaming place the child in regular classes where he may be uncomfortable or only marginally accepted?

The discussion of these issues with the parents cannot only help them in making the most appropriate decision, but can also serve as a vehicle for their developing a better differentiated understanding of their child's school difficulties and strengths.

The Involvement of Parents in Remedial Programs

Should parents help their own children with school work? If we alter this question to "*How* can parents help their children with school work?" we conjure up a more comprehensive and differentiated picture of parental involvement in remedial activities. In addition to direct instruction, there are a variety of services and emotional supports which parents can offer their children. These may include helping them set up and keep to a homework schedule, checking their work, listening to their compositions or oral reading, answering specific information questions, helping them locate reference materials, and so on.

Experience seems to show that most parents do not work well when they try to teach their children who are having school difficulties. Many who have tried it report that they stopped because they found themselves becoming impatient and taking it out on the children. Teachers frequently note that parents, in addition to getting upset, do not have enough information about how the material is being presented at school or what the teacher expects from the children. Not that some parents cannot do it well; there are many children whose parents have been their main or only teacher, usually because schools have refused to accept the child or have taken him but maintained that he could not learn. One example is Nigel Hunt's (Hunt, 1967) mother, a teacher by profession, who taught him to read at home after being told that he could never learn.

While most parents should not be involved in direct teaching if there is any other alternative, there is an important role for the parents in supporting the learning efforts of their child. This involves the same supports one gives any child: taking an interest in school happenings; praising good efforts; asking if there is homework to do; helping to plan time to do it without losing all play time; and being available to answer questions and to provide ongoing reinforcement for persisting until the work is finished.

In addition, some parents are able to provide more direct help in accordance with teacher suggestions or requests. They may drill the child on his reading or arithmetic flash cards or listen to his spelling words. They might check arithmetic computations or mark spelling errors in compositions. There are many tasks parents might take on, but they should act more in the role of teacher aides, who assist in carrying out assignments rather than as teachers, who plan what is to be taught and how it is to be presented. In sum, the goal is to help the child carry out what his teacher has asked him to do, and to avoid making parent-initiated demands which may be inappropriate.

Two examples of parent involvement that illustrate how well, and how poorly, parents can influence learning follow.

Cal had shown signs of a reading disability in second grade, and though he was making progress, he was moving slowly. He was not getting much reading practice in class. His teacher could not spend enough time with him alone, and he avoided reading whenever possible. Most recently, he had been delaying finishing one reader, fearful of beginning the next. His mother asked if she ought to practice with him at home. She met with the teacher and school psychologist and they agreed it was worth a try so long as Cal was interested and fairly willing. The teacher gave him a number of books at his level, and he chose one. The mother and teacher agreed on this particular procedure: Cal was to read a page a day, more if he wished. Any time he did not know a word, his mother was to write it on a list that he would go over later on and be asked to read the next day. If he missed more than six words on a page, it was to be taken as a sign that the material was too difficult (six was an arbitrary number, the teacher's way of relieving the mother of having to make qualitative decisions about the reading). In that case, the teacher would help Cal find another book. Cal agreed and they read daily. After about three weeks the teacher asked how things were going, and Cal's mother reported that it was going well. He read willingly, but never more than the prescribed page per day. He missed few words, and he always knew them the following day. Most encouraging was the mother's story of how, after missing a day of reading, Cal had come to her the following day with the book, announcing: "Today I'll do two pages to make up for yesterday." His taking the initiative in increasing the day's allotment was a welcome sign that he was not only not avoiding reading, but was eager to keep the system on track. There was the further implication that he believed that he was thereby being helped, and helping himself, to be a better reader. Without his mother's assistance, this development would have been, at best, delayed.

Ethan, at 12, had a life-long history of serious emotional and learning problems, and attended a small special school which maintained very close communication with the family. The mother had tried in earlier years to teach him, but she knew that she could not do so without becoming very frustrated and had given up trying. One holiday, an adult friend visited and brought a large chocolate bar for Ethan, who was out at the time. The friend then attached a simple note, which read "Hello Ethan—Happy Holiday—Your Friend Sam." When Ethan got home his mother showed him the candy and asked him to read the note. He glanced at it and said he could not read it. The mother insisted that he could, and Ethan continued to protest that he could not, until the mother finally announced, "Okay, no reading—no chocolate."

Within the same week, Ethan came home from school one day with a note saying that part of his assignment was to go to the nearby store and buy envelopes. At supper time he was asked if he had gotten the envelopes yet, and he began to whine that he was tired, he didn't want to go out, and so on. The parents insisted briefly, and then dropped it.

In these two events in Ethan's week, the parents had reversed potentially helpful approaches. When the child was presented with a school assignment requiring their support in holding firm on his responsibility to carry it out, they backed off. When he was presented with a freely offered gift, the mother turned it into a compulsory reading chore, with punishment for noncompliance. While the parents did not create Ethan's learning problems, they are, in these two instances, having a negative influence on their remediation.

Monitoring Remedial Programs

The previous examples illustrate the importance of ongoing communication between those concerned with the child's academic progress. Planning and instituting a program in no way insures success. At most, it represents the best understanding of the child combined with the best use of available resources at the time of assessment. The sources of error and the potential magnitude of error are great. Among the sources are errors in interpreting assessment data; changes in the child stemming from growth or external situations; changes in the educational program such that it does not provide the anticipated personnel, curriculum, or class composition; and events at home which affect the parents' ability to support the program. Not all sources of error or obsolete programs are bad. Children often make exceptional bursts of progress and no longer require a program as intensive as the one designed. A new educational facility may become available which better suits the child—a method, a teacher, a class, a school.

It is impossible to accurately anticipate how any program segment will work out. One must make decisions according to the best available information and understanding, try it, and then be prepared to reassess and change. For this reason, many people find it useful to build into the program some system of monitoring, such as periodic follow-up visits with the clinician or school conferences involving parents, teacher, and clinicians. In some instances older children may benefit from and contribute a good deal to such conferences.

Follow-up visits and conferences are to find out if the established remedial program seems to be working, by having parents and teachers, and sometimes the child, offer their evaluations of the program to the others. There may be small difficulties that have not been mentioned before because they did not appear serious enough to warrant a note or a phone call. There may be information from one person which will shed light on heretofore unexplained events or behavior observed by someone else. Frequently, a parent or teacher receives confirmation that what he or she has been doing has had a positive effect on the child's response in both home and school. Most children do not wish to attend such meetings. However, it is helpful to them if someone, usually the parents (or perhaps the clinician if he or she is still actively involved with the child), offers to present his or her feelings or wishes at the meeting. "There's going to be a meeting at school next week to talk about how things have been going. Is there anything you would like me to bring up, anything you'd like me to tell them about? Are there any special problems they should know about, or changes that you want to suggest?" Such questions may elicit no response or seemingly trivial requests, but they occasionally bring forth worries about school that had not been mentioned before. "Will I be promoted?" "One of the bigger boys sometimes teases me." "Do I have to stay in that special reading group?" "I don't have time to finish my work." Raising such concerns at a meeting sometimes results in specific changes and, in any event, should foster better understanding about the child and between parents and teachers.

A FINAL NOTE

Some states, and more recently the federal government, have mandated programs for all children with special educational needs. One immediate result of such action is the identification, at earlier ages, of increasing numbers of children who require special services. Parents are being actively encouraged to appeal to the schools for service, and public schools are required to provide programs. Theoretically it would no longer be possible for severely handicapped children to be denied an education, or for children like Jacob to sit through six or eight years of school, unable to progress without special help and unable to obtain it. Of course, passing a law does not educate children; but even so, it is already apparent that the laws have served to stimulate many programs which would not otherwise have been created. And more children are being served all the time.

However, the obligation to provide programs, and even the existence of programs, will not insure appropriate placement or successful education. As Kessler (1977) commented in an editorial addressed to psychologists:

> The recent federal legislation (P.L. 94–142) guaranteeing public educational services for all labeled handicapped children from 3 to 21 years, complete with individual educational plans reviewed annually with parents, least restrictive placement and guaranteed due process, promises more than we can probably deliver. (p. 2)

The demand for individual assessment will grow, and the need for clearly stated reporting to parents and for realistic recommendations about schooling will be more important than ever. Because parents are now in a better position to obtain programs for their children, they need the clearest possible understanding of what will be most beneficial.

Feeling the pressure from government legislation and from parents, local school systems will naturally attempt to provide programs that serve as many children as possible, with the least unnecessary duplication and the most economical expenditure of personnel. The clinician plays a critical, though not solitary, role in determining what program is likely to be most appropriate for a child, in monitoring the accuracy of that determination over time, and in recommending changes as they become necessary. While the individual clinician cannot make significant changes in the capacity of society to implement large-scale federal programs such as P.L. 94–142, he or she can help see to it that the opportunities afforded by such programs are used to the best advantage by those children and families for whom the clinician has professional responsibility.

APPENDIX I[1]

POSSIBLE QUESTIONS TO TEACHERS REGARDING THE CHILD'S SCHOOL BEHAVIOR AND ACADEMIC PERFORMANCE

I. *Behavior during lesson and nonlesson periods*
   A. *Strengths*
      1. In what school subjects, activities, and settings does the child operate best?
      2. Where is he most likely to achieve success, to behave appropriately, and to enjoy himself?
      3. Can he become actively involved in a book, an assignment, or a project, maintaining interest and completing it to his and to the teacher's satisfaction?
   B. *Weaknesses*
      1. Where is he most likely to experience difficulty, frustration, and failure?
      2. How does he express his distress? For example, withdrawal, temper tantrums, tears, attempts to deny or cover the failure, aggressivity (against teacher, children, self, materials, or furniture?), refusal to try again, demands for or refusal of help?
   C. *Interests*
      1. Are there topics or activities of special interest to the child that could be used as a core for various skill-building or socializing activities?
   D. *Special Problems or Skills*
      1. Are there special problems or skills apparent during noninstructional periods such as recess, lunch, or school assemblies?
   E. *Responsibilities*
      1. Can he handle responsibilities such as being room monitor, carrying messages, helping another child,

---

[1]Some of the material in this section was previously published in a different form in M. Sanders, *Guidelines for the Educational, Social and Psychological Assessment of Children in Special Educational Need* (Cambridge, Mass.: Research Institute for Educational Problems, 1973). Permission to reproduce this material is gratefully acknowledged. See discussion in chapter 5.

patrolling school crossings? (In this connection, it is not uncommon to hear the teacher say "I don't know, I've never tried having him do that. I'll try it this week." Once again this demonstrates what clinicians recognize from their diagnostic work in other settings; namely, that questions raised during the diagnostic process can lead to a spontaneous revision of attitudes and behavior with therapeutic results.)

II. *Ability to work in various groupings*
   A. *Independence*
      1. Can he work independently?
      2. How long and with what success, compared to the rest of the class? With small children this might mean completing a few arithmetic problems or a drawing; with older ones, long homework assignments and term projects.
   B. *Participation*
      1. Can he concentrate and participate in total class activities and discussions? What role does he usually play?
   C. *Cooperation*
      1. Can he work cooperatively with a small group of students, with or without teacher supervision?
   D. *Individual Help*
      1. Is he frequently in need of individual instruction?
      2. Can it be done by a student teacher, and aide, an older or abler child?
      3. Can he use it as a base for subsequent independent work?

III. *Relationships with children and adults in the school setting*
   A. *Children*
      1. Does he have friends among his schoolmates, among problematic or steady children? If so, are the relationships fairly standard, or is there a measure of caretaking or undue domination involved?
      2. How do students in general respond to him? Is he casually accepted in work or social groupings, like any other child, or does his handicapped status lead the others to make special concessions or be especially tolerant? Is he actively rejected or isolated? Under what circumstances?
      3. Are there ways in which he is exploited or taken advan-

tage of by other students? Are there ways in which he exploits or takes advantage?

B. *Adults*
1. Is there some general response to teachers—hostile, dependent, respectful, fearful, eager to please at all times?
2. What reactions have been noted with specific teachers? Does he become increasingly dependent on a special class or on a certain resource teacher, or does he become more confident and independent? Does he work better with teachers who are warm and lean in a permissive direction or with those who are more rigorous in maintaining standards for performance and self-discipline?
3. To what extent does he depend on the teacher to control his behavior, protect him from other children, do his work, etc.?
4. Has he developed a relationship with any of the non-teaching staff: administrative, guidance, custodial, secretarial, etc.? How does it help or hinder his school adjustment and performance?

IV. *Current academic functioning*

A. *Reading*
1. How technically skillful is the child, compared to others in the class, in such things as attacking unfamiliar words, possessing a reasonably wide sight vocabulary, reading with speed and smoothness?
2. What is his level of reading comprehension? Where is it in relation to the class level and to his own technical reading ability?
3. Are there any recent standardized test scores in these areas?
4. Where in the academic day is reading required? If the child has a reading problem, in what subjects is it particularly handicapping? Are there alternate ways for him to get the material, such as someone reading to him, from films, or tapes?
5. Has he had any special reading instruction?

B. *Spelling*
1. What kind of spelling mistakes does the child make? Are they common ones such as doubled consonants (*accross* or *across*), vowel substitutions (*optomist* or *optimist*),

vowel reversals (*seize* or *sieze*)? Are they apparently idiosyncratic and unintelligible?
   2. Has the class, or the child individually, been taught any spelling rules (use of silent *e*, the *i* before *e* rule, etc.)? Has he ever had any special help with spelling?
   3. Can he ever find his own spelling mistakes?
   4. Does the class take regular spelling tests? Does he do better at such times, with a specific learned list, than in spontaneous writing?
   5. Does it make any difference if he's given time to think about each word, rather than having to hurry along (as in writing from dictation)? Does he attempt to think about how a word is spelled, or does he rush through in order to finish as fast as possible?
   6. Is he penalized for spelling errors in some subject areas?
C. *Handwriting*
   1. If the teacher is actively teaching handwriting, what is the child's response to the lessons, what progress has he made, and what difficulties does he have? If the teacher is not teaching him, does he get help from any other source?
   2. What factors characterize his poor writing—inability to remember the form of letters, inability to form them properly or legibly, difficulty in maintaining proper spacing between letters and between words, difficulty in adjusting to wide- or narrow-ruled paper, etc.?
   3. Does he hold the pencil properly and easily? Does he sit properly and comfortably when he writes? Is the paper usually positioned properly? Does he tire quickly when writing; that is, does the writing start out relatively good but then deteriorate or fade out?
   4. To what extent does the writing improve if he has very little to write and is actively trying to do well?
   5. Does he have trouble copying work from the blackboard? (This is often a result of reading and spelling problems, rather than writing difficulties, but it shows up when writing is required.)
   6. If the child is older or known to have serious motor coordination problems, has a typewriter ever been tried? With what results?
D. *Arithmetic*
   1. What is the class currently working on in arithmetic, and what is the child's relative standing?

2. Are there outstanding gaps in his arithmetic background, either in concepts, computation or both?
3. Can he read directions and problems and numerical and symbol notations (e.g., 35,076, +, =) at the class level?
4. Can he set up problems correctly on paper? Can he copy them correctly from the blackboard?
5. Is his computation generally accurate?
6. Does he know number facts by heart, as well and as many as the average class member? If not, can he figure out what he cannot remember, by such devices as using his fingers, or adding 12 + 12 when he cannot remember 6 × 4?
7. Can he solve word problems at the class level? If not, can he solve them at lower levels?

APPENDIX II

DESCRIPTIONS OF THE ITPA, THE DETROIT TESTS, AND THE FROSTIG DEVELOPMENTAL TEST OF VISUAL PERCEPTION

The ITPA

The Illinois Test of Psycholinguistic Abilities (1968) consists of twelve subtests, with norms for children aged 2-4 through 10-3. The subtests are listed below, though not in the order of presentation to the child, with a brief statement of the rationale and a description or examples of easy and difficult items for each. (For a fuller discussion and examples, see Kirk and Kirk, 1971; and Kirk, McCarthy, and Kirk, 1968.)

1. Auditory Reception—the ability to derive meaning from auditory symbols (in this case words).
    Description: The child is asked questions such as "Do dogs fly?" and "Do wingless birds soar?"
2. Visual Reception—the ability to derive meaning from visual symbols.
    Description: Each item consists of two cards presented to the child. The first bears one picture and the second four. From the second he must choose the one picture that represents another instance of the picture he saw on the first card. There is no visual matching involved; even on the simple items, such as a dog on the first card and a dog and three other objects on the second, it is not the same dog on the second card. More difficult items deal with abstract concepts such as wetness and leverage.
3. Auditory Association—the ability to relate concepts presented orally.
    Description: The child is asked to complete sentences like "Grass is green, sugar is_____." and "Houses have architects, books have_____."
4. Visual Association—the ability to relate concepts presented visually.

Description: For each item, the child is shown a card with one central figure and four peripheral figures from which he must choose the one that "goes with" the central figure.

5. Verbal Expression—the ability to express concepts verbally and vocally.
    Description: The child is shown a common object and asked, "Tell me all about this." He is scored according to the number of meaningful attributes he mentions, including name, color, size, shape, function, composition, and others. Items include a ball, a block, an envelope, and a button.
6. Manual Expression—the ability to express ideas manually.
    Description: The child is shown pictures of a telephone, a guitar, a knife and fork, a pencil sharpener, etc. In each case he is asked, "Show me what we do with a (telephone, guitar, etc.)."
7. Grammatic Closure—the ability to make use of the redundancies of oral language in acquiring automatic habits for handling syntax and grammatic inflections.
    Description: The child is shown pictures corresponding to a verbal statement which he must complete, such as:
    "Here is a dog. Here are two _____ (dogs)."
    "Here is a mouse. Here are two _____."
8. Visual Closure—the ability to identify a common object from an incomplete visual presentation.
    Description: There are four items. In each, the child is shown a picture of an object (e.g., fish), which he must then locate approximately 15 times in a complex drawing where the object appears in incomplete or partially hidden form.
9. Auditory Sequential Memory—the ability to reproduce sequences of auditory symbols from memory.
    Description: The child is presented digit sequences in ever-increasing lengths, similar to Digits Forward on the Wechsler Scales. However, here rote recall is aided because the digits are given more quickly, at half-second rather than full-second intervals.
10. Visual Sequential Memory—the ability to reproduce sequences of nonmeaningful figures from memory.
    Description: The child is shown a card illustrating a sequence of small tiles, each bearing a complex design. He is then given the corresponding tiles, and with the card removed, asked to reproduce the sequence. The figures are intentionally so complex that they do not lend themselves to label-

ing, thus preventing the child from developing an auditory sequence to remember, rather than recalling visual images.
11. Auditory Closure—the ability to identify a word from an incomplete oral presentation.
Description: The child must tell what word is intended when he hears the following: airpla—; —ngernail; cho—late; —ype—iter.
12. Sound Blending—the ability to integrate a sequence of syllables into a recognizable word.
Description: The child must integrate the sequence of syllables in, for example, f-oot and k-e-tch-u-p.

In addition to consisting of subtests tapping specific functions, the test is also constructed so as to highlight three *dimensions* of cognitive abilities.

Channels of Communication. These are the routes through which the content of communication flows, beginning with the sensory modality receiving the input (e.g., vision or hearing) and ending with the form of expression (e.g., motor or speech) in which the response is made. Although the combinations of receptors and expressors are numerous, the test focuses on two channels, the visual-motor and the auditory-vocal. (These two channels are of major importance in many learning skills, but it should be noted that they do not reflect the major route involved in reading, which is visual-vocal; nor one of the important channels for spelling, which is auditory-motor.) Because the test separately taps each part of the processing—reception, association, and expression—it is possible to note whether an entire channel is being affected or perhaps only a sensory or response mode. Among children with learning problems, the test frequently reveals a significant weakness in either the visual-motor channel or the auditory-vocal channel, indicated by the scores on tests 1, 3, and 5 being consistently lower or higher than those on 2, 4, and 6. The same weakness may have been reflected in clinical, rather than statistical, interpretation of the intelligence and academic test performances.

Psycholinguistic Processes. Here the authors are referring to the processess of reception, organization or association, and expression. In some children, difficulties can be located in one part of the sequence, irrespective of which sensory mode or expressive form is involved. This dimension of cognitive abilities is one that has been referred to in the psychoanalytic literature (Liss, 1955; Blanchard,

1946; Pearson, 1952). Inhibitions in the intake, assimilation, or expression of information are regarded as analogous to inhibitions in the digestive process, and they are interpreted as neurotic expression of fear and aggression. To suggest neurogenic determinants for process difficulties is not to gainsay psychodynamic determinants. On the contrary, it enriches the general diagnostic picture, adding greater possibilities for a sensitive and balanced assessment. The most common problem found in this dimension is one of expression, reflected in particularly low scores on tests 5 and 6, relative to other subtests. However, difficulties may also occur in the reception or organization processes.

Levels of Organization. Two levels are postulated in the test, the representational and the automatic. The representational level includes cognitive behavior requiring extensive mediating processes, the use and manipulation of symbols which carry meaning, and quite conscious judgment and reasoning. The automatic level includes communication behavior requiring highly organized and integrated patterns of reception and response, less conscious and voluntary than representational level cognition. The automatic level comprises such skills as rote memory, perceptual speed, auditory and visual closure, memory for visual and auditory sequence, visual and auditory retention. We operate at the automatic level as we go through the mechanics of driving a car or the mechanics of reading and writing, "without thinking" as it were, after we have completed the earlier stages of learning and mastered these skills by consciously thinking about them. Some research studies indicate that classic dyslexic cases do less well on automatic-level tasks of the ITPA (Kirk & Kirk, 1971).

In addition to the three dimensions discussed by the test authors, the clinician will also find ITPA scores useful for checking specific functions. For example, if visual processing is in general a weak area, it will be evident in a number of low scores on those tests depending on visual input: Visual Reception, Visual Association, Visual Sequential Memory, and Visual Closure. If auditory processing is suspect, one would look to the six tests which are based on auditory input: Auditory Reception, Auditory Association, Auditory Sequential Memory, Auditory Closure, Sound Blending, and Grammatic Closure.

The Detroit Tests of Learning Aptitude

The Detroit Tests consist of 19 separate tests which tap a variety of learning aptitudes. They were developed in 1935 for use in the

Detroit Public Schools, and are surprisingly in tune with today's perspective on learning disabilities (although the lack of a more recent standardization means results must be interpreted cautiously). Unlike the ITPA, which is a single test all of whose parts add up to an integrated profile, each of the 19 tests in the Detroit is quite independent of the others. The clinician chooses to administer only those tests he or she needs in each individual assessment. Each test has its own age range and mental age norms.

Below is a list of the 19 tests, with the age range for each (rounded off to the nearest year):

Pictorial Absurditites	3–10	Free Association	5–19
Verbal Absurdities	5–16	Memory for Designs	3–16
Pictorial Opposites	3–9	Auditory Attention	
Verbal Opposites	5–19	Span for Related	
Motor Speed	4–18	Syllables	3–19
Auditory Attention		Number Ability	3–11
Span for Unre-		Social Adjustment B	3–18
lated Words	3–19	Visual Attention Span	
Oral Commissions	3–8	for Letters	6–16
Social Adjustment A	3–13	Disarranged Pictures	5–17
Visual Attention Span		Oral Directions	6–19
for Objects	3–19	Likenesses and Dif-	
Orientation	3–13	ferences	7–19

The clinical child psychologist will note that many of the test names are analogous to Stanford-Binet items. Like Binet items, the Detroit tests may be used in the learning assessment to check specific aspects of intellectual functioning, when routine testing has raised questions or requires additional support or refutation. The authors of the Detroit Tests see each test as being related to one or more "specific mental faculties": reasoning and comprehension, practical judgment, verbal ability, time and space relationships, number ability, auditory attentive ability, visual attentive ability, and motor ability. (Baker and Leland, 1967). Although the eight mental faculties listed are neither a comprehensive list nor a set of same-order variables, the psychologist may find them useful as he attempts to conceptualize the cognitive strengths and weaknesses of the child. It will be noted that these categories are similar to Wechsler subtests and also to various groupings of primary mental abilities (e.g., Thurstone & Thurstone, 1962).

The Detroit Tests offer a number of practical conveniences. They are very conveniently packaged in two handbooks—one for the examiner and one containing pictorial material. They do not cost much, are easily and quickly administered for the most part, and are comprised of interesting and entertaining material. The Detroit is more of an omnibus, do-it-yourself test than is the ITPA, which is more closely structured and organized around a theoretical model of information processing. Both can be useful clinical tools in learning assessment, as the clinician learns to discriminate the conditions under which to apply them.

The Frostig Developmental Test of Visual Perception

The Frostig test consists of five subtests, each related to some aspect of visual processing. Frostig labels them as follows:

  I. Eye-Motor Coordination. The child draws a line to connect two figures or points, sometimes with guidelines and sometimes without.
 II. Figure-Ground. Against increasingly "noisy" and distracting backgrounds, the child must find and outline a given figure.
III. Form Constancy. The child must discriminate circles from ovoids, and squares from other four-sided figures.
 IV. Position in Space. The child must match identical pictures, maintaining a clear sense of directionality. The wrong choices involve identical forms in rotated or reversed orientations.
  V. Spatial Relations. The child is shown a straight-line figure drawn on a dotted grid. On an adjacent empty grid, he must reproduce the same figure.

Subtests I and V tap visual-motor integration, while II, III, and IV relate to various aspects of visual perception and discrimination. Where visual processing is suspect the test is very useful in sorting out which processes in particular are deficient, since the test provides norms and scaled scores for each of the five tests. For children who are deficient in many or all areas, the total test result, expressed as Perceptual Quotient (PQ), is a useful measure to compare with the child's IQ. Norms extend only through age 8, but the test is also useful for older children with severe visual processing difficulties. Another advantage of the Frostig test is the available remedial material that has been keyed to it (Frostig, Horne, &

Miller, 1972), and which provides remedial training in all five areas at three different levels of difficulty and complexity.

Users should be aware that (1) factor analyses indicate the five subtests do not measure independent skills; (2) there is yet no evidence that the test aids in differential diagnosis of *specific* reading disability; and (3) the standardization group did not include minority culture children (Chissom, 1972). This does not mean that clinicians will not find the tests useful for individual assessments when they want to look closely at the visual skills required in each subtest.

REFERENCES

Achenbach, T. M. The Children's Associative Responding Test: A possible alternative to group IQ tests. *Journal of Educational Psychology*, 1970, *61*, 340-348.

Achenbach, T. M. Stanford-Binet short-form performance of retarded and non-retarded persons matched for MA. *American Journal of Mental Deficiency*, 1971, *76*, 30-32.

Achenbach, T. M. *Developmental psychopathology*. New York: Ronald Press, 1974.

Ames, L. B. Learning disabilities: The developmental point of view. In H. R. Myklebust (Ed.), *Progress in learning disabilities* (Vol. 1). New York: Grune & Stratton, 1968.

Anastasi, A. *Psychological testing*. (3rd ed.). New York: Macmillan, 1968.

Baker, H., & Leland, B. *Detroit Tests of Learning Aptitude*. Indianapolis, Ind.: Bobbs-Merrill, 1967.

Bakwin, H. Reading disability in twins. *Developmental Medicine and Child Neurology*, 1973, *15*(2), 184-187.

Bannatyne, A. *Language, reading and learning disabilities*. Springfield, Ill.: C. C. Thomas, 1971.

Beem, H. L., Van Egeren, L. F., Straissfuth, A. P., Nymen, B. A., & Leckie, M. S. Social class differences in maternal teaching strategies and speech patterns. *Developmental Psychology*, 1969, *1*, 726-734.

Beery-Buktenica Developmental Test of Visual-Motor Integration. Chicago: Follett, 1967.

Bell, E. F., & Vogel, N. W. The emotionally disturbed child as the family scapegoat. In E. F. Bell & N. W. Vogel, *A modern introduction to the family*. Glencoe, Ill.: Free Press, 1960.

Bender, L. A visual motor Gestalt test and its clinical use. The American Orthopsychiatric Association, Research Monograph no. 3, 1958.

Bender, L. Childhood schizophrenia. *Psychiatric Quarterly*, 1953, *27*, 663-681.

Bender, L. Problems in conceptualization and communication in children with developmental alexia. In P. M. Hoch & J. Zubin. *Psychopathology of communication*. New York: Grune & Stratton, 1958.

Bender, L. Specific reading disability as a maturational lag. *Bulletin of the Orton Society,* 1963, *13,* 25–44.

Bernstein, B. Social structure, language and learning. *Educational Research,* 1961, *3,* 163–176.

Birch, H. G., & Gussow, J. D. *Disadvantaged children: Health, nutrition and school failure.* New York: Grune & Stratton, 1970.

Blanchard, P. Psychoanalytic contributions to the problems of reading disabilities. *Psychoanalytic Study of the Child,* 1946, *2,* 163–187.

Boder, E. Developmental dyslexia: Prevailing diagnostic concepts and a new diagnostic approach. In H. R. Myklebust (Ed.), *Progress in learning disabilities* (Vol. 2). New York: Grune & Stratton, 1971.

Brodie, R. D., & Winterbottom, M. R. Failure in elementary school boys as a function of traumata, secrecy and derogation. *Child Development,* 1967, *38,* 701–711.

Bruner, J. S. *The process of education.* Cambridge, Mass.: Harvard University Press, 1960

Bryan, T. H., & Bryan, J. H. *Understanding learning disabilities.* Port Washington, N. Y.: Alfred Publishing, 1975.

Butcher, H. J. *Human intelligence: Its nature and assessment.* London: Methuen & Co., 1968.

Buxbaum, E. The parents' role in the etiology of learning disabilities. *Psychoanalytic Study of the Child,* 1964, *19,* 421–447.

Cancro, R. (Ed.). *Intelligence: Genetic and environmental influences.* New York: Grune & Stratton, 1971.

Carroll, J. B. Review of the Illinois Test of Psycholinguistic Abilities. In O. K. Buros (Ed.), *The seventh mental measurements yearbook* (Vol. 2). Highland Park, N.J.: Gryphon Press, 1972.

Cassler, L. Perceptual deprivation in institutional settings. In G. Newton & S. LeVine (Eds.), *Early experience and behavior.* Springfield, Ill.: C. C. Thomas, 1968.

Cattell, R. B. *Personality.* New York: McGraw Hill, 1950.

Cazden, C. B. Problems for education: Language as curriculum, content and learning environment. *Daedalus,* 1973, *102,* 135–148.

Chalfant, J. C., & Scheffelin, M. A. *Central processing dysfunc-*

tions in children: A review of research. Washington, D.C.: National Institute of Neurological Diseases and Stroke, 1969.

Chassagny, C. *Manual pour la rééducation de la lecture et de l'orthographie* (3rd ed.). Paris: Editions Neret, 1966.

Chissom, B. S. Review of Frostig Developmental Test of Visual Perception. In O. K. Buros (Ed.), *The seventh mental measurements yearbook* (Vol. 2). Highland Park, N.J.: Gryphon Press, 1972.

Chomsky, N. *Reflections on language.* New York: Pantheon Books, 1975.

Clark, K. B. The cult of cultural deprivation: A complex social phenomenon. In H. A. Solan (Ed.), *The psychology of learning and reading difficulties.* New York: Simon & Schuster, 1973.

Clements, S. D. *Minimal brain dysfunction in children.* (National Institute for Neurological Diseases and Stroke Monograph No. 3, U.S. Public Health Service Publication No. 1415). Washington, D. C.: U.S. Government Printing Office, 1966.

Cohen, J. The factorial structure of the Wechsler Adult Intelligence Scale between early adulthood and old age. *Journal of Consulting Psychology,* 1957, *21,* 283-290.

Cohen, J. The factorial structure of the Wechsler Intelligence Scale for children at ages 7½, 10½, 13½. *Journal of Consulting Psychology,* 1959, *23,* 285-299.

Cohen, H., & Weil, G. R. *Tasks of Emotional Development Test.* Lexington, Mass.: D. C. Heath, 1971.

Columbia Mental Maturity Scales (3rd Ed.). New York: Psychological Corp., 1972.

Connors, C. K. Drugs in the management of children with learning disabilities. In L. Tarnopol (Ed.), *Learning disorders in children: Diagnosis, medication and education.* Boston: Little, Brown, 1971.

Covington, M. V. Stimulus deprivation as a function of social class membership. *Child Development,* 1967, *38,* 607-613.

Crosby, R. M. *The waysiders.* New York: Delacorte Press, 1968.

deHirsch, K. The concept of plasticity and language disabilities. *British Journal of Disorders of Communication,* 1965, *8,* (1).

deHirsch, K., Jansky, J. J., & Langford, W. *Predicting reading failure.* New York: Harper & Row, 1966.

Denckla, M. B. Research needs in learning disabilities. *Journal of Learning Disabilities*, 1973, 43–49.

Denhoff, E., & Tarnopol, L. Medical responsibilities in learning disorders. In L. Tarnopol (Ed.), *Learning disorders in children: Diagnosis, medication and education.* Boston: Little, Brown, 1971.

Detroit Tests of Learning Aptitude. Indianapolis: Bobbs-Merrill, 1967.

Deutsch, C. Environment and perception. In M. Deutsch, I. Katz, & A. Jensen (Eds.), *Social class, race and psychological development.* New York: Holt, Rinehart & Winston, 1968.

Deutsch, M. *The disadvantaged child.* New York: Basic Books, 1967.

Douvan, E. Social status and success striving. *Journal of Abnormal & Social Psychology*, 1956, 54, 219–223.

Dunn, L. M. *Expanded manual, Peabody Picture Vocabulary Test.* Minneapolis: American Guidance Services, 1965.

Dykman, R. A., Ackerman, P. T., Clements, S. D., & Peters, J. E. Specific learning disabilities: An attentional deficit syndrome. In H. R. Myklebust, *Progress in learning disabilities* (Vol. 2). New York: Grune & Stratton, 1971.

Eisenberg, L. School phobia: A study in the communication of anxiety. *American Journal of Psychiatry*, 1958, 114, 712–718.

Eisenberg, L., Berlin, C. I., Dill, A., & Frank, S. Class and race effect on the intelligibility of monosyllables. *Child Development*, 1968, 39, 1077–1089.

Ekstein, R., & Motto, L. (Eds.). *From learning for love to love of learning: Essays on psychoanalysis and education.* New York: Bruner/Mazel, 1969.

Elashoff, J. D., & Snow, R. E. *A case study in statistical inference: Reconsideration of the Rosenthal-Jacobson data on teacher expectancy.* Stanford, Calif.: Stanford Center for Research and Development in Teaching, 1970.

Erikson, E. H. *Childhood and society* (2nd ed.). New York: Norton, 1963.

Friedman, R. Structured family interviewing in school disorders assessment. In R. Friedman (Ed.), *Family roots of school learning and behavior disorders.* Springfield, Ill.: C. C. Thomas, 1973.

Frostig, M., Horne, D., & Miller, A. *Pictures and patterns.* (rev. ed.). Chicago: Follett Educational Corporation, 1972.

Frostig, M., Lefever, D. W., & Whittlesey, J. R. B. *The Marianne Frostig Developmental Test of Visual Perception.* Palo Alto, Calif.: Consulting Psychologists Press, 1964.

Frostig, M., & Maslow, P. *Learning problems in the classroom.* New York: Grune & Stratton, 1973.

Gardner, H. *The shattered mind.* New York: Knopf, 1975.

Geschwind, N. Disorders of cortical function in children. *Clinical Proceedings of Children's Hospital National Medical Center*, 1972, *28*, 262-272.

Glasser, A., & Zimmerman, I. *Clinical interpretation of the Weschler Intelligence Scale for Children.* New York: Grune & Stratton, 1967.

Goldman-Fristoe-Woodcock Test of Auditory Discrimination. Circle Pines, Minn.: American Guidance Service, 1970.

Gordon, E. W. Problems in the determination of educability in populations with differential characteristics. In J. Hellmuth (Ed.), *Disadvantaged child* (Vol. 3). New York: Bruner/Mazel, 1970.

Gray Oral Reading Tests. Indianapolis: Bobbs-Merrill, 1967.

Green, O. C., & Perlman, S. M. Endocrinology and disorders of learning. In H. R. Myklebust (Ed.), *Progress in learning disabilities* (Vol. 2). New York: Grune & Stratton, 1971.

Grossman, H. J. (Ed.). *Manual on terminology and classification in mental retardation* (3d ed.). American Association on Mental Deficiency, Special Publication Series, No. 2, 1973.

Grunebaum, M. G., Hurwitz, I., Prentice, N. M., & Sperry, B. M. Fathers of sons with primary neurotic learning inhibitions. *American Journal of Orthopsychiatry*, 1962, *32*, 462-472.

Gunzberg, H. C. Mental deficiencies. In B. Wolman, *Manual of child psychopathology.* New York: McGraw-Hill, 1972.

Haggard, E. A. Social status and intelligence. *Genetic Psychology Monograph*, 1954, *49*, 141-186.

Harris, I. *Emotional blocks to learning.* Glencoe, Ill.: Free Press, 1961.

Heber, R. *A manual on terminology and classification in mental retardation* (2d ed.). American Journal of Mental Deficiency, Monograph Supplement, 1961.

Hellmuth, J. (Ed.). *Disadvantaged child* (Vol. 3). New York: Bruner/Mazel, 1970.

Hinshelwood, J. *Congenital word-blindness.* London: H. K. Lewis, 1917.

Hobbs, N. (Ed.). *Issues in the classification of children.* San Francisco: Jossey-Bass, 1975.

Holt, J. *How children fail.* New York: Pitman Publishing Corp., 1964.

Hunt, N. *The world of Nigel Hunt.* New York: Garrett, 1967.

Jansky, J., & deHirsch, K. *Preventing reading failure.* New York: Harper & Row, 1972.

Jensen, A. R. How much can we boost IQ and scholastic achievement? *Harvard Educational Review*, 1969, 39, (1).

Johnson, D. J., & Myklebust, H. R. *Learning disabilities: Educational principles and practices.* New York: Grune & Stratton, 1967.

Kaufman, A. S. Factor analysis of the WISC-R at 11 age levels between 6½ and 16½ years. *Journal of Consulting and Clinical Psychology*, 1975, 43, 135-147.

Kawi, A. A., & Pasamanick, B. Association of factors of pregnancy with reading disorders in childhood. *Journal of American Medical Association*, 1958, 166, 1420-1423.

Kazdin, A. E., & Bootzin, R. R. The token economy: An evaluative review. *Journal of Applied Behavior Analysis*, 1972, 5, 343-372.

Kessler, J. W. *Psychopathology of childhood.* Englewood Cliffs, N.J.: Prentice Hall, 1966.

Kessler, J. W. A problem of absorption. *APA Monitor*, 1977, 8(3), p. 2.

KeyMath Diagnostic Arithmetic Test. Circle Pines, Minn.: American Guidance Service, 1971

Kirk, S. A. *Educating exceptional children.* Boston: Houghton Mifflin, 1962

Kirk, S. A., & Kirk, W. D. *Psycholinguistic learning disabilities: Diagnosis and remediation.* Urbana: University of Illinois Press, 1971.

Kirk, S. A., McCarthy, J. J., & Kirk, W. D. *The Illinois Test of Psycholinguistic Abilities* (rev. ed.). Urbana: University of Illinois Press, 1968.

Knobloch, H., & Pasamanick, B. (Eds). *Gesell and Amatruda's Developmental Diagnosis* (3d ed.). Hagerstown, Md.: Harper & Row, 1974.

Koppitz, E. M. *The Bender Gestalt Test for young children.* New York: Grune & Stratton, 1964.

Lawson, L. J. Ophthalmological factors in learning disabilities. In H. R. Myklebust (Ed.), *Progress in learning disabilities* (Vol. 1). New York: Grune & Stratton, 1968.

Leiter International Performance Scale. Chicago: Stoelting Co.

Lerner, J. W. *Children with learning disabilities.* Boston: Houghton Mifflin, 1971.

Liss, E. Motivations in learning. *Psychoanalytic Study of the Child*, 1955, *10*, 100-116.

Littell, W. The Wechsler Intelligence Scale of Children: Review of a decade of research. *Psychological Bulletin*, 1960, *57*, 132-156.

Malone, C. A. The psychosocial characteristics of children from a developmental viewpoint. In E. Pavenstadt (Ed.), *The drifters.* Boston: Little, Brown, 1967.

Mattick, I., & Murphy, L. B. Cognitive disturbance in young children. In S. G. Sapir & A. C. Nitzburg (Eds.), *Children with learning problems.* New York: Bruner/Mazel, 1973.

Mattis, S., French, J. H., & Rapin, I. Dyslexia in children and young adults: Three independent neuropsychological syndromes. *Developmental Medicine and Child Neurology*, 1975, *17* (2), 150-163.

McCarthy Scales of Children's Abilities. New York: Psychological Corp.

McGlannan, F. Familial characteristics of genetic dyslexia: Preliminary report from a pilot study. *Journal of Learning Disabilities*, 1968, *1*, 185-191.

Mercer, J. R., & Lewis, J. F. *System of Multicultural Pluralistic Assessment (SOMPA).* New York: Psychological Corporation, 1977.

Money, J. Two cytogenic syndromes—psychologic comparisons: I. Intelligence and specific factor quotients. *Journal of Psychiatric Research*, 1964, *2*, 223-231.

Morgan, W. P. A case of congenital word-blindness. *British Medical Journal*, 1896, *2*, p. 1378.

Myers, P. I., & Hammill, D. D. *Methods for learning disorders* (2d ed.). New York: Wiley, 1976.

Myklebust, H. R. *Auditory disorders in children: A manual for differential diagnosis.* New York: Grune & Stratton, 1954.

Myklebust, H. R. Learning disabilities: Definition and overview. In H. R. Myklebust (Ed.), *Progress in learning disabilities*. New York: Grune & Stratton, 1968.

O'Leary, K. D., & Drabman, R. Token reinforcement programs in the classroom: A review. *Psychological Bulletin*, 1971, *75*, 379–398.

Ong, B. The pediatrician's role in learning disabilities. In H. R. Myklebust (Ed.), *Progress in learning disabilities* (Vol. 1). New York: Grune & Stratton, 1968.

Orton, S. T. Word blindness in school children. *Archives of Neurology and Psychiatry*, 1925, *14*, 581–615.

Orton, S. T. *Reading, writing and speech problems in children.* New York: W. W. Norton, 1937.

Orton, S. T. Specific reading disability, strephosymbolia. *Journal of the American Medical Association*, 1928, *90*, 1095–1099.

Osgood, C. E. A behavioristic analysis of perception and language as cognitive phenomena. In J. S. Bruner (Ed.) *Contemporary approaches to cognition.* Cambridge, Mass.: Harvard University Press, 1957.

Pavenstedt, E. (Ed.). *The drifters.* Boston: Little, Brown, 1967.

Pearson, G. *Psychoanalysis and the education of the child.* New York: Norton, 1954.

Peller, L. The school's role in promoting sublimation. *Psychoanalytic study of the child*, 1956, *11*, 437–449.

Piaget, J. *Psychology of intelligence.* Patterson, N.J.: Littlefield, Adams & Co., 1960. (Originally published, 1947.)

Quay, L. C. Language dialect, reinforcement, and the intelligence test performance of Negro children. *Child Development*, 1971, *42*, 5–15.

Rabinovitch, R. D. Reading problems in children: Definitions and classification. In A. Keeney & V. Keeney (Eds.), *Dyslexia*. St. Louis: Mosby, 1968.

Riessman, F. *The culturally deprived child*. New York: Harper & Row, 1962.

Rosenthal, R., & Jacobson, L. *Pygmalion in the classroom: Teacher expectation and pupils' intellectual development*. New York: Holt, Rinehart & Winston, 1968.

Sanders, B., Zigler, E., & Butterfield, E. Outer directedness in the discrimination learning of normal and mentally retarded children. *Journal of Abnormal Psychology*, 1968, *73*, 368–375.

Sanders, M. *Two motivational patterns of high school achievement: Intellectual involvement and behavioral compliance*. Unpublished doctoral dissertation, Harvard University, 1964.

Seashore, H. Difference between verbal and performance IQs on the Wechsler Intelligence Scale for Children. *Journal of Consulting Psychology*, 1951, *15*, 62–67.

Shaffer, J. A specific cognitive deficit observed in gonadal aplasia (Turner's syndrome). *Journal of Clinical Psychology*, 1962, *18*, 403–406.

Silver, A., & Hagin, R. Maturation of perceptual functions in children with specific reading disabilities. *The Reading Teacher*, 1966, *19*, 253–259.

Spache Diagnostic Reading Scales. Monterey, Calif: CTB/McGraw Hill, 1972.

Sperry, B. M., Staver, N., Reiner, B. C., & Ulrich, D. N. Renunciation and denial in learning difficulties. *American Journal of Orthopsychiatry*, 1958(a), *28*, 98–111.

Sperry, B. M., Ulrich, D. N., & Staver, N. The relation of motility to boys' learning problems. *American Journal of Orthopsychiatry*, 1958(b), *28*, 640–646.

Sperry, R. W. Left-brain, right-brain. *Saturday Review*, August 9, 1975, pp. 30–33.

Stedman's Medical Dictionary (22d ed.). Baltimore: Williams & Wilkins, 1972.

Stein, M. E. *The thematic apperception test: An introductory manual for its clinical use with adults* (rev. ed.). Cambridge, Mass.: Addison-Wesley, 1955.

Strauss, A. A., & Lehtinen, L. L. *Psychopathology and education of the brain-injured child.* New York: Grune & Stratton, 1947.

Strickler, E. Family interaction factors in psychogenic learning disturbance. *Journal of Learning Disabilities,* 1969, *2,* 146–154.

Thurstone, L. & Thurstone, T. *Primary Mental Abilities Test* (rev. ed.). Chicago: Science Research Associates, 1962.

Torrey, J. W. Illiteracy in the ghetto. *Harvard Educational Review,* 1970, *40,* 253–259.

Turnure, J. E., & Zigler, E. Outer-directedness in the problem-solving of normal and retarded children. *Journal of Abnormal and Social Psychology,* 1964, *69,* 427–436.

Tyler, L. E. (Ed.). *Intelligence: Some recurring issues.* New York: Van Nostrand Reinhold, 1969.

Wallbrown, F. H., Blaha, J., Counts, D. H., & Wallbrown, J. D. The hierarchical factor structures of the WISC and revised ITPA for reading disabled children. *Journal of Psychology,* 1974, *88,* 65–76.

Wechsler, D. Cognitive, conative, and non-intellective intelligence. *American Psychologist,* 1950, *5,* 78–83.

Wechsler, D. Intelligence defined and undefined. *American Psychologist,* 1975, *30,* 135–139.

Wepman Auditory Discrimination Test. Chicago: Language Research Associates, 1958.

Wepman, J. Neurological approaches to mental retardation. In R. L. Schiefelbush, R. H. Copeland, & J. O. Smith (Eds.), *Language and mental retardation.* New York: Holt, Rinehart & Winston, 1967.

Wepman, J., Cruickshank, W. M., Deutsch, C. P., Morency, A., & Strother, C. R. Learning disabilities. In N. Hobbs (Ed.), *Issues in the classification of children* (Vol. 1). San Francisco: Jossey-Bass, 1975.

White, R. W. Motivation reconsidered: The concept of competence. *Psychological Review,* 1959, *66,* 297–333.

Whiteman, M., & Deutsch, M. Social disadvantage as related to intellective and language development. In M. Deutsch, I. Katz, & A. Jensen. *Social class, race and psychological development.* New York: Holt, Rinehart & Winston, 1968.

Winick, M., Rosso, P., & Waterlow, J. Cellular growth of cerebrum, cerebellum and brain stem in normal and marasmic children. *Experimental Neurology*, 1970, *26*, 393-400.

Winterbottom, M. R. The relation of need for achievement to learning experiences in independence and mastery. In J. W. Atkinson (Ed.), *Motives in fantasy, action and society*. Princeton, N.J.: Van Nostrand, 1958.

Zigler, E. Mental retardation: Current issues and approaches. In L. W. Hoffman & M. E. Hoffman (Eds.), *Review of child development research* (Vol. 2). New York: Russell Sage Foundation, 1966.

Zigler, E. The retarded child as a whole person. In H. E. Adams & W. K. Boardman (Eds.), *Advances in experimental clinical psychology*. New York: Pergamon Press, 1971.

Zigler, E., Abelson, W. D., & Seitz, V. Motivational factors in the performance of economically disadvantaged children on the Peabody Picture Vocabulary Test. *Child Development*, 1973, *44*, 294-303.

Index

Academic functioning:
   parent interviews, 124–126
   teacher interviews, 135–138
Academic skills tests, 168–174
Achievement:
   orientation, 86
   testing, 169–173
Adolescence, 67–69
Adults, 200–207, 225
Age:
   relative to assessment and remediation, 224–225
   relative to learning problems, 199
Aggression, 76–81, 99–100
   IQ and, 73, 78
   learning process and, 76–77
   subject matter and, 76, 77
   the teacher and, 76–78
Aphasia, 40
Arithmetic, 32, 42, 44–45, 229
   case examples, 215–219, 243–246
   subtest, WISC–R, 150, 153–154
   teacher interviews, 137–138
   tests, 172–173
Articulation, 39
Assessment (see also Clinical assessment, interviews; Clinical assessment, testing):
   use of the term, 8–9
Attentional-deficit syndrome, 28
Auditory processes, 36–38
   discrimination, 37
   memory, 37–38
   on WISC–R subtests, 156–157
   perception, 36–37
   sequence, 38
   test, 167
Authority of teachers, 72–73
Automatic-level functioning, 29–30, 31–32, 39, 44
   in case materials, 194, 199, 206, 216–217
   on WISC–R, 149, 158, 163
   vs. representational-level functioning, 232–235

Beery-Buktenica Developmental Test of Visual-Motor Integration (VMI), 165, 166
Behavior modification, 6, 217, 225–230
Bender Visual Motor Gestalt Test, 165–166
Binet, Alfred, 3, 4
Biological determinants, 17–50
   congenital contributions, 17, 27
   constitutional contributions, 17, 27–31
   four categories of, 17
   hereditary contributions, 17, 18
   innate contributions, 17
   maturational lag, 48–50
   mental retardation, 19–22
      cultural-familial group, 19–21
      IQ, 19–20
      outer-directed aspect of, 21–22
      pathological group, 19
Birth order, 95–99
   only child, 95–96
   sibling pairs, 96–99
   youngest child, 95–96
Block design subtest, WISC–R, 160–162
Brain, the, 17
   function of, 28
   injury (damage) to, 17, 22, 23
   minimal brain dysfunction syndrome (MBD), 24–25, 46

Case illustrations, 188–219
Cathecting school, 55–58

Index 287

Childhood and Society (Erikson), 8
Chromosomes:
  anomalies, 17, 20
  sex-determining, 27
  X, 27
Clinical assessment, interviews, 118–139
  parents, 121–130
    academic functioning, 124–126
    aspirations, 128–129
    developmental history, 124
    family interaction, 127–128
    health, 123–124
    heredity, 123–124
    hopes, 128–129
    medical background, 123–124
    play activities, 128
    projections, 128–129
    referral, 121–123
    remedial program and, 129–130
    scholastic strengths and weaknesses, 124–126
    school history, 126–127
    social activities, 128
  teachers, 130–139
    ability to work in groupings, 134
    academic functioning, 135–138
    children and adult relationships, 134–135
    home-school relationships, 139
    lesson periods, 133
    nonlesson periods, 133
    school behavior, 133–135
    school history, 132–133
Clinical assessment, testing, 142–185
  academic skills, basic, 168–174
  copying tests, 164–166
  expressive language skills, 166–168
  intellectual, 143–144
  learning disability, 174–178
  personality, 178–180
  referral, 180–185
  WISC-R, 143–164
    individual subtests, 152–164
    subtest clustering, 145–152

Coding subtest, WISC-R, 149–150, 163–164
Cole Animal Test, 179–180
Columbia Mental Maturity Scales, 143
Competition, 70–71
Comprehension subtest, WISC-R, 152–153
Conceptual development, intellective differential characteristics, 105–107
Congenital contributions, 17, 27
Constitutional contributions, 17, 27–31
Coordination of motor processes, 41–42
Copying tests, 164–166
Culture, the, 99–112
  attitude about school and education, 99–103
  conceptual development, 105–107
  differences among children starting school, 103
  the family and, 19–21, 99–112
  intellective differential characteristics, 103–107
    conceptual development, 105–107
    language, 103–105
    perceptual development, 105–107
  nonintellective differential characteristics, 107–112
    motivation, 111–112
    practice, 107–108
    rapport, 108–110
  perceptual development, 105–107
Curriculum, 113–115

Detroit Tests of Learning Aptitudes, 175, 178
  description of, 271–273
Developmental history, parent interviews on, 124
Digit span subtest, WISC-R, 157–158
Directionality, 42
Disadvantaged (*see* Subcultural groups)

288 Index

Discrimination:
  auditory, 37
  right-left, 32
  visual, 34
Down's syndrome, 17, 20
Drugs, 17, 183–184
Dyscalculia, 23 (see also Arithmetic)
Dysgraphia, 23, 42–43, 173–174
Dyslexia, 22–23, 27, 31
"Dyslexia in Children and Young Adults: Three Independent Neuropsychological Syndromes" (Mattis, French, and Rapin), 30

Ego, weak controls of, 58–61
Elaborated language, 104
Electroencephalogram (EEG), 183
Encephalitis, 17, 27
Environment, heredity and, 18
Epiloia, 19
Extension testing, 151–152
Eye-hand coordination, 32

Family, the, 85–99
  attitudes about school and education, 99–103
  the culture and, 19–21, 99–112
  father-child relationships, 90–92
  interactions, 92–95
    parent interviews, 127–128
  mother-child relationships, 85–90
  Oedipal rivalry, 88–92
  only child, 95–96
  sibling pairs, 96–99
  splitting tendency, 98
  youngest child, 95–96
Father-child relationships, 90–92
Foreign language learning, 48, 138
Formulation aphasia, 40
Frostig Developmental Test of Visual Perception, 32, 175
  description of, 273–274

German measles, 17
Goldman-Fristoe-Woodcock Test, 167
Gray Oral Reading Tests, 171

Handwriting, 42–43, 45 (see also Writing)

teacher interviews, 136–137
tests, 173–174
Harlem Youth Opportunities Unlimited (HARYOU), 115
Heredity:
  as a biological determinant, 17, 18
  environment and, 18
  parent interviews, 123–124
Hyperkinetic syndrome, 25

Illinois Test of Psycholinguistic Abilities (ITPA), 147, 148, 175–177, 183
  description of, 268–271
Independence, 86–87
  teacher-student relationship in remediation, 249–250
Information processing, 28–29, 150 (see also Automatic-level functioning)
  memory and speed in, 44
Information subtest, WISC-R, 152
Inhibition in learning, 70, 71, 76, 81
  of production, 91
Innate contributions as biological determinants, 17
Innovation, teacher-student relationship in remediation, 251–252
Intellective differential characteristics, 103–107
  conceptual development, 105–107
  language, 103–105
  perceptual development, 105–107
Intellectual assessment, 143–144
Intelligence, definition of, 18
Intermodal integration, 43–45
Interpersonal orientations, 71–76
Interviews, clinical assessment (see Clinical assessment, interviews)
IQ, 107–108, 143–149, 161, 177
  aggression and, 73, 78
  mental retardates, 19–20
Irradiation, 17

KeyMath Diagnostic Arithmetic Test, 172–173

Kibbutzim, 9-10, 88-90
Klinefelter's syndrome, 20, 27

Language:
  association, 146-147
  elaborated, 104
  expressive, 146-147, 166-168, 212
  intellective differential characteristics, 103-105
  problems requiring referral, 182-183
  receptive, 146-147, 211, 212-213
  restricted, 104
  subcultural groups, 103-105
Language processes, 38-41
  articulation, 39
  speech fluency, 39-40
  vocabulary, 40-41
Learning disabilities, 4-6, 8, 10-13, 18, 22-48, 67
  as a continuum, 46-47
  as deficits in degree, 47-48
  biological determinants of, 27
  definition of, 25-26
  relationship to other handicapping conditions, 45-46
  schematic history of, 22-25
  testing, 174-178
  use of term, 4-5
Leiter test, 143
Look-say words, 34

Malnutrition, 17, 20
Maternal illness, 17
Maternal malnutrition, 17
Maturational lag, 48-50
Memory:
  auditory, 37-38
  visual, 34-35, 174
Meningitis, 17, 27
Mental retardation, 19-22
  cultural-familial group, 19-21
  IQ, 19-20
  outer-directed aspect of, 21-22
  pathological group, 19
Microcephaly, 20
Minimal brain dysfunction syndrome (MBD), 24-25, 46
Minorities (*see* Subcultural groups)
Mongolism (*see* Down's syndrome)
Mother-child relationships, 85-90

Motivation, culture and, 111-112
Motor processes, 41-43
  coordination, 41-42, 174
  -spatial organization, 42-43
  -temporal organization, 43
Mutations, 17, 19, 20

National Institute of Neurological Diseases and Blindness, 24
Neurological inefficiency, 26, 46-47
Neurology, 183-185
Neuropsychological functions, 31-45
Nonintellective differential characteristics, 107-112
  motivation, 111-112
  practice, 107-108
  rapport, 108-110
Numbers, writing, 36

Object assembly subtest, WISC-R, 162-163
Oedipal rivalry, 88-92
Orientation:
  achievement, 86
  interpersonal, 71-76
  organization, 45
  spatial, 32-33
  task, 71-76
  time, 45
Overprotection, 86-87
Oxygen, blockage of, 17

Parents:
  interviews, 121-130
    academic functioning, 124-126
    aspirations, 128-129
    developmental history, 124
    family interaction, 127-128
    health, 123-124
    heredity, 123-124
    hopes, 128-129
    medical background, 123-124
    play activities, 128
    projections, 128-129
    referral, 121-123
    remedial programs, 129-130
    scholastic strengths and weaknesses, 124-126
    school history, 126-127
    social activities, 128

remediation
  involvement, 257-260
  reporting to, 252-254
Peabody Picture Vocabulary Test, 107-108
Perception, 22
  auditory, 36-37
  intellective differential characteristics, 105-107
  visual, 32-34
Personality testing, 178-180
Personalization of content, 58, 59-61, 157
Phenylketonuria (PKU), 17, 20
Physical education, teacher interviews on, 138
Physical handicap, effect on learning, 87-90
Picture arrangement subtest, WISC-R, 159-160
Picture completion subtest, WISC-R, 158-159
Play, parent interviews on, 128
Poison ingestion, 17, 20, 27
Psychological determinants, 52-81
  aggression, 76-81
    IQ and, 73, 78
    learning process and, 76-77
    subject matter and, 76, 77
    the teacher and, 76-78
  disturbances, 53-71
    intimately connected with basic issues, 69-71
    preventing cathecting school, 55-58
    related to specific aspects of school, 61-69
    weak ego controls, 58-61
  four categories of, 53
  interpersonal orientations, 71-76
  task orientations, 71-76

Rapport, culture and, 108-110
Reading:
  and maternal complications, 27
  comprehension, 207, 211-213, 235-236, 241-243
  examples of decoding problems, 33-34, 35-36, 63-64, 132, 191, 192, 194, 228, 237-238
  teacher interviews, 136
  tests, 170-171
Referral:
  clinical assessment testing, 180-185
  parent interviews on, 121-123
Remediation, 50, 222-262
  automatic versus representational information, 232-235
  basic issues, 223-235
  behavior modification principles, 225-230
  clinical issues in, 252-261
    adult patients, reporting to, 255
    children, reporting to, 255
    involvement of parents in, 257-260
    monitoring programs, 260-261
    parents, reporting to, 252-254
    varieties of programming, 255-257
  goals of, 223-225
  parent interviews, 129-130
  problems in, 223-225
  samples and approaches, 235-248
  teacher-student relationships, 248-252
    independence, 249-250
    innovation, 251-252
    reality-based support, 248-249
    structure, 250-251
  teaching to strengths versus weaknesses, 231-232
  two important dualities in, 230-235
Representational-level functioning, 29-30, 232-235
Restricted language, 104
Rhyming, 36, 228, 229
Right-left discrimination, 32
Rote memory, 41, 153, 154, 158
  (see also Memory)

Scapegoating, 94
School, the, 112-116
  behavior, teacher interviews and, 133-135

cathecting, 55-58
curriculum, 113-115
family attitudes about, 99-103
-home relationships, 139
intimately connected with basic issues, 69-71
specific aspects of, 61-69
teacher-pupil interaction, 115-116
School history:
parent interviews, 126-127
teacher interviews, 132-133
School phobia, 69
Sequence:
auditory, 38
visual, 35-36
Sex-determining chromosomes, 27
Sex of child, and learning, 95-99
only child, 95-96
sibling pairs, 96-99
youngest child, 95-96
Sibling pairs, 96-99
Sight-word vocabulary, 34
Similarities subtest, WISC-R, 154-155
Social activities, parent interviews on, 128
Social determinants, 84-116
the culture, 99-112
attitude about school and education, 99-103
conceptual development, 105-107
differences among children starting school, 103
intellectual differential characteristics, 103-107
language, 103-105
nonintellective differential characteristics, 107-112
perceptual development, 105-107
the family, 85-99
father-child relationships, 90-92
interactions, 92-95
mother-child relationships, 85-90
only child, 95-96
sibling pairs, 96-99
splitting tendency, 98
youngest child 95-96
the school, 112-116
curriculum, 113-115
teacher-pupil interaction, 115-116
Spache Diagnostic Reading Scales, 171
Spatial organization in motor processes, 42-43
Spatial orientation, 32-33
Speech fluency, 39-40
Spelling, 35, 36, 38, 43, 45, 201-203, 205-206, 233-235
teacher interviews, 136
test, 172
Splitting tendency, 98
Stanford-Binet test, 3, 143, 144
Strauss syndrome, 22
Subcultural groups, 6-7, 99-112, 144
attitude about school and education, 99-103
conceptual development, 105-107
differences among children starting school, 103
intellectual differential characteristics, 103-107
language, 103-105
motivation, 111-112
nonintellective differential characteristics, 107-112
perceptual development, 105-107
practice, 107-108
rapport, 108-110
Subject matter, aggression and, 76, 77
Subtests:
clustering, 145-152
individual, 152-164
Success, fear of, 70-71
Syntactical aphasia, 40
System of Multicultural Pluralistic Assessment (SOMPA), 144

Task orientations, 71-76
Tasks of Emotional Developmental Test, 179
TAT test, 77-79, 179, 180
Teachers:
aggression and, 76-78

292 Index

attaining more intimate relationship with, 73–74
authority of, 72–73
as a critical figure in the learning process, 72
the curriculum and, 113–115
interviews, 130–139
  ability to work in groupings, 134
  academic functioning, 135–138
  children and adult relationships, 134–135
  home-school relationships, 139
  lesson periods, 133
  nonlesson periods, 133
  school behavior, 133–135
  school history, 132–133
possible questions to, 263–267
-student interaction, 115–116
-student relationship in remediation, 248–252
  independence, 249–250
  innovation, 251–252
  reality-based support, 248–249
  structure, 250–251
Temporal organization of motor processes, 43
Time orientation, 45
Toxemia, 17
Turner's syndrome, 27
Twins:
  dizygotic, 27
  monozygotic, 27

Underachievement ratios, 81

Vision, 181–182
Visual-motor skills, 164–166
  (*see also* Visual processes, Motor processes)
Visual processes, 32–36
  discrimination, 34
  memory, 34–35, 174, 238–241
  on WISC–R subtests, 148, 157–164
  perception, 32–34, 175, 273–274
  sequence, 35–36
Vocabulary:
  biological determinants in, 40–41
  in language process, 40–41
  sight-word, 34
  subtest, WISC–R, 155–157
  tests, 107–108, 155–157
Vocational counseling, 120

WAIS, 145, 147, 156
Wepman Auditory Discrimination Test, 167
Wide Range Achievement Test (WRAT), 36, 170–172
WISC, 143, 145, 146, 151, 154, 156, 177
WISC-R, 143–164
  individual subtests, 152–164
  scale differences, Verbal and Performance, 145–149, 190–192
  subtest clustering, 145–152
Withdrawal behavior, 56–58
WPPSI, 145
Writing, 38, 41–43, 174 (*see also* Handwriting)
  numbers, 36